The Complete Idiot's Freshwater Aquarium Re...

Popular Tropical Fish for the Community Tank

Red Fire Gourami

Zebra Danio

Black Lyretail Molly

Red-Eye Tetra

Glass Catfish

Black Tetra

Yellow Rainbow

Neon Tetra

Blue Metallic Guppy

Albino African Frog

Cherry Barb

Gold Barb

Mickey Mouse Platy

Gold Nugget Pleco

Marble Angelfish

Skunk Catfish

alpha books

tear here

Popular Fish That Get Big!

Jaguar Cichlid

Tricolor Shark

Arowana

Red-Tail Catfish

Oscar

Red Devil

Fancy Goldfish   ## African Cichlids

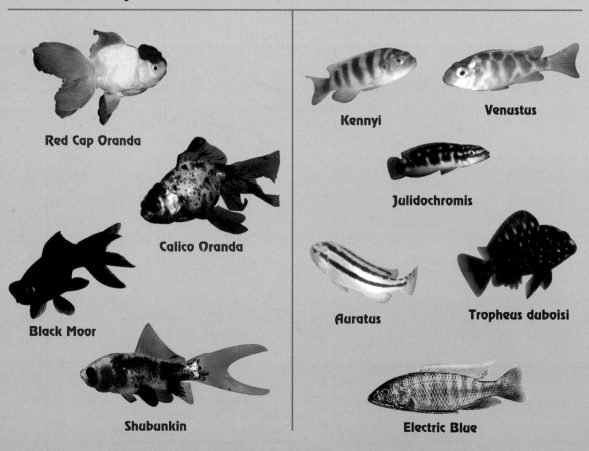

Red Cap Oranda

Calico Oranda

Black Moor

Shubunkin

Kennyi

Venustus

Julidochromis

Auratus

Tropheus duboisi

Electric Blue

2.00

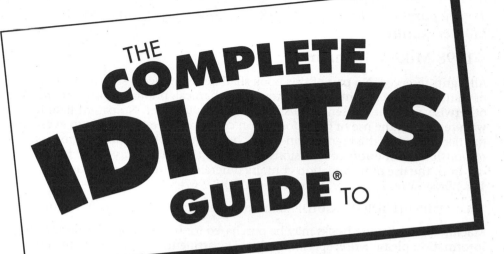

THE COMPLETE IDIOT'S GUIDE® TO

Freshwater Aquariums

by Mike Wickham

alpha books

A Division of Macmillan General Reference
1633 Broadway, New York, NY 10019

*To my parents, who have always been my biggest fans, and to
Mother Nature.*

©1998 Mike Wickham

Macmillan Publishing books may be purchased for business or sales promotional use. For information please write: Special Markets Department, Macmillan Publishing USA, 1633 Broadway, New York, NY 10019-6785.

International Standard Book Number: 0-87605-327-4

Library of Congress Card Catalog Number: 98-13987

00 99 98   4   3   2   1

Interpretation of the printing code: The rightmost number of the first series of numbers is the year of the book's printing; the rightmost number of the second series of numbers is the number of the book's printing. For example, a printing code of 98-1 shows that the first printing occurred in 1998.

Printed in the United States of America

Alpha Development Team

Publisher
Kathy Nebenhaus

Editorial Director
Gary M. Krebs

Managing Editor
Bob Shuman

Marketing Brand Manager
Felice Primeau

Senior Editor
Nancy Mikhail

Development Editors
Phil Kitchel
Jennifer Perillo
Amy Zavatto

Editorial Assistant
Maureen Horn

Production Team

Editor
Beth Adelman

Production Editor
Kristi Hart

Copy Editors
Susan Aufheimer
Lynn Northrup

Cover Designer
Mike Freeland

Cartoonist
Kevin Spear

Photos and Illustrations
Mike Wickham

Designers
Ruth Harvey
Glenn Larsen

Indexer
Chris Barrick

Production Team
Angela Calvert
Kim Cofer
Nicole Ritch

Contents at a Glance

Contents

Part 2: What Stuff Do You Need First?   33

4 Select Your Aquarium and Stand   35

5 Choosing Your Filter System   47

Part 3: Look at All Those Cool Fish and Plants!   117

11 Picking Your First Fish   119

12 Popular Fish for Beginners   131

Foreword

That you even have this book in your hands is a testament to your wisdom. It is an axiom among experienced aquarists, and those who own or work in pet and aquarium stores, that most people who are interested in having an aquarium are not particularly interested in reading about them. This is probably nothing more than an extension of the widely held belief that only if all else fails does one read the instructions.

But let's face it, no one is born knowing how to keep fish alive and healthy in a container. Yes, it does seem almost too simple—a glass box, some water, and fish. Ironically, the basics of this endeavor are neither complicated nor difficult, but without knowing at least that bare minimum, the odds of success are dismally small. Once you know these "secrets," however, maintaining an aquarium and the fish in it is easy.

What really makes the aquarium hobby so interesting are the many ways there are of being involved in it. In fact, to a beginner, the choices may seem somewhat overwhelming—with dozens of tanks filled with many kinds of fish. And the multitudes of equipment and supplies filling shelves and hanging from pegboards can seem intimidating. But a little knowledge goes a long way—which is why reading this book is such a wise investment, one that gives so much in return.

The quality of a book like this is directly proportional to the knowledge and expertise of the author, and Mike is very experienced both as a hobbyist and also as a retailer who has guided thousands of customers to fishkeeping success. His advice is practical and it works. This matters more than you might think. When it comes to aquariums and fish, there's often more than one way to accomplish the same goals, so you want simple, reliable information to get you started. Later, when you have some experience, you can forge your own path.

Read this book first to learn about what to do and how to do it. And then, use it as a reference as you find your interests expanding. A lifetime of fishkeeping begins with the first aquarium. Good luck, and have fun!

Edward Bauman
Editor, *Aquarium Fish Magazine*

Introduction

I got my first aquarium in 1964. I was just a kid and it took me several months to save up enough money for a little five-gallon starter kit. My parents didn't want me to buy it, because they thought I would quickly lose interest. I suppose they also feared they would get stuck caring for it!

Still, it was my money, so they let me make the purchase. As it turns out, my parents also got interested in my little aquarium. A local dime store was running a special on 10-gallon starter kits, and my mom surprised me by offering to buy one for me. She really shocked me, though, when we got to the store and she said, "What the heck, let's get two!" Before we knew it, we had over 40 aquariums in the house and a little fish breeding business.

Fishkeeping has turned out to be not only a life-long hobby, but also a profession for me. Yes, I kept my interest in those dazzling denizens of the deep. The hobby offers many niches, and over time, most aquarists progress through several of them. New hobbyists usually keep small, peaceful "community tank" fish. Some move on to a phase where they keep larger, aggressive varieties. Others find fun in watching fish spawning and rearing the babies. Who knows? You may end up doing all of the above and more!

How to Use This Book

As you read *The Complete Idiot's Guide to Freshwater Aquariums*, you will soon recognize that it is very much like your aquarium—it is structured like an ecosystem. In an ecosystem, if you change a parameter (by adding or removing a species, for example), it will affect something else. Everything is interconnected.

The information in this book is very similar. Just about every fact in every chapter relates in some way to the information in other chapters. Skip something and you may change the complete picture in your tank. Change something and you may find unexpected consequences. It's a ripple effect.

Anyway, as you read this book, you will find a few topics are interwoven through many chapters. So many things are interrelated, and it is impossible to separate them entirely. Still, I came up with a logical plan. The book is divided into five parts. The topics are laid out in the order you will most likely need to learn them.

Part 1: Introduction to Fishkeeping. I start by telling you some things you need to know before you buy your first aquarium.

Part 2: What Stuff Do You Need First? I'll follow with detailed instructions on purchasing equipment and assembling it into a functional aquarium.

Part 3: Look at All Those Cool Fish and Plants! The real fun begins as we talk about fish and plants. If an aquarium is the steak, then fish and plants are the sizzle!

Part 4: The Tank Is Running; Now What? Water is the lifeblood of your aquarium, so I'll start by telling you everything you ever wanted to know about water, but were afraid to ask. Heck, 10 bucks says I'll tell you a few things about water that you never would have thought of asking! Discussion of water leads perfectly into routine maintenance—including partial water changes. I'll also throw in fun things, though, like breeding fish and propagating plants.

Part 5: Problems in Paradise. Part 5 is the problem section. We will talk about some common problems that hobbyists encounter, how you can prevent them, and how to deal with them if you didn't prevent them.

How much would you pay for a book like this? You might expect to pay a jillion dollars, but not with this special offer! But, wait . . . don't get out your checkbook yet, because there's more! That's right! If you act today, I'll also throw in a table of contents, an index, and several informative . . .

Appendices! I end the book by pointing you toward other sources of information, giving you some sample shopping lists, and telling you how to find a local aquarium society if you'd like to join a club.

Now, how much would you pay?

But, Wait! There's More!

As you read this book, be sure to check out the little boxes. They give you extra pointers by highlighting various important and interesting tidbits of information. Watch for these boxes:

Fish Tales

Look in this box for miscellaneous interesting fishy facts.

Fish and Tips
Check here for helpful hints that save you time and money, and make fishkeeping easier.

Fish School
Look here for definitions of unfamiliar words. There is also a glossary at the back of the book.

Something's Fishy
When something is not quite right, we say that something's fishy. These boxes contain warnings and safety tips.

You can also expect a few things thrown in just for giggles, like this:

You know you are too much like your fish when . . .

. . . you can't pass a pile of rocks without moving a few.

. . . you spit your food out a couple of times before eating it.

. . . you keep smashing into the sliding glass door and think nothing of it.

. . . you eat your children without blinking an eye.

. . . you die a week after moving into a new home.

. . . you don't take baths—you take freshwater dips.

Acknowledgments

Special thanks to Dennis Hare and Richard Graham of the Aquarium Center in Randallstown, Maryland. Thanks also to Denise Petty, DVM, Ed Bauman, Ashli Williams, Joe Lora, Dave Doolittle, Diane Shiflett, Greg Randell, Bill Greene, and Melody DeLong. Extra thanks to the gang at CompuServe's FishNet Forum. Finally, a big ol' hug to my editor, Beth Adelman, for thinking of me to do this project, and putting up with me when I procrastinated!

Part 1
Introduction to Fishkeeping

You probably can't wait to get started purchasing your aquarium and supplies, setting everything up, and then stocking the tank with spectacular fish. Before you do that, though, let's talk about the reasons people get into the hobby, and what benefits you can expect from it. There are many ways to enjoy aquariums and fish!

You want to be happy with your choices, so I'll point out some things you need to consider before you pick a size and style of aquarium. I'll also teach you how to choose a good dealer—perhaps your best resource as you get started.

Chapter 1

Why Keep Fish?

Picture a pebbled, rock-strewn stream. Ribbons of dark-green eel grass sway in the crystal-clear current. Clumps of water wisteria reach lush, fingery fronds of chartreuse toward the light. Against the green background, the blades of a ruby swordplant make a bold accent. To one side, a catfish peers from beneath a gnarled driftwood stump. In the dappled light, a school of neon tetras hangs near the edge of the foliage, their fluorescent colors living up to their name. A male guppy spreads red and yellow fins and dances to court a nearby female, as pygmy sucker cats diligently rasp algae from large, smooth stones. Near the surface, a school of zebra danios plays tag.

Scenes similar to this occur every minute of every day in an aquarium. There is always something going on and always something to watch. Exotic tropical fish provide an endless array of shapes and colors. And they tantalize us with spectacular exhibits of interesting behaviors.

A beautifully decorated aquarium. (Courtesy All-Glass Aquarium)

We're Not Number One, but We Should Be

Believe it or not, fishkeeping is not the number one hobby in the United States. We aquarists must settle for second place. Photography lays claim to being the number one hobby.

But, if you ask me, fish have made photography what it is today. Think about the pictures that people take. How about those vacation pictures on the beach? What's that in the background? That's right—an ocean full of fish! Let's say some friends go on a cruise. What's that on the buffet in the picture they took? That's right—salmon. If your friends take a trip to Yellowstone National Park, don't you think they'll go trout fishing and bring back a picture of themselves proudly displaying the fish they caught? And what is the groom wearing in those wedding pictures? An outfit named after the tuxedo platy—a fish! Anyway, I think you see my point. If it weren't for fish, there would be no need to take pictures.

Be an A"fish"ionado

So, what is it that attracts so many of us to fishkeeping? What is so special about these slimy, cold-blooded creatures that makes us want to fork out our hard-earned dollars for them? What is it that makes us want to fawn over them like they are our own children? Okay, well, maybe we don't fawn over them like they are our children. At least, I don't. Well, maybe just a little.

Living Furniture

There are lots of reasons people are drawn to fishkeeping. But when asked, the most common reason given is that they think the aquarium will look good in their home. A properly lit and attractively decorated aquarium can add natural beauty to any room. And these days you can buy stands and canopies that are furniture quality and will fit right in with any decor. The aquarium becomes a piece of living furniture.

Your aquarium is live art! It is like a picture frame that holds an ever-changing portrait of Mother Nature. It adds a window to the outside world that is unaffected by weather or season or geography. Properly maintained, your tank will always provide you with a breathtaking scenic view.

An aquarium can be a small tank on a countertop, or it can dominate an entire wall. Some people even build them into the wall or use them as room dividers. You get to be artistic and decide what contribution your aquarium will make to the room.

Mellow Out

One great benefit of this hobby is a subliminal one. Fishwatching is relaxing. It is known that petting a dog or cat will lower a person's blood pressure. The same thing happens when you watch fish. Except, of course, when you see your $2 fish trying to kill the $50 one!

Fish Tales

A recent study conducted by Drs. Katcher and Beck at the University of Pennsylvania showed that watching an aquarium for 20 minutes did a better job of relaxing dentists' patients than hypnosis.

Learn About Nature and Science

Fishkeeping is educational. Your aquarium is a miniature ecosystem. It will give you an opportunity to learn about interrelationships among species—both plant and animal. You will learn how the inhabitants are affected by their environment. You will have an opportunity to delve into or dabble in ichthyology, microbiology, chemistry, horticulture, aquaculture, taxonomy, and numerous other fields.

But don't let those big words scare you off. You don't have to be a genius or a scientist to be successful with your aquarium. Even a complete idiot can do it, with a little preparation. I'm living proof!

The good news is that you are reading this book. The fact that you are reading any aquarium book at all puts you 20,000 leagues above 95 percent of the people who keep fish. It also puts you in the group that will have the highest success rate. Way to go! Smart move!

You are going to learn a lot. This book will teach you all the basics. It will also offer some topics that are a bit more advanced. Believe me, though, if you so desire, there is a lot more that can be learned about fish than can be learned in this one book. That's why there's a reading list at the end.

Build your own aquatic library!

Learn Respect for Living Things

Before you buy a car, it helps to take a driver's education class. Before you buy your aquarium, do a little reading. The more you know, the better your chance of success. You want your fish to live. Your fish want you to want them to live. They depend on you. You can't write them off as dependents on your tax return, though. Sorry.

Fish are perishable, but do not think of them as expendable! Often, I have seen customers want to buy fish against my recommendation. I let them know there is a good chance that the specimen they've chosen will not survive with their other fish, but they buy it anyway. "What the heck," they say. "It's only 99 cents. If it dies, I'll just get something else." I get annoyed when this happens. While 99 cents may not be much to you or me, I bet the fish would consider its life to be worth much more than that. You should, too.

If you don't show respect for the fact that fish are living beings—if you consider them to be expendables—then you really should forget fishkeeping and take up stamp collecting or some other hobby. Maybe you should buy a camera and just take pictures of fish, instead. It's the number one hobby.

Lights! Aquarium! Action!

Okay, I have listed many reasons why people enjoy the science and art of fishkeeping. But for me, the biggest appeal is that properly decorated aquariums, with the right mix of fish, are just plain beautiful. They have living color. They have fluid motion.

A good aquarium will have all the elements of a never-ending movie. In your tank, you will find comedy, drama, and suspense. You'll laugh. You'll cry. You'll fall in love. Just kidding—you won't laugh or cry.

Sometimes you'll watch your aquarium for fun and sometimes you'll watch it to wind down. Try this some evening: Turn out the room lights, switch off the television, erase the 1-900 numbers from your speed dialer, and just sit there for a bit, watching the fish. Feel the tension slipping away? Try it some time when you are having trouble falling asleep. It can work wonders.

If It's Not Easy, You're Doing It All Wrong

Fishkeeping is easy, but fish plus water does not necessarily equal success. You need to learn a few things to succeed. And, if you want, you can learn lots.

It surprises me how many people walk into a fish store, ready to buy fish, knowing only that fish live in water. They have no idea what it takes to keep a fish alive. They don't even have the tank purchased or set up yet. It doesn't dawn on them that some fish won't get along, or that fish need a certain amount of room to swim, or that they don't all eat the same thing, or that unconditioned tap water can kill the fish. These people mistakenly think, "I can drink the water, so it must be safe, right?"

They don't know what temperature is required, or that rapid temperature changes can kill a fish. In fact, unless a fish is floating upside down—dead, bloated, and stinky—they wouldn't be able to tell if it is healthy or not. By the way, if you're reading this thinking to yourself, "Uh oh . . . that's me he's describing," don't worry. It is not a problem, because you bought this book, which means you are taking steps to learn. For some people, learning would be too much trouble. Their tanks are destined to end up collecting dust in the attic or garage. Yours is not.

Fish and Tips
If you have to spend more than five to 10 minutes per week maintaining your tank, you are probably doing something wrong. Seriously. How many hobbies do you know with that kind of work-enjoyment ratio?

Fish and Tips
Another easy thing about fishkeeping is dealing with the fish when you go on vacation. They can be left for two or three days with no food and no harm will be done. If you plan to be gone longer, it would be wise to buy an electronic fish feeder to dispense food automatically while you are away.

You don't have to take a college course to learn how to keep fish. There are a few basic rules to follow, and if you stick to them things will go well and you will spend lots more time enjoying your tank than maintaining it. It should take you less time to maintain your tank, than it would take to drop off a roll of film to be developed.

Fish Are Amazing

Did you know that kissing gouramies really do kiss? Or, that some species of fish show parental care and guard their young? Did you know that there are fish that keep their eggs and babies in their mouths for safety? There are fish that can travel across land to the next pond, and fish that can survive a drought, dried up in the mud. You'll find fish that have live babies, and fish that jump out of the water to stick their eggs on overhanging leaves. There are fish that build nests out of plant leaves. There are fish that make sounds. You can even find a fish that catches overhead insects by shooting them down with spitballs!

Interesting fish behaviors provide many good reasons for a person to want to keep fish. You will find that fish have personalities, too. They will come to recognize you and to look forward to your presence—well, either your presence or the presence of the can of fish food in your hand. It's hard to tell.

Fish can display intelligence. I've heard of large fish learning to splash their owners when they want to be fed. Fish will do things that make you laugh. The first time you see one swimming nonchalantly around with a long string of poop trailing behind, you will laugh. When the string finally breaks free, and every fish in the tank tastes it a couple of times to see if it is food, you'll laugh again. Yes, fish also can display stupidity.

Be a Voyeur

Another reason to keep fish is because they are fun to breed. Yes, you can watch your fish breed, and no one will think you are a pervert—unless all the fry are born looking like *you*. Be sure to check out the chapter on breeding fish to see some of the many interesting ways that fish reproduce.

Fish School
Baby fish, singular or plural, are called *fry*. A fish fry isn't just something you have on Friday night.

Breeding fish is easy. Well, at least breeding some species is easy. In fact, just try to stop them. Guppies, mollies, and other popular livebearing species are known for their ability to reproduce quickly. Under the right conditions, many species of egglaying fish are even more prolific. Imagine hatching a thousand or more eggs from a single spawn.

Breeding fish can even be profitable. Your dealer may be interested in buying some of the fish you raise. But if your goal is to make money at it, be sure to ask the dealer beforehand what kind of fish would interest him. Some species are so prolific that you'll have trouble giving them away. And some species are so cheap that it wouldn't be worth the bother.

Before I scare you off, note that you probably don't have to worry about having your fish breed to overpopulation. Unless you take steps to raise the fry in separate tanks, few will survive. Most will get eaten by the other fish—a nutritious treat—and some will starve, get sucked up by the filter system, and so forth. A properly maintained aquarium will achieve a healthy, balanced population.

The real reasons I like to keep fish are . . .

. . . it's fun to have spitting contests with archer fish.

. . . swordtails make great cat treats.

. . . I love kissing gouramies.

. . . it counts as community service, in lieu of serving jail time.

. . . fish geeks get all the good-looking babes.

Reasons Not to Keep Fish

Frankly, I can't think of a single reason fish shouldn't be kept, but I can think of several reasons why a person would not deserve to keep them. It all boils down to being responsible. Fish are living things, and though they require a very small commitment on your part, they do require a commitment. If you are not a responsible person, and you are not willing to do the tiny little bit of work required to keep the fish fed and the water changed—or, if you would look at your tank so rarely that you wouldn't spot disease until it was way too late—then you really should forget about getting an aquarium. It is not fair to make the fish suffer.

Alternately, there are companies that provide aquarium maintenance services. Many dealers offer this service, and you also may find individuals or aquarium service companies listed in the Yellow Pages.

Now that I've listed reasons why you may or may not want to keep tropical fish, let me end this chapter by saying welcome to an interesting hobby. Whether you keep a single small tank for the kids, a larger one to decorate the living room, or you become so involved with fish that your basement fills up with aquariums or you open an aquarium shop of your own, there is something in the hobby of fishkeeping for everyone. Enjoy!

The Least You Need to Know

➤ Aquarium-keeping is the second most popular hobby.

➤ An aquarium is living art.

➤ The hobby teaches about nature and science.

➤ It is very relaxing to watch fish.

➤ Fish are a commitment, and you must be willing to care for them.

Chapter 2

What Kind of Tank Do You Want?

In This Chapter

➤ Freshwater vs. saltwater

➤ Big bruisers vs. peaceful pygmies

➤ Mother Nature vs. polypropylene

There are many ways to set up an aquarium. You may already have a vision of what your aquarium should look like, based on tanks you've seen set up before. Perhaps you like the way a friend's tank looks, or maybe you saw a nicely decorated aquarium on display in a restaurant or doctor's office. Perhaps the aquarium in Captain Picard's ready room on *Star Trek: The Next Generation* caught your eye, or maybe you really liked the one in that Mel Gibson movie, before Mel put several bullets through it. (Geez, and Mel was supposed to be the good guy.)

However, it is possible that you have never seen an aquarium before, or haven't paid much attention to the ones that you have seen. It might be the interest of a son or daughter that has you buying this book. But no matter where you got your notion to set up a tank, before you go out and buy one, you need to make some decisions about what type of aquarium you want to set up.

So, take note of your friends' aquariums to see what you like, what you tolerate, and what you hate. Perhaps you can visit some public aquariums—and by public aquariums I mean fish zoos, such as the National Aquarium in Baltimore or the John G. Shedd Aquarium in Chicago. Now, you won't be able to set up an aquarium like many of the ones you'll see at these attractions—they are way too big, and you won't be able to keep killer whales at home, for example—but you will find some smaller, nicely decorated tanks to give you some ideas.

In fact, most of the species shown in public aquariums can be purchased at your local tropical fish store. You might be surprised to learn that those two-inch pacus at the local shop are the same species as those three-footers on display at the public aquarium. The little ones are just a bit younger.

Also, check out the local pet shops for some ideas. Most stores that sell tropical fish will have at least one, and probably several aquariums set up as "display only." That is, the fish in them will not be for sale. The tanks are decorated to give you an idea of what you can do to make your tank look nice at home.

The National Aquarium in Baltimore. (Photo © National Aquarium in Baltimore, Ron Haisfield)

Usually, the tanks your dealer sells his fish from will be decorated poorly or not at all. So don't use those tanks to form an opinion of how an aquarium should look. A dealer generally keeps his aquariums devoid of decorations to make it easier to catch the fish for sale. The decorations can make it more difficult to net the fish, and can get disturbed, broken, or damaged. Live plants, particularly, can take a beating from a fish net.

Check other books for ideas, too. You should be able to find pictures of attractively decorated aquariums in almost any aquarium book. In fact, there are even a few books in print that contain nothing but photos of gorgeous aquarium setups. Amano's *Nature Aquarium World* series (three volumes), published by T.F.H. Publications, contains beautiful displays of decorated aquariums of all sizes.

Even if you already have an idea what an aquarium should look like, I'm going to discuss the many things you should consider before deciding. Perhaps you'll get some ideas that hadn't already occurred to you—if not for your first tank, then for your next one.

Freshwater or Saltwater

This is your first major choice. Freshwater is relatively salt- and mineral-free. It is the type of water that we drink. Freshwater isn't always fresh, though. If you constantly overfeed your fish, your nose may soon tell you just how true that statement is.

Freshwater is the type of water that starts out as rain, and eventually wends its way to the ocean. On its way there, it travels through rivers, streams, and lakes, picking up trace amounts of salts and minerals as it goes.

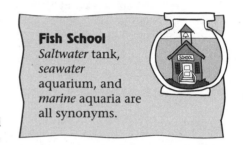

Fish School
Saltwater tank, *seawater* aquarium, and *marine* aquaria are all synonyms.

Saltwater, or seawater, is what we find in the oceans. The ocean is like a big dead-end lake—the water flows in, but only leaves via evaporation. So, all the dissolved salts and trace minerals deposit there and have built up to high levels over millions of years.

Anyway, all water has some salts and minerals in it, but there is a big difference between how much you will find in freshwater and in seawater. You could almost think of saltwater as highly concentrated freshwater, or of freshwater as greatly diluted seawater.

All of this is a roundabout way of saying that freshwater fish and saltwater fish require much different water chemistry. You cannot just plop any old fish into your tank and expect it to live. Besides the water chemistry difference, there are other differences as well. Let's talk about the differences that will concern you most.

Why Your First Aquarium Should Be Freshwater

Except in this chapter, you won't find me discussing marine aquariums anywhere else in this book. I only tell you about them now, so that you will know all the choices available to you, and maybe to give you something to aspire to. But your first aquarium really should be a freshwater aquarium. Why? For several reasons.

First, freshwater aquariums are easier. You don't have to pre-mix seawater in a separate container when you do water changes. You won't have anywhere near the same amount of salt deposits building up on equipment, so you will have less cleaning to do. And you won't have to monitor salinity in your freshwater tank.

Next, freshwater tanks have more margin for error. If you are a beginner, that extra margin could make the difference between success and failure, until you get some experience. The water chemistry in a freshwater tank can fluctuate a bit more before it causes problems. Freshwater holds more oxygen, and the fish can stand a bit more range in pH. Also, the toxicity of ammonia, which is excreted by the fish, rises with the pH of the tank water. Since saltwater has a normally high pH, the risk is greater.

Saltwater fish are more expensive. Though there is a whole range of prices, the most popular freshwater fish will cost you between $1 and $2 each. Marine fish, on the other

Fish School
Salt creep can be 1) unsightly mineral deposits that build up where water splashes and dries; 2) affectionate slang for a saltwater aquarium hobbyist.

hand, will average closer to $20 each. So it is probably a good idea to learn the ropes of fishkeeping with something a bit cheaper. Also, you will require more equipment for most saltwater setups, and some of it will be quite pricey.

Availability is another factor. Your dealer will stock many more varieties of freshwater fish. In fact, unless you live in a larger metropolitan area, your dealer may not stock marine fish at all. It takes a larger investment in equipment and knowledge to keep saltwater fish, and your dealer may not be able to justify it to serve what is typically a very minor percentage of his clientele. After all, he has to turn a profit, or he will disappear.

Fish Tales

About 11 percent of all American households keep freshwater fish, while just 0.6 percent keep saltwater fish, according to a survey by the American Pet Products Manufacturers Association.

Don't Stop Reading!

Just because I said that your first aquarium probably should be a freshwater one, and that this book will have a freshwater emphasis, doesn't mean you should stop reading. Except information relating to specific species, almost all of the information in this book will apply to saltwater tanks, too. Think of freshwater fishkeeping as a way to master the basics of aquarium keeping. You are now taking Fishkeeping 101. Saltwater is more advanced, and you will need to learn a few *more* things to do it right. Think of this book as the prerequisite before you move up to Fishkeeping 201—marine aquaria.

Size Counts

The next step in planning your tank is deciding what size fish you plan to keep. Big fish eat little fish. With rare exceptions, you cannot mix large fish with small ones. That is, not unless you want the small fish to be bait for the lunkers—the big fish in your small pond.

Fishy snacks aside, the size of fish you keep will determine what size aquarium you need to buy. Do you want to keep small fish? If so, you can keep a few in a small aquarium, or many in a large tank. However, if you want to keep jumbo fish, you will need to buy a large tank right off the bat.

You cannot crowd your fish, or they will die. Big fish require more gallons of water per inch of fish. In the chapter on picking your first fish, I will give you some detailed guidelines on how to determine how many fish will fit in your tank. Those guidelines can also help you determine what size tank to buy.

Something's Fishy
Big fish eat little fish. Even big *peaceful* fish eat little fish.

Peaceful Community or Wrestling Ring

Some people like to watch fish to relax. They like to view the graceful movements and enjoy the ebb and flow of motion. The serenity attracts them.

I fall into that category of person. I prefer to see the plants swaying in the current, schools of fish flitting by like a flock of birds, and catfish grazing along the bottom like contented cows. I like my aquariums to be pastoral, even when I plant them like a jungle. Yes, the community tank is for me. It also happens that the community tank is what most people keep.

Fish School
An aquarium containing a mixture of small peaceful fish is called a *community tank.*

Other people prefer action and drama. They want to see an assault here and there, and maybe even some serious bloodshed. One thing about Mother Nature is that she offers it all, and it is no different in the aquarium. A tank can be set up to provide this kind of setting, too.

Fill your aquarium with African cichlids and they will chase each other in and out of the rocks all day long. Occasionally, someone will get severely beaten . . . or maybe even killed. Now, I don't much like replacing murdered fish, or playing doctor to injured ones, so that style of tank is not really my cup of tea. But African cichlids are quite beautiful and the action appeals to many.

Aggressive fish have evolved to behave that way, so there is nothing wrong with keeping them and enjoying them for doing what they do naturally. Just because I'm the expert doesn't mean you have to like what I like. Besides, some of my best friends are "cichlidiots." Cichlid clubs abound, and there is even one for women only—Babes In The Cichlid Hobby. Their acronym says it all.

Or, maybe you want to keep a tank of piranhas. Even I have to admit that it is fun to watch them snarf down a bunch of goldfish. Piranhas mostly sit around all day doing nothing. But drop a fish into the tank, and things change. A piranha will chase down a fish and, if it will fit in its mouth, eat it whole. Otherwise, the piranha will use its razor sharp teeth to bite chunks out of the fish until nothing remains but a few scattered scales sparkling in the current. Cool, huh? Most everyone thinks so, except the poor goldfish.

Fish Tales

Piranhas aren't really as nasty as they are made out to be in the movies. In the aquarium, you will usually find them to be very shy fish—especially if you just have one. They do have the dentition to dismantle any fish, though—and your fingers, too, so be careful. However, it is highly unlikely that they would ever try to bite you, and is normally quite safe to work inside the tank around the fish. Be very careful when handling them in a net, however. In fear, they will bite right through it and get your fingers.

Do You Want to Fool Mother Nature?

How do you visualize your aquarium? Is it filled with driftwood, natural rocks and gravel, and live plants swaying in the current? Or do you prefer having a six-inch plastic diver bubbling next to a four-inch plastic shipwreck, with plastic palm trees sprouting stiffly from fluorescent pink gravel?

Seriously, everyone has their own preferences. It is your tank, so you get to decide how it will be decorated. Don't let anyone berate your choice of decorations, no matter how strange or silly they are. But choosing between natural decorations and artificial ones is a choice you must make.

Obviously, my preference is for the natural aquarium. I am a bit of a purist; I like my aquariums to look like something you might find in nature. To my knowledge, fish have not evolved to enjoy living around fluorescent pink gravel and plants they can't eat. I prefer to set up my aquariums in a way that is most likely to make the fish feel at home. An advantage of this is that the fish feel more secure and show their coloration to the fullest.

But this is America, and when that guy in *The Graduate* said he could sum up the future in one word—plastics—he wasn't far off the mark. In fact, if you want, you can buy every kind of decoration in plastic. There are plastic plants, plastic rocks, pieces of plastic driftwood, and of course, plastic castles and treasure chests. You can even buy plastic fish. Heck, even Goofy and Mickey Mouse are available in diving gear to decorate and aerate your tank.

Plastic decorations are an American phenomenon. In Europe, and elsewhere in the world, natural decor is preferred. In fact, European aquariums may contain few or no fish. They put a greater emphasis on aquatic horticulture, tending to plant heavily. European aquariums often do not have covers. Instead they have suspended lighting and allow the plants to grow right up out of the tank. It is almost as if they add the fish as an after-thought.

Plastic Pluses and Minuses

The heavily planted European style aquarium—often called the *Dutch aquarium* because the style first became popular in Holland—and the American style aquarium each have their advantages and disadvantages.

Plastic rocks and driftwood won't leach any substances into the water, so you don't have to worry about them changing the pH or hardness of your water, and some plastic rocks even lock together so that you don't have to worry about them caving in on your fish.

Plastic plants don't die and they don't need to be trimmed. There is no need to worry about how much light they get, or to bother offering fertilizer to them. All in all, they are fairly maintenance free. But the downside is that they don't compete with algae for nutrients, so you are more likely to have algae to scrub in a tank that has plastic plants instead of live ones.

While plastic plants may not die, they also do not grow. Once you set up a scene, there is nothing dynamic about it. Unless you physically move the plants around, you will have a static display. Every leaf will be in the same place tomorrow as it is today. There will be no new stems, no new leaves, and no new runners.

Of course, live plants do have some disadvantages. They may shed some leaves, giving you a bit more debris to clear away. Also, they may grow to the point where you need to spend time pruning and replanting. (However, if you give your plants proper care, you may be able to sell extras back to your dealer for credit on supplies.) And, of course, if you do things wrong, live plants may rot and die. Some fish love to eat plants, too. If you plan to keep a tank full of silver dollars, for example, you may find that plastic plants serve you better.

> **Fish and Tips**
> The kind of fish you keep may influence your decor choices. If you keep large fish that like to dig, you will have a hard time keeping live plants with them. Plastic plants may work better, because they can stand continual abuse and uprooting.

Mix It Up

Another option is to mix. Often, aquarists will have both live and plastic plants in their tanks. Plastic plants are used in place of delicate species, or instead of species that are easily munched. It is a useful compromise that lets the live plant-loving aquarist enjoy species he or she might otherwise be unable to keep.

By the way, most of the plastic plants sold in aquarium stores are fashioned after actual species of aquatic plants. You also will probably find nonaquatic species such as plastic marijuana plants, and stuff like that. Hey, they may not be aquarium plants, but if customers buy them, dealers happily line up to sell them. You can't blame a dealer for finding a way to take your money.

Whether you go plastic or *au naturel*, you will create a habitat for your fish. So let's talk about some of the various habitats you can establish in your tank.

Aquariums With Style

Obviously, there are many ways to set up an aquarium, and you need to pick what suits you most. Here are some typical styles of freshwater aquaria that might fit your needs.

Heavily Planted

This is my favorite style. I like to make my tank look like a jungle, with some room left over for the fish to swim. Mixing in a few rocks and pieces of driftwood makes an even more natural appearance. Admittedly, a similar decor can be set up using plastic plants, and some look quite nice, but that is not for me.

Rock Pile

This style is especially popular with African cichlid fans. Few, if any, plants are put in the aquarium. These fish tend to eat most plants, anyway. Instead, a large thick, wall of rocks is built, with plenty of shelves, ledges, caves, and holes. The fish chase each other in and out all day, and the tank is always full of action.

Wide Open Spaces

Some hobbyists go very light on the decorations and leave lots of swimming space. Usually, this style of tank looks naked to me, but there are times when it has its uses. Large fish may constantly knock over and move decorations around the tank, especially species that dig a lot. In that situation, the plants would all end up floating and the rocks would all end up buried by gravel, anyway.

When it comes right down to it, all tanks should have some wide open space though. If you put plants and rocks right up to the glass, you may not get to see the fish much. And if you keep schooling fish, they like to have some space to chase each other around.

Paludarium

These swamp aquaria contain both land and water. The lower part of the tank is a typical aquarium with plants and fish and so forth, but driftwood, rockwork, and plants continue to grow right up out of the water into a terrarium set-up. Sometimes, the units are designed to be open on top, so that the plants can grow as tall as they want. In other set-ups, the top portion is enclosed. That way, tree frogs, geckos, and anole lizards can be housed inside, too. (Without the top cover, they'd get loose.)

A paludarium is half terrarium, half aquarium. Paludarium means swamp tank.

Theme Tanks

This often grotesque category can contain a real hodgepodge of styles. A popular version would have several aerating ornaments with a common theme bubbling away. Or, it may be something as simple as setting up a tank that only contains species of rainbows or barbs. I've seen theme tanks set up with assorted plastic divers doing various treasure-hunting chores. Piranha tanks with piles of ceramic skulls in them are a popular choice. I even have seen patriotic theme tanks that had red, white, and blue plastic plants as the only decor.

Years ago, I saw a theme tank set up to mimic the bottom of the Cuyahoga River—in the days when it was highly polluted. Ceramic beer cans, spare tires, boots, bricks, and concrete blocks made up the decor. Small carp swam happily inside. All I can say is egads. I would never want to set up a tank that ugly! But I also realized that the tank was set up to make a point, and it did so quite well. Ironically, I also have to admit that it may have been the most "natural" tank I've ever seen.

Brackish Aquaria

Many species of fish live in coastal areas and have evolved to tolerate large ranges of salinity. They can survive in freshwater, saltwater, and anything in between. The "in between" is brackish water. Many species sold as brackish are really juvenile saltwater fish. They belong to species that spawn in the coastal waters. The youngsters then live in the tidal estuaries and mangrove lagoons until they are large enough to move out to sea.

Pure freshwater has no salt. Seawater has a specific gravity—measured with a device called a hydrometer—of around 1.023. That is approximately 24 teaspoons of salt per gallon. So a brackish tank is kept somewhere between those two extremes. Some hobbyists keep as little as two teaspoons of salt per gallon in their brackish tanks, but anywhere up to 12 teaspoons per gallon is suitable.

Obviously, you cannot throw any species into a brackish tank. You must pick suitable species, and I'll list a few in the chapter on popular fish and critters. Another consideration with brackish tanks is that, depending on the salt level you keep, most plants won't survive. Plastic plants will probably be your only option.

Biotopes for Purists

I have already said that I much prefer to set up my aquariums with natural plants, rocks, and driftwood. Some hobbyists take this a step further by creating natural biotopes. A *biotope* is a sample of a particular type of environment.

Unlike most aquariums, which are set up with a mix of compatible fish and plants from Asia, Africa, and North and South America, the purist might strive to match plants and fish that would be found together in the wild. They might go for a region as large as Southeast Asia, or limit themselves to species from a particular country, and ideally to a particular habitat. For example, some species prefer still ponds and others fast-moving streams. The two would not be found together in the wild, although their habitats may be found within a few hundred yards of each other.

Setting up a biotope isn't always easy. Your dealer is probably not going to label each species with its wild point of origin. Probably, your dealer won't even know more detailed information than what continent the species comes from.

However, if you want to set up this style of aquarium, you can be reasonably accurate with a little research. There are many aquarium atlases on the market, which will give information about country of origin, preferred pH, and other details for individual species. Recently, some biotope books have appeared on the market, as well. These books may even give you a shopping list for some sample biotope setups.

Most hobbyists who try to accurately match wild biotopes do it just for fun, or for the sake of accuracy. However, closely matching natural surroundings is often a way to get a difficult species to breed. Maybe you could be the first to have a captive spawning of a species!

The Least You Need to Know

➤ Start with a freshwater tank. There is more margin for error.

➤ Big fish eat little fish. Even big *peaceful* fish eat little fish. Big fish also need big aquariums.

➤ Your choices for aquarium decor are limited only by your budget and good taste.

Chapter 3

Finding a Qualified Dealer

In This Chapter

➤ How to determine if your dealer is a doofus

➤ Learn which is more important: quality, selection, or price

➤ I tell you where to go . . . shopping

You can make it easier on yourself if you find a good place to shop—a place with helpful, knowledgeable staff. Your dealer can play a big part in your success. It is important to find a dealer who can serve your needs, and is willing to do so.

Now, some of you won't be lucky. You will find yourselves living in towns that are too small to support more than one pet store or aquarium shop. You may have to travel some distance to find just one store to serve your needs, and even then, the selection might be quite limited.

Many of you will be much luckier. If you live in a major metropolitan area, you are likely to find many stores where you can buy fish, aquariums, and supplies. You will find a better selection, and more competitive prices. Lucky you.

But whether you live in the city or a rural area, you need to find a good dealer. You need to find someone who sells the equipment you need, who stocks the fish you covet, and who can offer advice when you need it. You need to find a dealer who you can think of as a friend in the business.

How do you find such a person? I'm glad you asked.

Dead Fish Stink

I put this at the top of my list, and for a very good reason. A dealer whose tanks have many dead fish is a dealer who probably doesn't know how to properly care for them. If he can't keep his own fish alive, how is he going to be able to offer advice that you can trust to keep your own fish alive? Further, do you want to risk buying from tanks that are full of dead and diseased fish?

Avoid stores where there are lots of dead fish. They are bad news, pure and simple. Now, having said that, let me qualify this a little. Fish are livestock. Livestock is perishable. That means fish can die. Eventually, even healthy fish will die—of old age or accident, or maybe some other healthy fish will decide to have them for lunch or beat them to death. So it is unreasonable to expect that you will never see a dead fish in your dealer's tanks, even if he is the best dealer in the whole wide fishy world.

Fresh Fish

Avoid buying new arrivals. Your dealer has new shipments of fish coming in all the time, and that means he has new shipments of stressed-out fish arriving constantly. Stressed fish are fish that tend to get sick.

Imagine being crammed into a plastic bag with up to a thousand other fish, and then put into a dark box that gets tossed around, roasted and chilled in transit. Imagine being locked up that way, without food, for up to 48 hours. That is what many fish go through to get from fish farms in Asia to the tank in your home. Worse, they may have stressful stops on the way as they pass through the hands of transshippers and wholesalers.

The result is that some fish will get sick, especially if they are new arrivals. I can personally vouch for the fact that the tanks we have under treatment at my store, at any given time, are almost always the new arrivals. So don't hold it against your dealer if he has an occasional tank under medication.

Fish Tales

The painted glassfish really is painted. Fluorescent dyes are injected into this transparent fish to give it spectacular colors. However, the paint soon wears off. Don't be fooled.

Now, you are not going to be able to tell if a fish is a new arrival by looking at it—at least, not unless you are in the store so often that you can recognize a tank of fish that wasn't there previously. So the only way to know how long a fish has been in your dealer's stock is to ask. The longer your dealer has had a fish in stock, the safer it will be to buy it.

Do not buy from medicated tanks. Your dealer may treat tanks because the fish in them are obviously sick, or he may medicate new arrivals solely as a preventive. While it is true that fish receiving preventive medication are probably completely fine, you still should not buy from those tanks. The fact that your dealer has chosen to medicate preventively means he knows that species has a history of developing problems as an aftereffect of shipping stress. Let your dealer quarantine the fish for at least a couple of days to make sure they really are as healthy as they look.

Look for the Good Stuff, Too

Don't just look for dead fish. Your dealer may be lousy at keeping fish alive but very good at regularly searching out and discarding dead bodies. So it is also important to look for healthy stock. Look for fish with bright eyes and erect fins. Look for fish with energy.

Look for fish with an interest in life. When you approach the tank, do they come running for food? Now, you may think this is a bad sign, because they act like they are starving. But even fish that have their stomachs so stuffed with food that it looks like they are balancing on a basketball act like starving fish. So don't accuse your dealer of fish abuse, just because the fish appear hungry. The fact that they swim toward you, hoping for food, is a good sign they are well fed—that they get fed often enough to have learned that when people approach, munchies may be approaching, too.

Feel free to stick your hand near the front glass to see if the fish come running. However, please do not touch the glass or tap on it. Sound travels through water much easier than it travels through air. So tapping on the glass is like unexpectedly crashing cymbals in a fish's ears. It can frighten a fish very badly, and can cause injury. Besides, touching the glass leaves finger marks that make it harder to see the fish.

Fish and Tips
Dedicated pet and aquarium stores are usually much better sources for quality stock and supplies than are stores that simply wedge a pet department in between the shoes and the sporting goods.

A Predelection for Large Selection

There are thousands of species of fish available in the hobby. Your dealer won't be able to carry them all, but the more tanks he has, the better his selection will be.

A large aquarium store is likely to have a larger selection, making shopping more fun, but don't overlook the smaller stores. The most important consideration is the health of the livestock. Sometimes the largest store around has the most disease-ridden fish, because they are just too busy or lacking in expertise to give the fish the proper care.

Look for a large selection of dry goods, too. Does the dealer carry more than one brand of various items? It is good to see choices. However, sometimes there can be too many choices, making it confusing to decide which is right for you. I learned a long time ago that you can scare people away by giving them too much to think about. Still, my feeling is that a dealer who carries only one brand for most items is a dealer who doesn't understand that everyone's needs are not the same. Your dealer's recommendations are going to be very valuable, but there still should be some flexibility.

Ask the Experts

Your dealer can't help you if he doesn't know what he is doing. As a novice to the hobby, you are at a disadvantage because you don't know what you are doing, either.

Obviously, it would be foolish to assume that everyone who works in an aquarium or pet store is an expert. There are no academic degrees required to own or work in a fish store, and there aren't any official tests to pass. Even the best store with the most knowledgeable staff in the world has to hire people off the street to fill all the positions. So you not only have to look for a store that has a staff with expertise, but you also have to be sure the individual salesperson who is helping you is knowledgeable.

How can you tell if your particular salesperson knows his stuff? Some salespeople can be very good at bluffing their way through things. Often, the person who is the most full of baloney is able to serve it with such confidence that it is easy to believe it all. You need to be able to weed out the B.S. artists.

This may not be easy, especially since you are new to the hobby. The only way you will know if someone else knows what they are talking about is to arm yourself with a little knowledge beforehand. The more you know before you walk into a store, the better you will be able to tell what kind of advice you are getting. Since you are reading this book, I would say it's safe to assume you are already arming yourself with knowledge. If you at least know the basics, you will be able to tell if the information given to you by a salesperson agrees with what you already know.

Fish and Tips
There are many ways to skin a catfish. Getting different answers to the same question does not necessarily mean any of the answers are wrong. Rather, it may merely be a reflection of personal preference. For example, one dealer may prefer to use undergravel filters, while another may prefer to use outside power filters. Both methods will work, as long as you perform the proper maintenance.

Fortunately, the odds are good that the employees will at least know the basics. So even if you get a rookie to wait on you, you probably will be okay. However, if you feel a salesperson is not yet ready to answer your questions, don't be afraid to ask if there is someone with more experience available to help you—even if you have to come back later.

As you get answers to your questions, listen to how they are delivered. Does the person have an answer for everything? This may indicate a salesperson who likes to bluff his way through a conversation. You need someone who is willing to admit when he doesn't know something. Does the salesperson hesitate before each answer? This could be a sign that they don't really know their material or are making it up—particularly if the answer turns out to be vague.

Look for a consensus. Try asking a couple of different salespeople the same question. Try it in a couple of different stores. If you get similar answers, that's a good sign that you are probably getting good advice. However, be careful and don't do this too much—especially if you are asking different salespeople in the same store. I can personally vouch for the fact that this feels like an insult when it happens. When I spend time explaining something to a customer and I overhear them asking the very same questions of someone else, it makes me feel untrusted. It also makes me feel like I wasted my time with them, and doesn't give me much incentive to want to take time to talk to them again.

Service and More Service

You want a dealer who looks out for your interests, as well as his own. Hopefully, you will find salespeople who are not just trying to sell you something, but are hobbyists who also share your joy for the hobby. You don't want to be sold products that don't work, or items you don't need.

A good dealer will suggest additional products that you need or may find of use—items that you may not have considered—but he won't try to offer you a product for every little problem. Sometimes, there are simpler, cheaper, or even free ways to solve your problems, and your dealer should be willing to volunteer that information.

Besides courteous service, a good dealer will offer additional professional services. Some of these will be freebies, some not. For example, your dealer may offer free water testing. You bring in a sample from your tanks, and they'll do a quick workup for you. (That doesn't mean you shouldn't regularly monitor your water quality on your own.)

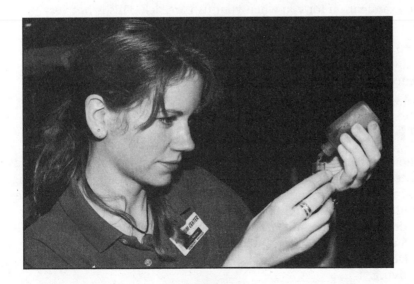

Some dealers offer water-testing services. Here, Alexandra runs a pH test.

Some dealers will offer free repair service on pumps, filters, heaters, and other equipment—charging only for parts. Be aware that you may have to leave the item for repair at their convenience, and you may have to wait for parts to be ordered. Most dealers don't carry much in the way of replacement parts, and their distributors probably only offer them a spotty selection of repair parts.

If your dealer offers free instructional seminars, take advantage of them. Usually they will be on topics suited for beginners, but advanced topics may be covered as well. Sometimes guest speakers who are well-known in the trade may be brought in. It is a great way to learn, have fun, and maybe even make some new friends.

Another service your dealer may offer is aquarium drilling. Yes, most glass can be drilled with the proper tools. More and more people are having holes drilled in their tanks to allow for under-tank plumbing.

Some stores will offer custom-built aquariums and cabinets for sale. These items are more expensive, but are designed to your specifications.

Your dealer also may offer aquarium servicing. This is where you pay your dealer to come to your home to do the installation or routine maintenance on your aquarium. The service may be performed on equipment that you own, or you may lease the aquarium from the dealer. There are many ways this can be done, tailored to each customer. You may even set it up so that the service occasionally swaps fish and decorations in your tank, so you have something new to look at. Most aquarium service companies will ask you to sign a contract that explains your obligations and theirs.

All tropical fish stores offer free advice on treatment of fish diseases. Granted, some are much better at it than others. You may even get lucky and find a store that is willing to do some microscopic examination for you when your fish are sick. This is not very common, though.

Another sign of a good store is the availability of live foods. It is highly entertaining to watch fish feed the way they do in nature. Goldfish, guppies, brine shrimp, and blackworms are the most common live foods, but there are others, and an exceptional dealer will have them available for sale, too.

How Much Is That Fishy in the Window?

It is a Saturday afternoon and you are shopping for aquarium supplies at Super Duper Tropicals, your favorite aquarium store. Today, you happen to be thinking about setting up another aquarium, so you are looking at the various filters that are available. Let's say you find two similar filters, of two different brands. Both are rated at the same number of gallons per hour, are designed for the same size aquariums, but use different types of filter media. One filter is $5 more than the other. Interestingly, the cheaper filter can be bought for $1 less at D&D Tropicals down the street. (By the way, in this story D&D stands for "dead and dying.")

Of the two brands of filters, which is better? Which one will you buy? Since it appears that the dingy store down the street may sell at a lower price than your favorite store, will you go there to buy it?

Every dealer has a different method of pricing his merchandise. So as you shop around, you may find a large range of prices for the same items. Prices will vary from store to store and by geographic region. Welcome to the real world.

Now, everyone loves to get a good deal. None of us wants to pay more for an item than we need to. I hope that you find a good bargain every time you go shopping. But keep this in mind: Price is not everything.

Fish and Tips
Don't be ruled solely by price. Quality and service are more important.

When you look at the price of an item, take a minute to think about what you are getting for your money—it's not just what is inside the package in your hand. In the above example of the two filters, did your dealer take time to explain why one is a much better choice than the other? Did he give you advice on how to set it up? Has he helped you in the past, even when you weren't making a purchase? In my example, I stated that you were making this comparison in your favorite dealer's store. Why is he is your favorite dealer?

All these things must be factored into the price you are willing to pay for merchandise. If your dealer is helpful, be willing to pay a little extra for that. A dealer whose advice keeps you from killing expensive fish is saving you a lot more money in the long run. A dealer who explains that the more expensive filter will be cheaper long term because it uses less expensive replacement media is also saving you money. When you are lucky enough to find a good dealer, help keep him in business by shopping there. Don't reward the joker down the street with your dollars.

I'll Tell You Where to Go

There are many places to shop for fish and supplies, and I don't just mean dedicated fish and pet stores. Let's talk about some of these choices, and the advantages and disadvantages of each. I will admit up front that I'm about to stereotype some of these options for you, but my descriptions will be based on what you would commonly find. However, let me emphasize that every seller should be judged individually. There are good ones and bad ones of every type.

Pet Stores

Most of you will be buying your fish and supplies from pet stores. These stores will sell other animals in addition to fish. While a pet store doesn't specialize in fish, the aquarium and fish departments typically count for half the business in a neighborhood pet store. So there is a very good chance that there will be staff on duty who know their stuff when it comes to fish.

Tropical Fish Stores

The best place to buy your aquariums, fish, and supplies is from a dedicated tropical fish store. Unfortunately, there are not many of them out there, except in the larger cities.

The great thing about the dedicated aquarium store is that the people working there are the most likely to know what they're doing. They are there because they like keeping fish. When people like something, they learn about it. So you are most likely to get good advice, find the best equipment, and the healthiest fish in this store. Count your blessings if you've got one nearby.

Superstores

This is a relatively new category. In the last few years, the pet business has changed a lot. Smaller mom-and-pop stores used to be the norm, but many have disappeared with the appearance of gigantic retail pet superstore chains that have sprung up around the country. These chains move into a market and, due to their size and buying power, run many existing smaller stores out of business with prices that are temporarily lower. The superstore chains have recently started gobbling each other up. At present, they have pretty much whittled themselves down to two major players.

These superstores emphasize an inventory of low-overhead dry goods, particularly dog and cat foods, and carry little in the way of high-maintenance livestock. In other words, they gear their business toward selling supplies, not fish or pets.

What are the advantages and disadvantages? One thing I must give the superstores credit for is that they have brought a degree of professionalism to the pet business. The stores are large, nicely laid out and merchandised, and the selection is good. Since they are actual pet stores and not just pet departments, there is a semi-decent chance that you could find the equipment you need and someone to help you.

However, the odds of that are not as good as they could be, because the stores' emphasis is on dry goods, especially dog and cat food. These stores were designed to be low maintenance, self-serve operations. They have livestock, but no one ever seems to buy any of it.

There are very few dedicated tropical fish superstores around the country, but the ones I've seen have been well worth the trip. It's a lot of fun to walk into a huge store and find upwards of 600 aquariums full of fish to pick, supplies galore, and wall-to-wall fish geeks.

Mass Merchandisers

These days, most of the mass merchandisers (that is, the various XYZ-Marts) have pet supply departments. Some of them even carry a few pets and fish. If you know your stuff, you may find some good deals there.

However, if you are new to the hobby I recommend that you avoid these places. You need to be able to get good advice to get started right. Unfortunately, the pet departments in these stores are almost always staffed by employees who have insufficient training. As I like to say, "They don't know the difference between cichlids (pronounced SICK-lids) and sick fish." If you don't know the difference either, that only proves my point that you need to find a store that has an experienced and knowledgeable staff available.

Also, the mass merchandisers tend to have less selection, and will be more likely to carry inferior lines of merchandise and have less healthy fish.

Mail Order

If you live in a rural area, you may not have an aquarium shop anywhere nearby. You may have no other choice than to order supplies through the mail. There are a few places around the country that sell through the mail, often at very good prices. In fact, I've sometimes seen stuff for sale at prices less than what your dealer pays through his distributor.

So yes, there is the possibility of finding some very good bargains via mail order. However, there is a downside. First off, you need to be familiar enough with the products to order them sight unseen. There is no way a person can describe all the choices of filters over the phone, or how to assemble them.

Another disadvantage of buying through the mail is that you have to wait. Do you really want to spend the next few days running to the door every time you hear a truck, to see if it's the U.P.S. delivery? Don't forget to factor in the cost of shipping your purchase, and the cost and time that will be involved if you need to return or exchange any merchandise. Of course, that assumes that everything you ordered arrived in the first place, and there were no back orders.

Mail-order suppliers mostly sell dry goods. There isn't much livestock available via mail, and most of that is the more expensive saltwater livestock.

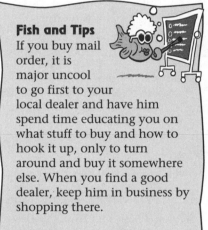

Fish and Tips
If you buy mail order, it is major uncool to go first to your local dealer and have him spend time educating you on what stuff to buy and how to hook it up, only to turn around and buy it somewhere else. When you find a good dealer, keep him in business by shopping there.

Something's Fishy
There is no warranty on used equipment. It is common for people to buy boxes of used equipment, only to find that some of it doesn't work, or is missing pieces. Plus, you don't know if grandma unwittingly washed the tank with toxic soap to clean it up for the sale.

Garage Sales

Aquariums are often offered for sale in the classified ad section of your local newspaper. You will find them in the occasional garage sale, too. Depending on how much you know, you could get a really good deal, or waste a lot of money. It is risky to buy this way.

Also, when people sell used equipment, it is usually because they failed to keep their fish alive. Granted, this may be because they didn't know how or didn't keep up with the general maintenance. However, it also may be because they bought inferior equipment. If you buy used equipment, make sure it is the same stuff you would have bought had you gone to a dealer. Until you know more about fishkeeping, I recommend that you avoid used equipment.

It's Guaranteed

Sometimes things go wrong. When they do, you may be able to take advantage of a dealer's or manufacturer's warranty. Most dealers offer some type of guarantee on their livestock, and most dry goods will have a manufacturer's warranty.

Warranties are there to protect you from product defects. They don't cover your negligence. Before trying to collect a guarantee when something goes wrong, you need to consider if the problem really was a defect or if it was due to something done incorrectly on your end.

Fish and Tips
Always open packages carefully and in a way that you can easily reseal them. If you need to return an item because it's the wrong size or style, you won't be able to do so if you shredded the package when you opened it.

For example, if you buy a glass canopy and find that it has a crack when you get home and open the box, your dealer should be happy to replace it. On the other hand, if you buy a glass canopy and accidentally drop it on the floor, you shouldn't expect the dealer or manufacturer to pay for it.

Likewise, a fish that dies of disease or unknown reasons within the warranty period should be readily replaced by your dealer. However, if the fish died because you forgot to cover your tank and it jumped out, or because your ammonia levels are sky high, then it really isn't fair to ask for someone else to pay. The fish has already paid with its life.

Warranties usually don't cover changes of heart. If you buy something and change your mind, you may be stuck with it. Most dealers will give refunds or credit on dry goods returned within a certain period—in new condition with all packaging intact, of course. Dealers are usually much less willing to take back fish that you decide you don't want.

Why the difference? Merchandise is merchandise, isn't it? Well, not really. Your dealer can tell the condition of returned dry goods by looking at them. With fish, there is no way to know if they were exposed to temperature extremes, poor water quality, toxins, or disease that will affect them later. So it is riskier for the dealer to take back a fish.

Typical Guarantees

Every manufacturer has a different guarantee, and so does every dealer. So there is no way that I can explain this topic fully. However, I can tell you about some typical guarantees. You probably will find similar guarantees at your local shops.

➤ *Aquariums.* Smaller aquariums usually have a 90-day warranty. Larger models may have warranties of one, two, five, or up to 15 years. Occasionally, I've seen tanks offered with lifetime warranties. Be sure to ask for details, because sometimes the extended warranty requires that you buy the manufacturer's aquarium stand at the same time you purchase the tank.

The guarantee on your aquarium will be very specific. It will cover leaks and pressure cracks. We define a pressure crack as a *single-line* crack, extending from one edge of a pane to another, with *no chips* at either end. The guarantee does not cover abuse or damage caused by you or family members. Chips on corners denote impact. They are not guaranteed. Several cracks radiating from one point like a spiderweb also indicate impact or external pressures, and are not guaranteed. Aquariums are glass. Handle them carefully!

➤ *Dry goods.* Warranties on packaged merchandise will vary by item. Heaters usually have a 90-day or one-year warranty. Air pumps, filters, and lights (the fixture, not the bulb) often have a one-year warranty. Most other items only guarantee that they are not broken when you buy them. It is a good idea to save receipts for your major pieces of equipment, and to save copies of the manufacturer's warranty. Sometimes it is printed on the box, sometimes it is printed on a slip of paper inside. Other times you won't be able to find a warranty printed anywhere.

➤ *Fish and plants.* Check with your dealer for details on his livestock guarantee. Every dealer's guarantee is different. Some give 24 or 48 hours and some give a full week. Others give no guarantee at all, or guarantee freshwater fish but not saltwater fish. The guarantee may be for full replacement, half-price replacement, or (rarely) full refund.

How to Collect

Always remember that you catch more flies with honey. A smile, a pleasant attitude and a desire to get help (rather than to point blame) go a long way. A dealer is going to be more amenable to merchandise returns when the customer is polite and willing to accept advice. Confrontational people get stubborn responses.

To collect on a fish guarantee, you usually will need three things:

1. *An identifiable dead body.* It is proof of death, and the dealer needs to see it to identify the species. He'll also take a quick look to see if there were bites taken out of the fish, suggesting that aggression was the cause of demise.

2. *Your sales receipt.* The sales receipt proves that you are within the time limit of the guarantee and that you didn't buy the fish at another store.

Something's Fishy
Always inspect your aquarium before you buy it. Chips on corners indicate damage and are weak points where cracks may develop. Reject any aquarium that has chips.

3. *A water sample from your tank.* Keep it separate from the dead body! Most dealers will want to run a quick test of your water to see if they spot any problems. If they find problems with the water, dealers usually will still guarantee the fish, but will recommend that you take a credit slip instead of a replacement. It would be better to fix the problem before adding more fish.

Fish and Tips
When returning merchandise, take your itemized cash register receipt. Unitemized charge card slips won't do.

Please note that fish guarantees are rarely "no questions asked." Frankly, I would avoid any store that doesn't try to find out what went wrong. It could be a sign that they don't care or, worse, that they expect you to lose fish. When you try to collect on a fish guarantee, a good dealer is going to ask you several questions about your tank and its care. The questions may make you feel like he is trying to shift the blame from himself to you. He isn't! Or, at least . . . he shouldn't be.

Instead, he is trying to help you solve problems. If something is wrong in your tank, wouldn't it be better to find out before you put replacement fish in there? While it is true that your dealer would prefer not to replace a fish for you, his main concern is that he not have to replace the replacement. It makes more sense to find and fix problems before they compound themselves.

Here is a quick checklist for you to follow when returning packaged merchandise:

✔ Before exercising a guarantee, review its terms. Be sure you are within the allowable time limit, and be sure it is a defect, not misuse, that caused the problem.

✔ Does the guarantee say to return the item to your dealer or to send it to the manufacturer?

✔ Gather your sales receipt to establish proof of purchase and date of purchase.

✔ Gather the merchandise that you want to return. If you are returning new merchandise that is the wrong size or style, be sure you have the original, undamaged package and any warranty sheets and instruction cards that came inside. Your dealer needs to be able to resell this unused item.

The Least You Need to Know

➤ Avoid dealers with sick and dying stock.

➤ Find a dealer who is knowledgeable.

➤ Seek dealers who are courteous and are willing to spend time with you.

➤ Quality is most important, followed by selection and price.

➤ It's usually best to shop in a dedicated aquarium store, but a good pet store will suffice. Evaluate each dealer individually.

➤ Keep your sales receipt.

Part 2
What Stuff Do You Need First?

The whole point of keeping an aquarium is to admire the gorgeous fish and plants, but you can't keep them alive without the proper equipment. So prepare yourself to receive lots of advice on selecting the proper equipment to do the job. There are many choices, though, and the result will be up to you. I've also included some sample shopping lists in Appendix A at the back of this book.

Knowing what to buy is one thing. Knowing how to put it together is another. The last chapter in this part, "Some Assembly Required," will give you detailed, step-by-step instructions. I even drew some illustrations to guide you.

Select Your Aquarium and Stand

Aquariums come in many shapes and sizes. You are probably familiar with the typical rectangular aquarium, but did you know there are also pentagons, hexagons, spheres, and triangular tanks? Did you know that standard aquariums range in size from one gallon up to 300 gallons? Or that custom built tanks could go even larger? Before I talk about how to choose specific pieces of equipment, there are some important considerations.

Make Sure It Will Fit

Before buying an aquarium, you should decide where you are going to put it. Take time to measure the space. You don't want your tank to stick too far into a hallway or block a doorway. Measure how tall the tank and stand together can be. You want to be sure they won't block access to a window or electrical circuit panel, or bump into overhead shelves or cabinets. Allow a bit extra so there is room to open the lid to maintain the aquarium.

Also measure how wide your tank can be (from front to back). Remember that you may need to leave a bit of space behind for any hang-on-the-back filters. Minimally, you need to allow enough room for electrical cords, air lines, or filter hoses to run behind the tank. Write down all these measurements and take them with you when you go shopping. That way, you will be able to pick an aquarium and stand that fit into the space you've chosen.

Fish and Tips

To determine if your floor is strong enough, figure that a filled aquarium weighs roughly 10 pounds per gallon. So a 10-gallon tank would weigh around 100 pounds, a 75-gallon tank weighs around 750 pounds, and a 300-gallon tank weighs a ton and a half!

While you are measuring, it is also a good idea to consider the strength of your floor. Some older homes may not have strong enough floors to hold a large aquarium. If your floor bounces a lot when you walk on it, it probably is best not put a really large tank there. Bouncing is not very good for aquariums anyway, as it can twist and crack your tank.

Don't let the weight frighten you. Most sizes of tanks should be safe in every house. It is only when you get into the larger tanks—say, 75 gallons or larger—that it could get a bit iffy, and even then I'd say it is probably only a problem in buildings older than 30 years. If the floor joists are 2 × 8s, 2 × 10s, or 2 × 12s, I doubt there is need to worry. Some older homes may only have 2 × 6 or even (gasp!) 2 × 4 floor joists. I'd stick to smaller tanks in those situations.

Acrylic May Be Idyllic

When you go shopping for your aquarium, you will need to decide if you want glass or acrylic. Oddly, you may find this decision was made for you, because your dealer will often stock only one or the other. Both types have their advantages and disadvantages, though. So if you want acrylic, and your dealer only stocks glass, either find another dealer or see if you can place a special order.

Many people prefer acrylic tanks. They have a different look than glass tanks, and often it is the look alone that will be the deciding factor. After all, an aquarium with fish is a work of art, and everyone has their own ideas of what it is that constitutes art. Acrylic tanks have a "cleaner" look than glass tanks. That is, acrylic is clearer than glass, and acrylic tanks are usually manufactured using single-piece construction—one sheet of acrylic is heated and bent to form the front and sides of the aquarium. So the corners are seamless, rounded, and completely transparent. Acrylic tanks also have the more modern look of space-age plastics.

One downside is that acrylic is a bit more flexible than glass. So once the tank is full and water presses outward on the sides, the material bows slightly. This happens with glass, too, but it is not as pronounced. Now, don't get me wrong. This bowing is only slight and doesn't pose any strength problems. The disadvantage is that this slight distortion presents more curved surfaces to reflect light from the room. So depending on your room lighting, there may be more curvy reflections to interfere with your viewing.

Acrylic tanks have a clean, modern look.

One advantage of acrylic is that it is lighter than glass. It will take only one or two people to move an empty acrylic aquarium around, where it may take up to four to move a glass tank of the same size. Acrylic is also stronger than glass. Yes, it can be cracked or shattered, but it takes quite a bit more force to do it. Also, typical construction involves using solvents to weld the seams together at the molecular level. So an acrylic tank is effectively a one-piece deal with seams that are difficult to split. I would like to add a caveat here: It depends on the manufacturing technique. There are some brands that use thick acrylic glues to bond the panels, instead of the thin liquid solvent. Those tanks aren't as strong.

Anyway, the added strength of the acrylic tank has made acrylic more popular on the West Coast. Why? Well, partly, it's just a California sense of style, but another big factor is that acrylic tanks hold up better in earthquakes. Being a bit more flexible than glass, they can take more bouncing and twisting before they crack.

Acrylic tanks can also be purchased with solid-colored backs—usually blue or black—eliminating the need to buy a separate background. These tanks have colored acrylic rear panels, instead of the typical clear back. Of course, an acrylic background is there to stay, and you can't change to a different color or scene later.

Fish and Tips
You can drill acrylic with typical household tools. So if you want to install plumbing for through-the-wall or through-the-bottom filtration, you can do it yourself.

Something's Fishy
You need to be more careful when scrubbing algae on your acrylic tank. It is not safe to use razor blades on acrylic, and even some algae pads are too rough and can cause damage. Be especially careful not to get bits of gravel between the acrylic and the scrubber pad.

SNIFF! SNIFF!

37

Acrylic tanks have an integral welded top that helps to strengthen the sides of the tank. It is clear, just like the bottom, but has cutouts to allow access for filters, heaters, feeding, and maintenance. So there is no need to buy a separate glass cover. The integral top also prevents much of the mineral build up that you could get at the edge of a glass cover.

Still, acrylic isn't perfect. It has its disadvantages, too. For starters, acrylic is softer than glass, so it scratches more easily. If you or your fish are prone to knocking large rocks against the sides, you may soon find your tank scratched.

Is Glass First Class?

Personally, I prefer glass tanks. I like the appearance of acrylic better, but I worry about scratching the sides. I've seen many scratched-up acrylic tanks. In fairness, there are kits you can buy to polish out scratches in acrylic, but I find them to be a pain. Some involve liquid polishes for fine scratches and various size abrasive screens for deeper scrapes.

Glass is not as strong as acrylic, but it is plenty strong enough. (Probably not in an earthquake, though.) Glass gives a slightly greenish cast to the aquarium, especially on larger tanks where the glass is thick. However, there has recently been a move toward manufacturing tanks with glass that is more optically clear.

Glass tanks are made by gluing panes together with silicone rubber sealant. Of course, the corners are not transparent because of this, and are not smooth and rounded like acrylic. Rather, glass tanks have sharp angles on the corners—polished, so that you don't get cut on them. Since the corners aren't rounded, you don't get the funhouse mirror distortion that you get on the corners of acrylic tanks.

Glass aquariums come with glued-on plastic frames on top and bottom. Usually, the frames come in basic black, dark or light woodgrain finishes (referred to as walnut or oak), or a gray granite-type finish. There are other, less common, colors that you may stumble across, as well. The tanks are identical, except for the color of the frames. You typically choose the color that will match your aquarium stand and the decor of your home.

Glass aquariums are usually clear on all four sides, but there are some brands that have solid-colored acrylic backgrounds glued inside. Also, you may occasionally find models with integral mirror backs. These tanks reflect the decorations inside the tank to make it appear twice as deep. Pretty cool, huh? Of course, the downside of a mirror background is that you may see the reflection of a familiar fool looking back at you!

Glass aquariums can sometimes be drilled for through-the-wall plumbing of filters. It depends on the type of glass. We'll talk about that in a moment, but first I want to mention that both glass and acrylic tanks are often available pre-drilled, with plumbing installed, ready to connect to the proper filter. These tanks are commonly referred to as "reef ready" because reef tank hobbyists tend to prefer to put their filters in the cabinet underneath the tank. They can be used for freshwater or saltwater, though.

Plate Glass or Tempered?

There are two types of glass used to make aquariums—plate glass and tempered glass. Most tanks are made of plate glass. Some larger tanks are manufactured all or in part with tempered glass. Tempered glass is manufactured in a process that makes it stronger than an equal thickness of plate glass. This means that thinner sheets of glass can be used to keep the cost down, resulting in a cheaper and lighter aquarium. An advantage of tempered glass is that it is harder to break than plate glass.

Fish Tales

There are two types of plate glass. "Rolled" glass is more commonly used in windows than in aquariums. The liquid glass passes between rollers to make the sheets of glass. "Float" glass, the type usually used in aquariums, is manufactured by pouring liquid glass onto a bed of liquid mercury. The glass floats on top and cools to form the smoothest, most perfect type of glass. Rolled glass is a bit more wavy than float glass.

The downside of tempered glass is that, if it does break, it will shatter into a million pieces. You will lose every drop of water in the tank. So you cannot drill tempered glass. On the other hand, plate glass only cracks where it breaks. So depending on where the crack, or multiple cracks occur, you may not lose all the water from the tank. If the bottom of a plateglass tank cracks, you will lose all the water; but if only a top corner cracks, just a little water will leak out.

Usually you won't have a choice, anyway. Certain sizes of tanks may be available only as plate glass, and others may be available only as tempered glass. Which should you choose? If you want to drill the aquarium, tempered glass is out of the question. Otherwise, it comes down to deciding whether you think your tank will take a hard enough whack to break tempered glass. If you think it will, get plate glass because, although it breaks somewhat easier, there is less chance of losing the entire contents of your tank on the floor.

Personally, I prefer plateglass tanks.

Shapes and Footprints

Aquariums come in all shapes and sizes. Which shape is best? There are a couple of things to consider. First, an aquarium with flat sides is best. Fortunately, that includes most tank shapes. It really only rules out spheres and those tanks with slanted fronts that have recently hit the market. Rectangles, hexagons, and pentagons are fine. Flat-sided tanks are best because they maximize the surface area of your tank.

Some typical aquarium shapes. (Photos courtesy of Perfecto Manufacturing)

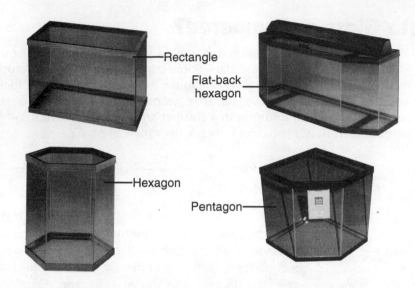

Rectangle

Flat-back hexagon

Hexagon

Pentagon

Wide, low aquariums are also better than tall, narrow ones. Again, this maximizes the surface area per gallon. As an example, let's take two aquariums. One is 20 inches long by 10 inches wide by 10 inches high. The other is 10 by 10 by 20. Both have the same volume of 2,000 cubic inches (length × width × height). However, the first tank will have a bigger footprint (how much space the tank takes up on a table), providing it with a water surface of 200 square inches (length × width). The second tank will have a water surface of only 100 square inches (length × width), or only half as much!

Both tanks hold the same amount of water, but one has a footprint and surface area that are twice the size of the other. Why is this important? First, oxygen and carbon dioxide exchange at the surface, so the larger the surface area, the better the aeration of the tank. Second, a tank with a larger footprint provides more room for fish to swim—fish prefer swimming back and forth to up and down—and also provides more bottom territory for fish to stake out. In other words, your fish will be more comfortable in the wide, low aquarium than in the tall, narrow one.

This does not mean you can't buy a tall, narrow tank, if that is what you really like. Please feel free. Just buy fewer fish for the tank, and be sure they are members of a less territorial species.

Aquarium Sizes and Dimensions

Shape	Gallon Size	Length × Width × Height (in Inches)
Rectangle	2.5	12 × 6 × 8
	5.5	16 × 8 × 10
	10	20 × 10 × 12
	15	24 × 12 × 12
	20	24 × 12 × 16
	29	30 × 12 × 18
	30	36 × 13 × 16
	40	48 × 13 × 16
	44	22 × 22 × 24
	45	36 × 13 × 24
	55	48 × 13 × 20
	58	36 × 18 × 21
	75	48 × 18 × 21
	89	36 × 24 × 24
	90	48 × 18 × 24
	100	72 × 18 × 18
	110	60 × 18 × 24
	120	48 × 24 × 24
	125	72 × 18 × 22
	135	72 × 18 × 24
	150	72 × 18 × 28
	180	96 × 18 × 24
	180	72 × 24 × 24
	200	84 × 24 × 25
	220	84 × 24 × 25
	265	84 × 24 × 30
Hexagon	10	14 × 12 × 18
	14	14 × 14 × 20
	20	18 × 16 × 20
	27	23 × 20 × 24
	45	22 × 22 × 24
	60	22 × 22 × 30
Flat-Back Hexagon	18	24 × 12 × 16
	23	24 × 12 × 20
	26	36 × 12 × 16
	33	36 × 13 × 20
	52	48 × 13 × 20

Bigger Is Better

Always buy the biggest tank you can afford that will fit in your designated space. Bigger is better because a big tank provides a more stable environment. It is safer for your fish. A couple of extra flakes of food can pollute a tiny tank, but have no effect on a larger one. A larger tank is less subject to temperature fluctuations. Besides, it takes almost the same amount of time to maintain a small tank as it does a large one. A larger tank also gives more maneuvering space for the fish, should a fight break out. The loser can't get away if there is nowhere to run.

The best reason to buy the biggest tank you can afford is because you will quickly wish that you had more room to keep more species of fish! As a dealer, I hear this lament all the time. You will be surprised at how fast you can fill an aquarium, given all the choices of interesting species that are available.

Fish and Tips
Aquariums are sold in standard sizes and dimensions, but the stated size of the tank in gallons is based roughly on external dimensions. To calculate the *true* volume of your aquarium, measure the *inside* length, width, and height (all in inches), multiply them together, and divide by 231 to get gallons. So if a tank had inside dimensions of 30 × 10 × 10, multiplying gives you 3,000. Divide by 231 to get 12.98 gallons. True gallon capacity is almost always less than the capacity stated on the label.

Avoid mini tanks. They will severely limit how many fish you can keep. I consider anything under 10 gallons to be a mini tank, and most are closer to one or two gallons in size. Some come in novelty shapes, fashioned to look like gum-ball machines, Garfield the Cat, or giant crayons, for example. Others are miniature hexagon aquariums. Some have no filters, others have the light unnaturally positioned *under* the tank. Sheesh! Anyway, unless your space is severely limited, or you at least have some fishkeeping experience under your belt, please avoid these fish-torturing tanks.

Fish bowls are even worse. They come in sizes even smaller than mini tanks and rarely include filters. If each inch of fish should have one gallon of *filtered* water, how many one-inch fish do you think you can safely fit in an *unfiltered* one-quart fish bowl?

Fish and Tips
Some of the most popular sizes for starter tanks are 10, 29, 55, 75, and 125 gallons. Choose the largest that will fit your budget or space.

If you are thinking you would rather start out small to see how things work out, and then move up to something larger, consider that your chances of success are much less with a small aquarium. It's better to get the big tank and enjoy it than to get a mini tank that will end up collecting dust in the attic.

Starter Kits vs. Complete Outfits

Often the easiest way to get started is to buy one of the complete kits that your dealer offers. They often include a break on the price. But before we talk in detail about what such a kit would include, let me define my terminology. I define a "complete" aquarium kit as one that includes everything you need to set up the tank—except your choices of decorations and livestock. Those items will need to be purchased separately. A "starter" kit is anything less than that.

Unfortunately, you will often see starter kits labeled as complete kits, although they are missing many necessary items. Now, don't get me wrong. There is nothing wrong with buying a starter kit, if you know what other items you need to buy and actually do buy them. It's just that I've seen too many consumers buy kits that they thought were complete, only to learn (often the hard way) that they need to buy more stuff. This problem is more frequent with kits purchased somewhere besides a dedicated aquarium or pet store, though it does happen there, too.

Here is a shopping list of items that I believe make up a *really* complete aquarium kit:

➤ Aquarium
➤ Full hood with light
➤ Filter system
➤ Heater
➤ Thermometer
➤ Gravel
➤ Gravel vacuum
➤ Food
➤ Net
➤ Water conditioner
➤ pH, ammonia, and nitrite test kits
➤ Beginner's book (*this one!*)
➤ Aquarium stand

Something's Fishy
Avoid mini tanks! Most have room for only one or two fish. *I don't care how many fish are pictured on the box!*

Something's Fishy
You will not find complete aquarium kits for $19.99 or even $29.99. Cheap setups are going to be incomplete and contain inferior items. The equipment needed to properly set up a 10-gallon tank probably will cost you somewhere between $75 and $100, without a stand. I've seen people kill off $100 worth of fish trying to save $20 by buying inferior equipment!

If your budget is tight, you could get the gravel vacuum later. You won't need it for a few weeks, anyway. If your dealer provides a free water-testing service, you may be able to skip the test kits, as well—although I don't recommend doing so. Also, if you have a counter or shelf strong enough to hold your aquarium, you may not need the aquarium stand at all. For those of you who need a stand, read on.

Taking a Stand

Your aquarium stand *must* be strong, flat, and level. Remembering that a full aquarium will weigh around 10 pounds per gallon, you can see that this may be no easy task. While people often do put aquariums on shelves, tables, and countertops, these items are usually not designed to hold that kind of weight. If the stand wobbles or twists, your tank will break.

Usually your best bet is to buy a commercial aquarium stand. Fortunately, there are many styles of them available, all designed to match the finishes on the various styles of aquariums that your dealer sells. They'll also fit well with your household decor.

Angle-Iron Stands

The least expensive variety is the simple angle-iron stand. These come with either a black or copper finish to match the frames on most aquariums. (The copper is similar to both the oak and walnut finishes, its color falling somewhere between.) These stands are fully welded and pre-assembled.

Something's Fishy
Your angle-iron stand may be made from aluminum or iron. Iron versions will be heavier and can rust if water is left standing on them.

You can buy angle-iron stands at the typical 30-inch height (or thereabouts), or you can buy the "lowboy" version. Lowboy stands are only about a foot high. The full-size stands are usually double stands. That is, they can hold a tank on top and have a lower shelf where you can put another tank with the same size footprint. Lowboy stands also have a lower shelf, but it won't leave enough room for another aquarium.

Wrought-Iron Stands

Also called "deluxe" stands, these are a fancier version of the angle-irons. They have decorative scroll work instead of straight legs, and cost just slightly more. Other than that, the features are the same as angle-iron stands.

Knock-Down Stands

Knock-down stands are similar to angle-iron stands in utility, but they look like wood. Today's knock-down stands typically consist of two wooden shelves and two wooden side panels. The stands come with bolt sets, and you assemble them at home in just a few minutes. Usually made of particle board, they have an applied woodgrain laminate finish. Knock-down stands are doubles, so you can also put a tank on the bottom shelf.

In some regions of the country, there are commercial knock-down stands made of stained 2 × 4 lumber. Though not fancy, these stick-built stands can be sturdy and quite inexpensive.

Cabinet Stands

These stands are completely enclosed, with doors on the front and room for a single tank on top. They come in a variety of finishes to match the various styles of aquariums and room decor. I've seen black, white, oak, walnut, granite, black oak, whitewashed oak, and other styles. Your dealer may even be able to special order custom finishes for you.

Some cabinet stands are made of particle board with a laminate finish. Others are made of wooden panels or planks. The latter are a much better choice, because they are not as easily damaged by water.

There are also acrylic cabinet stands designed to match the various colors of acrylic aquariums. Black, white, and blue are common, but you'll also find various finishes of marble and granite. The glossy finish of these stands sets them apart from wooden stands.

Cabinet stands will cost a bit more than other styles, but they make the best choice because there is room underneath to store food, nets, and other supplies. Plus, the cabinet hides any electrical cords, air lines, or filter hoses that run down the back of the tank. The open design of other stands does not provide these benefits.

Enclosed Stands

These are the fanciest, most impressive aquarium stands. Enclosed stands consist of a cabinet stand and a matching canopy. Often they will be designed as one piece, with side supports. The tank slides in from behind. All you see is the aquarium's glass, and the cabinetry. The aquarium frame is completely hidden. I have even seen versions that have matching cabinets above and below. With those, you pop open the top doors to access the tank for maintenance.

Enclosed stands are the best crafted stands you can buy, but they are not easily found in stores, and they are not cheap.

> **Something's Fishy**
> SNIFF! SNIFF!
> One disadvantage of knock-down stands and some cabinet stands is that, being made of particle board, they can be damaged by water. If your tank ever leaks or a filter hose pops loose and soaks the stand, there is a very good chance the stand will warp and be ruined.

> **Fish and Tips**
> Modern aquariums rest on their bottom plastic frames. So they don't touch the stand in the center, but only around the perimeter. Because of this, you may find stands that are open on top, with no central support. That is perfectly fine, and comes in handy if you ever want to plumb through the bottom of the tank or see what is hiding under your undergravel filter.

45

Homemade Stands

Some people buy lumber and build their own aquarium stands. Serious hobbyists often build fish rooms, lining the walls with racks that can hold several rows of tanks. I've also seen simple stands made by stacking concrete blocks and threading some 2 × 4s through the holes to support the tank. All I can say is, if you build your own stand, make sure that you know what you are doing and make it sturdy, flat, and level enough to support your aquarium properly.

Some popular stands. (Photos courtesy of All-Glass Aquarium)

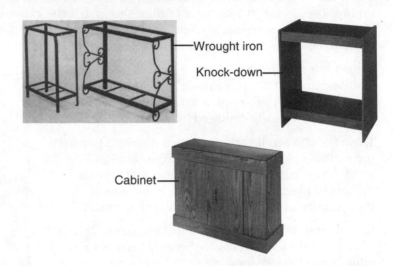

Wrought iron

Knock-down

Cabinet

Canopies

We will talk some more about these in Chapter 7, but I think it's a good idea to mention here that you can often buy canopies that match the finish of your aquarium stand. The canopy is an added furniture-like piece that sits on top of the aquarium, hiding the top frame and your lighting system. It gives a nicer architectural look to your aquarium setup. Canopies open on top to access the tank. Please note that these are wooden or acrylic, like the stands, and are different from glass canopies, which are the lids for your glass aquarium.

The Least You Need to Know

➤ Measure your space before selecting an aquarium size.

➤ Buy the biggest tank you can afford.

➤ Avoid fish bowls and mini tanks.

➤ Long and wide aquariums are better than tall and narrow ones.

➤ Starter kits are seldom complete, and you will need to buy more stuff.

➤ Your aquarium stand must be flat, level, and strong.

Chapter 5

Choosing Your Filter System

Your filter system acts like the internal organs of your aquarium. It functions like the heart, lungs, liver, kidneys, and intestinal tract of your tank. It is thanks to filtration that we are able to keep fish in such small spaces. Without filtration, you would have to greatly reduce the number of fish you keep in your aquarium. You would also have to increase the frequency of water changes.

Your filter is your aquarium's best friend. Don't forget, though, that filters are equipment. They need to have regular maintenance or they will fail to function. Your filter helps clean the tank, but *you* have to clean the filter. I will talk about that more in Chapter 20 on routine maintenance.

Also, don't even begin to think that your filter can remove all types of waste. It can't! There are many dissolved wastes that will only be removed by keeping up with your regular partial water changes. Additionally, those water changes help replenish lost trace elements. Filters do not eliminate the need for water changes.

The Basics of Filtration

There are many brands and styles of filters, and they work in many ways. It may take one or more to do the job satisfactorily. There are three basic types of filtration that your filter system needs to provide:

➤ Mechanical filtration

➤ Biological filtration

➤ Chemical filtration

Mechanical Filtration

Mechanical filtration is what the typical person thinks of when they think of filtration. With a mechanical filter, particles of solid waste are physically removed by passing the water through filter media. Most types of filters provide some degree of mechanical filtration. Undergravel filters collect debris that has settled in the gravel. Most other filters collect debris in removable or disposable filter media.

Biological Filtration

Bio-filtration is probably the most important type of filtration. It works by using helpful bacteria to break down fish waste, particularly ammonia, that the fish excrete. Be sure to read Chapter 16 for full details on cycling your new tank.

All filters provide some biological filtration, but some are better at it than others. Two things determine how well a filter performs this function. First, the more filter area there is, the better. That is because the helpful bacteria live on all the solid surfaces in the tank. The more surface area provided by your filter media, the more room there is for these bacteria to colonize.

Second, disposable filter media affect biological filtration. Disposable media are less preferable than media that can be rinsed and reused. You see, every time you throw away your filter media, you throw away all the helpful bacteria living on it, too. So the new medium must be re-colonized with helpful bacteria before it works at maximum efficiency.

Chemical Filtration

Chemical filtration means using a chemical compound to collect certain types of dissolved waste. Granular activated carbon (GAC) is the most common chemical filter medium used, but there are also various resinous beads used to soften water and to remove copper, phosphates, organics, and other metabolites. Also, zeolite (ammo-chips) is sometimes used to remove ammonia, nitrates, and phosphates.

The chemical filter media are almost always disposable. That is, after some use, it will no longer be able to adsorb the impurities that you want to remove. In fact, if it becomes fully loaded with waste and your pH changes, the chemical filter medium could release some nasties back into the aquarium. So always change your chemical filter medium on schedule. I recommend that you replace activated carbon monthly. Zeolite and resinous beads (some are re-chargeable) should be recharged or replaced monthly. Follow the manufacturer's instructions.

There are some chemical filtration products on the market that claim to be good for up to six months. While these are excellent products, you should never try to stretch their useful lives to that point, unless you have an unusually low bioload. Rather, replace these products every month or so.

Sifting Through the Choices

Your dealer probably will offer a perplexing array of filters in many brands, shapes, and sizes. Don't be afraid to ask for his advice in picking the right filter or filters for your tank.

Undergravel Filters

For many years these were the most popular choice, and still are for many people. The good feature of undergravel filters is that you don't have to replace any filter media, so they are very cheap to operate. Rather, use a gravel vacuum to siphon debris out of the gravel when you do your partial water changes.

Fish and Tips
In addition to removing dissolved waste, chemical filtration helps keep the water clear. Without the use of activated carbon, your water may be quite transparent but may develop a yellow cast from the build-up of dissolved organic materials.

Something's Fishy
Activated carbon is not rechargeable. You may hear people say that you can recharge it by baking it in an oven. However, that is not true—not unless you have a special super hot, low oxygen oven. (You don't!) After a month, throw away the old carbon and buy new.

Undergravel filters work on a simple principle. The filter consists of a perforated platform that sits under the gravel in your tank. Rising from the filter are one or more lift-tubes. These days, they are usually one-inch diameter tubes, and they have an air line with a small air diffuser hanging inside. Outside the tank is an air pump that drives the filter.

Air is pumped down the center of the filter lift-tube(s), and as the bubbles rise from the bottom, they push water ahead of them. The effect is that water gets pulled down through the gravel, pulled through the slots in the filter plate, and then pulled from under the platform and pushed up the lift-tube back into the tank, where the cycle begins again.

As the water is pulled through the gravel, debris gets trapped between the stones (me-chanical filtration). Also, helpful bacteria living on every particle of gravel will break down ammonia that is excreted by the fish (bio-filtration). Some models have small activated-carbon cartridges atop the lift-tubes. These provide minimal chemical filtration.

I think undergravel filters are great for most tanks. You must remember, though, that the gravel is the filter medium. Like all filters, you must clean the media regularly, or it will become too clogged to function. If you keep up your regular partial water changes and use a gravel vacuum, the undergravel filter may be the only filter system you need. However, it also helps to add a small outside power filter to provide additional chemical filtration.

Fish and Tips
For the undergravel filter to function properly, you need the right amount of gravel. Gravel is the filter media in this system. Use a one and a half to two-inch deep layer. If the gravel isn't deep enough, it will have a very hard time trapping debris.

Pick gravel that has the correct particle size. One-eighth to one-quarter inch diameter particles are good. If the particles are too large, the spaces between them will be too large to trap debris. Worse, the spaces would be large enough to let food fall into the gravel and become trapped, where it can't be reached by the fish. Do not use sand, as it will sift down through the filter plate and clog the filter.

There are some situations where undergravel filters aren't a good choice. One situation would be in a tank that has large piles of rocks, such as an African cichlid tank. In this setup, you will be unable to perform proper maintenance because the rocks will impede use of your gravel vacuum. Additionally, some species, including African cichlids, like to dig a lot. If they dig and expose the filter plate, the filter won't function fully. You see, water takes the path of least resistance. So if slots in the filter plate become uncovered, water will tend to take that path, rather than filtering down through the gravel where the filtration takes place. Also, digging fish will keep stirring the trapped debris out of the filter bed.

Finally, instead of an air pump, a powerhead may be used to run an undergravel filter. I will tell you about powerheads and air pumps shortly.

A typical undergravel filter (left) and outside power filter.

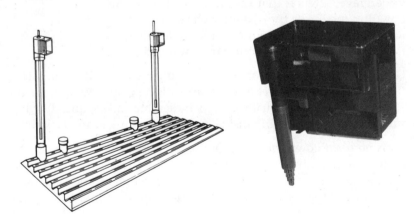

Outside Power Filters

These motorized plastic boxes hang on the back of your aquarium. Changeable filter media go inside the box. There is an intake tube that hangs into the tank, and the motor draws water directly up through it. The water then flows through the media, where mechanical, biological, and chemical filtration all take place. The water is then typically returned to the aquarium via a waterfall chute. Since there is a built-in motor, no additional pumps are required.

Outside power filters are great and provide all three types of filtration. Some are a little better than others, though. I recommend the models that use a sponge as one type of filter medium. The sponge collects debris, but also provides a place for helpful bacteria to colonize. When it gets dirty, you rinse it out and reuse it, retaining many of your helpful bacteria. Other models use disposable cartridges made up of a sandwich of polyester filter media and activated carbon.

Some recent versions include something called a Bio-Wheel. This is a paddle boat-like wheel suspended above the filter box. As water flows through, it rotates the wheel, alternately wetting it and exposing it to the air. Helpful bacteria grow on the wheel. Since there is 30,000 times as much oxygen in air as there is in water, and since these bacteria require oxygen to break down waste, they are quite efficient in this setup.

Fish and Tips
When buying an outside power filter, be sure to follow the recommendations of your dealer. Not only do you need to choose a model that is adequate for the size of your tank, but you need to be sure you get one that will fit the frame of your brand of aquarium. Some tanks have thicker frames, requiring a slightly larger filter.

Canister Filters

Over the years, these have become my favorite filters because they are so versatile. Canister filters resemble miniature wet-vacs, and can provide all three types of filtration—mechanical, biological, and chemical. There is a canister that sits underneath your aquarium and connects to the tank via input and output hoses. Inside are various styles of filter media. The built-in motor pumps the water through the filter.

These filters are great for tanks with lots of plants, rocks, or other decorations. With an outside power filter, you have no choice where the output will be. With canister filters, you can install the output hose so that it pumps the water where you want it, and you can even tee it off so that it pumps to more than one location (in the same aquarium). The output can be set up to spray the water back in a single large jet, or through a perforated spray bar that has many small jets.

The brands I like best use three types of filter media, and have separate inner compartments for them. Typically, the first compartment will contain ceramic noodles. These evenly channel the water flow, trap larger particles of debris, and provide space for helpful bacteria to colonize. The second chamber will be used for activated carbon or other chemical filter media, and the third chamber contains a sponge. The chemical filter media is the only media that you replace. When dirty, the ceramic noodles and sponge get rinsed and reused, retaining helpful bacteria. Other brands of canister filters use polyester sleeves, pleated cartridges, and other types of filter media.

Something's Fishy

If you buy a canister filter, be sure your model comes with shut-off valves for each hose, or you could have water back-siphoning onto your carpet when you disconnect the filter for cleaning.

One other consideration with canister filters is that some are easier to change than others. You may want to ask your dealer's advice on this topic.

I also should mention "internal" canister filters. These combine features of canister, outside power, and box filters. I don't much like them, because they take up space inside the tank, and are ugly. Still, they do have uses. Many people use them in turtle and amphibian tanks, where the water level is too low for other types of filters. The motor is built in, and as long as the water is about three inches deep, the filter will function.

Trickle Filters

Also called "wet-dry" filters, these are more commonly used in the saltwater trade, but they work quite well in fresh water. The trickle filter is a large acrylic box that sits under-neath your tank. An elaborate overflow system—that can be plumbed directly through the glass, if your tank can be drilled—draws water from the tank above. The water trickles down through various types of filter media, suspended above the water in the acrylic box. A water pump then returns the water from the acrylic filter box to the tank above.

Something's Fishy

All filters should be installed as designed. Do not waste your time trying to hybridize them to make them better. Doing so could result in disaster. For example, do not try to replace the overflow system on a trickle filter with a siphon, or try to plumb a canister filter to run more than one tank. If you do, the result *will* be a flood, or a burned out pump. Or both!

A polyester filter pad on top collects particles of debris (mechanical filtration). Beneath that, the media is more porous stuff, designed to let plenty of air flow through with the water. Bioballs or DLS (double-layer spiral) filter media are typical types of filter media. Helpful bacteria grow on the bioballs or DLS, and since the trickle action exposes them to both air and water, they are quite efficient at biological filtration. Placing net bags of activated carbon or resins in the acrylic chamber provides chemical filtration.

Fluidized Bed Filters

This style of filter is new to the aquarium trade. They work well, but I don't recommend them for most people. The reason is that they are quite expensive and must be used with other filtration. The fluidized bed filter usually consists of a sand-filled chamber that hangs on the back of your tank. There are some larger free-standing models, though. A powerhead is placed into your tank and used to pump water into the bottom of the chamber, up through the sand. The water then exits through a tube and returns to your tank.

These filters work by keeping the sand in suspension. Each particle of sand then provides space for the colonization of helpful bacteria. There is a lot of surface area on that sand, so fluidized bed filters do a great job at biological filtration. Unfortunately, that is all they do. They don't filter out debris (mechanical filtration), and they don't provide any chemical filtration. So you will need an additional filter to finish the job. My feeling is why spend a ton of money on one of these fancy filters, when there are plenty of cheaper effective alternatives? One good use might be on heavily overstocked systems, such as tanks holding feeder fish.

Diatomaceous Earth Filters

These filters are specially designed for "polishing" the water. They come in both hang-on-the-back and canister style models. Diatomaceous earth (DE) filters work by forcing the water through a very fine, porous powder—diatomaceous earth. This powder consists of the silica skeletons of microscopic organisms called diatoms (pronounced *DYE-uh-toms*). The pores in the diatoms are so fine that they filter out particles down to one micron in diameter.

DE filters are great for quickly clearing a tank of cloudiness. They are even able to filter out ich (a fish disease), although you can't depend on this filter to cure a tank of it.

However, they are not designed for continuous use. When a filter is capable of collecting particles as small as this one is, it tends to clog very quickly. By quickly, I mean within minutes or hours. Then, the filter must be cleaned and recharged with fresh powder before it can be reused.

If you want my opinion (and since you bought this book, I assume you do), don't waste your money on a diatomaceous earth filter. If you perform proper maintenance, any cloudy water problems that you have (if you get them at all) will be quite temporary. However, if you have a cloudy tank and want it to be perfectly clear when company comes over, a DE filter can do the job fast.

> **Fish and Tips**
> When purchasing filters, first compare features. Then compare prices. Be sure to factor in the regular cost of any replacement filter media that may be needed. Sometimes cheaper filters use more expensive media, and end up being more costly in the long run.

Box or Corner Filters

This is the oldest style of filter. It consists of a small plastic box into which you put polyester filter floss and activated carbon. An air pump drives water through the device. While box filters do have their uses, they are ugly, have limited capacity and really aren't the best choice. They do provide all three types of filtration, though. You may commonly find box filters in cheap starter kits, to keep the price low.

Internal Cartridge Filters

There are a couple styles of these. None are good choices. One is a cross between a box filter and an outside power filter. Its shape is more like a box filter, and it is also powered by an air pump, but it uses a filter cartridge similar to those in outside power filters. It provides low levels of all three types of filtration.

The other type of cartridge filter is merely a replaceable slotted cartridge with chemical filter media inside. It is designed to be used as a supplementary filter in small tanks.

Box (left) and sponge filters have limited uses.

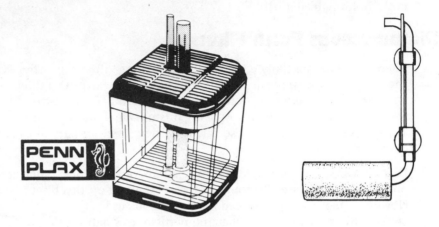

Sponge Filters

These also have limited use in most tanks. I love to use them in quarantine and fry tanks, though. They do a very good job of biological filtration, and they don't trap baby fish the way all other filters do. They are not very good at collecting debris, though. Also, they go inside the tank, so they are ugly to look at. There are models that stick to the side with suction cups, and models that rest on the bottom. You need a small air pump to drive this filter. They don't do chemical filtration.

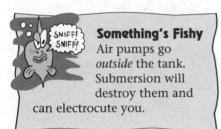

Something's Fishy
Air pumps go *outside* the tank. Submersion will destroy them and can electrocute you.

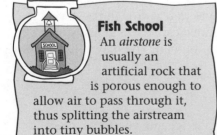

Fish School
An *airstone* is usually an artificial rock that is porous enough to allow air to pass through it, thus splitting the airstream into tiny bubbles.

Air Pumps

Air pumps are mainly used to drive various types of filters. But they can also be used to power decorative airstones and ornaments. Air pumps come in many sizes, which includes not only varying degrees of power, but varying numbers of outlets.

You must pick the right size pump for the job, and this can be difficult because the packaging will often say good for tanks "up to X number of gallons." That information is fairly useless, because you should not pick your air pump based on the size of your tank. Instead, you should pick it based on what you want it to run. For example, it would take a large air pump to run the four outlets on the undergravel filter of a 55-gallon tank. But it would take a very small air pump to place one of those bubbling treasure chests in the very same tank.

So choose your air pump based on your needs, not the tank size. Your dealer should be able to advise you regarding the various brands and models.

Most air pumps available for fish tanks are diaphragm pumps. That is, they have a plunger-shaped rubber diaphragm that vibrates 60 times per second, pumping air. As the diaphragms age and wear, they may crack. There are other parts, including rubber valve flappers, that may wear or get dirty and clogged. Your dealer sells repair kits for when this happens, and may even offer repair service.

> **Fish and Tips**
> If you find your air pump only works in shallow water, but not when you put the air line to the bottom of the tank, your pump has a cracked diaphragm. Your dealer sells replacement parts.

 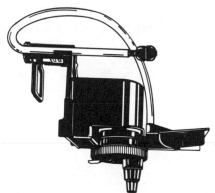

Air pumps (left) and powerheads can be used to power undergravel filters.

The best way to extend the life of your air pump is to make sure your airstones or filter outlets aren't clogged. Back-pressure from clogged outlets is the chief cause of wear on diaphragms. The built-up pressure is what stretches and cracks them.

You will need an air line to go with your air pump, and may also need gang-valves to increase the number of outlets you can run. We'll talk more about those items in the chapter on choosing supplies.

> **Something's Fishy**
> Should the power fail, there are instances where the water can bounce up through the airline and back-siphon out through the air pump. To prevent this, either position your air pump higher than the water line in your tank, or install a *check-valve*.

Powerheads

Powerheads are small water pumps that can be used to power an undergravel filter, instead of using an air pump. The powerhead sits on top the undergravel filter lift-tube and draws water directly. It has an adjustment that lets you control the flow to some extent, and an adjustment that lets you draw outside air into the mix.

Some people like powerheads. Some like air pumps.
I honestly can't say that one has real advantages over the other. They do the same job.

You can also use powerheads for stand-alone circulation. They can be suction cupped to the inside glass, or clamped to the tank frame, and you direct the flow where you want it. So some people use them in addition to their filter systems to provide extra current.

The Least You Need to Know

➤ Filters don't eliminate the need for regular partial water changes.

➤ You need mechanical, biological, and chemical filtration.

➤ For best results, choose undergravel, outside power, canister, or trickle filters.

➤ You may need an air pump or powerheads to drive your filter.

Chapter 6

Hot Picks in Heating Systems

In This Chapter

➤ How to choose the right size heater for your tank

➤ Tips on evaluating common heater features

➤ Ways to prevent broken heater tubes

➤ Learn how your heater's thermostat works

➤ Picking the proper thermometer

Most of the fish we keep in aquariums are tropical fish. That means they come from warm climates. To keep them comfortable and healthy, we need to be sure their aquariums are warm enough. In other words, most of us will need to purchase aquarium heaters for our tanks.

Most tropical fish prefer to be kept at 75° to 78°F (24° to 26°C). But even if you keep cold-water fish, it can be a good idea to have an aquarium heater. It would not be impossible for a winter cold snap to drop temperatures below ideal levels. Even Florida gets freezing weather, sometimes. Further, if the furnace in your house malfunctions, an aquarium heater may be the only salvation for your fish. Aquarium heaters have built-in thermostats which, when properly set, will turn the heater on only when needed. So it should be safe to set the heater and feel secure that it will automatically kick on if required.

To find a good selection of aquarium heaters, you simply need to visit your local pet store. Your dealer will be able to hook you up with the proper size and style of heater to fit your tank and your budget.

Many things can influence your choice of aquarium heaters. Your budget may be the first thing. Aquarium heaters come in quite a range of prices. The hang-on-the-tank versions

Fish and Tips
You may not necessarily need an aquarium heater, for example, if you keep coldwater fish. Goldfish are happiest at 65° to 75°F (19° to 24°C). If the normal temperature of your room won't get too cold for them, you won't need supplemental heat.

are usually cheaper. Fully submersible models will cost more. Like most merchandise, the various brands and models will come with different features. Some features will affect the price.

Clip-On vs. Submersible

Is a submersible heater better than a hang-on-the-tank one? Usually, either style will do the job quite well. However, there are situations where one choice is better than the other. If you are on a limited budget, the hang-on-the-tank heater probably will be your only choice. Submersible heaters have some additional features that you may need or want.

Submersible heaters are fully submersible (of course!). That means you can place the entire heater under water, including parts of the cord. One good thing about this is that you can hide the heater behind some driftwood or rocks and hardly be aware that it is there. Don't hide the pilot light, though. You won't be able to tell if the heater is functioning! Submersible heaters come with suction cups that mount them to the side glass. Both vertical and horizontal mounting are possible.

If you've set up a specialty aquarium that is only partly full, say a tank for turtles or frogs, then submersibles are the best choice. That is because the hang-on-the-tank heaters hang only so far into the tank. If the water level is too low, they will be sticking out of the water and be unable to function. Hang-on-the-tank heaters should only be used where the water level is within an inch or so of the very top of the aquarium.

Fish and Tips
Submersible heaters are more childproof. They put the controls under water and out of reach.

Many submersible heaters are easier to calibrate, having built-in temperature settings for you to choose. However, you calibrate most heaters using a separate thermometer. I'll talk about calibration in detail in Chapter 10 on assembling your aquarium outfit.

Heater Styles

To help you choose between clip-on and submersible, let's look at the many styles available of both types. I'll start with the cheaper models and work up.

Mini-Tank Heater

You may run across dealers selling this small seven-watt submersible heater for tiny tanks. It is only six inches long and has no thermostat. So when you plug it in, it turns on and stays on. It is not a full-fledged automatic heating system. Rather, its purpose is to be a "better than nothing" alternative. However, it could be worse than nothing! Since it doesn't shut off, it could cause a problem. There are situations where it could provide too much heat for the job.

Economy Heater

These are the typical, inexpensive clip-on heaters that come with most aquarium kits. They are best-sellers because they are the cheapest. However, they are not the most dependable. Also, the thermostats are more prone to cause static interference on your radio. Most companies only make these in 25- to 100-watt sizes, and they only mount vertically. Typical prices are probably in the $5 to $10 range.

Deluxe Heater

This hang-on-the-tank heater looks physically very much like an economy heater. However, it has better circuitry or magnetic thermostats, to reduce the possibility of radio interference. It may be available in a larger range of sizes, too. The typical price may be around $20.

Submersible Heater

With this model the controls are encased in rubber, so the heater can go completely under water. The older styles of submersible heaters come with thermostats similar to deluxe heaters. In the last few years, models have become available that have built-in temperature adjustment scales. If you want to keep your tank at 78°F (26°C), you merely dial it with the control knob. Submersibles will usually run $20 and up.

Electronic Heater

These are the top-of-the-line heaters. Unfortunately, you won't find these heaters in many shops because they are fairly expensive—often in the $50 range. Electronic heaters have no moving parts in the thermostat, so they are the most dependable. Often, the thermostat mounts separately from the heater tube, giving more accurate readings. Later in this chapter, I'll talk about how thermostats work.

Heating Cable

Here is an item you probably won't see at all due to the cost—often several hundred dollars. I really only mention it because it is commonly recommended in popular aquarium books that have been translated from German (the Germans like to have very high-tech, expensive equipment). Anyway, you bury heating cables in the gravel. They're said to be particularly good for live-plant tanks, as warming the roots is beneficial.

Watts Hot?

Heaters come in several lengths, typically six inches, eight inches, 10 inches, 12 inches, and 15 inches. With heaters that hang down into the aquarium, be sure not to get a heater that is too long. The heater must usually be at least two inches shorter than the height of your tank. Three or four inches shorter than the tank height is even better. That allows plenty of room for gravel and rocks at the bottom of the tank.

Something's Fishy
Always unplug your heater and give it time to cool before removing it from your tank. Likewise, never plug in your heater before installing it. Aquarium heaters can get red hot! Without water to dissipate that heat, they can start a fire or burn you. If the heater is already hot when you put it in the cooler water, it will shatter.

Follow the same rule for submersible heaters, if you are planning to mount them vertically. If you plan to use a horizontal orientation, though, the length of the tank (rather than the depth) will limit the length of the heater.

You will find that aquarium heaters come in several standard sizes of output. Sizes are based on the number of watts they consume when running. Standard wattages are 25w, 50w, 75w, 100w, 150w, 200w, 250w, and 300w. Please note that all wattages aren't available in all brands. Additionally, anything over 200 watts would be available only in submersible models.

Usually, you can use a simple formula to figure out what size heater you need for your tank. The most commonly quoted rule is that you need five watts per gallon. So, a 25-watt heater would fit a five-gallon tank, a 50-watt model would fit a 10-gallon, and so on. Since larger tanks (those over 50 gallons) are more stable in temperature, many people say that three watts per gallon is a good rule to follow for them.

Still, how much heat you need depends on other things besides the simple volume of your aquarium. If you live where the winters are cold, and particularly if you set your house thermostat low, you will need a more powerful aquarium heater to make up the difference. In warm climates you may rarely need to heat your tank more than five degrees above room temperature, in which case a smaller heater would do.

You see, your heater is not really putting out, say, 78°F of heat. Rather, if the house is 70°F the heater needs to be able to heat that tank 8°F *above room temperature*; if the room is 75°F it only needs to be able to heat the tank 3°F above room temperature. So, to decide what size heater you truly need, you need to know what temperature you desire and what the minimum temperature of your room will be.

It always helps to have a little extra power, though. A bit too much is better than too little. If your heater is more powerful than you need, the only thing that should happen is it will turn itself off quicker. In other words, it will heat faster, not more. The thermostat controls when it comes on and goes off. On the other hand, an undersized heater could kick on and run continuously during cold times without being able to produce enough heat for the job.

The Right Size for the Job

Some recent research produced the following two tables. They give more accurate estimates of appropriate heater sizes. To use the first table, find the size of your tank in the top row. Then follow the column down until you find the number of degrees above room temperature that your tank may need to be heated. (For example, if you want a 78°F temperature and your room temperature is only 65°F, then you need to achieve 13°F of additional heat.) When you find the appropriate figure, look at the wattage in the far left column to determine what size heater you need.

Wattage Needed to Increase Water Temperature Above Room Temperature

Heater Watts	Aquarium Size, in Gallons				
	10	20	29	55	60
50	16°F	12°F	10°F		
75	19°F	17°F	15°F		
100	26°F	22°F	19°F	13°F	12°F
150	24°F	22°F	18°F	18°F	
200	30°F	24°F	20°F		
250	32°F	30°F	27°F		
300	38°F	34°F	29°F		

Table courtesy of Aquarium Systems, Inc., makers of Visitherm aquarium heaters.

There's another way to think about this. To use the next table, find your tank size at the top. Then, read down the column to see what size heater you need, based on the desired increase above room temperature, as listed on the left.

Heater Selection Guide

Desired Increase Above Room Temperature	Aquarium Size, in Gallons							
	5	10	20	25	40	50	65	75
9°F	25w	50w	50w	75w	100w	150w	200w	250w
18°F	25w	50w	75w	100w	150w	200w	250w	300w
27°F	75w	100w	150w	200w	300w	400w	500w	600w

Heaters are listed in watts.
Table courtesy of Aquarium Systems, Inc., makers of Visitherm aquarium heaters.

Heater Elements

The following elements make up most typical aquarium heaters:

➤ *Tank clamp.* Anchors the heater to the side of your tank.

➤ *Control knob or dial.* Turns the adjustment screw, pushing on the bi-metallic strip in the thermostat.

➤ *Tamper-reducing peg.* Not all heaters have this feature. You can find it beneath the control knob or dial on the ones that do. It matches with a tab on the underside of the dial, and prevents you from turning the control more than one full turn at a time. To turn more, remove and reseat the control knob.

➤ *Temperature-control gauge*. Some submersibles have this precalibrated scale. If so, merely dial the temperature you want.

➤ *Moisture seal*. Keeps water away from electric parts.

➤ *Thermostat*. Turns the heater on and off automatically, according to the current temperature in the tank and the desired temperature, as set by the control knob.

➤ *Adjustment screw*. The extension of the control knob.

➤ *Bi-metallic strip*. Made of two types of metal, back to back. Temperature changes make the two metals expand at different rates, causing the strip to bend—which turns the heater on or off.

➤ *Contact point*. When touched by the bi-metallic strip, it closes the circuit, allowing power to reach the heater coil.

➤ *Pilot light*. An orange light that glows when the heater is producing heat.

➤ *Heating coil*. Nickel-chromium wire that heats up when power is applied.

➤ *Glass tube*. Waterproofs the inner workings of the heater.

➤ *Electrical cord and plug*. Come on! I really don't have to tell you what this is for, do I?

The parts of a typical aquarium heater.

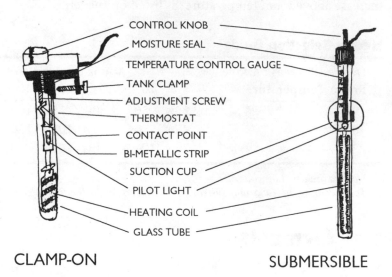

CONTROL KNOB
MOISTURE SEAL
TEMPERATURE CONTROL GAUGE
TANK CLAMP
ADJUSTMENT SCREW
THERMOSTAT
CONTACT POINT
BI-METALLIC STRIP
SUCTION CUP
PILOT LIGHT
HEATING COIL
GLASS TUBE

CLAMP-ON   SUBMERSIBLE

Look at That, a Thermostat

You will better understand what your heater can do if you understand how it works. Aquarium heaters are slightly complicated devices, but they work on very simple principles. Your heater needs to perform two functions. The obvious function is to produce heat. The built-in thermostat handles the less obvious function of deciding when to produce heat.

Your heater produces heat by passing electrical power through a coil of wire that glows red hot when current is applied. Controlling the output is the tricky part. You need your heater to kick on when the water cools, and turn itself off when the water reaches the desired temperature. This is the job of the thermostat. The thermostat works on a very simple principle, but it is a little complicated to explain.

Fish School
A *thermostat* is a device that automatically controls temperature. A *thermometer* is an instrument that measures temperature.

Without the thermostat, your heater would come on when you plug it in (completing an electrical circuit), and never go off again until you unplug it. That's not a workable solution. You can't stand around plugging and unplugging your heater all day. Enter the thermostat. The thermostat replaces part of the electrical circuit with a couple of simple parts. One part is a stationary contact. The other part is usually a bi-metallic strip.

The Bi-Metallic Strip

The bi-metallic strip is made of two different kinds of metal sandwiched together. You may remember from physics class that metals expand and contract with changes in temperature, and different metals expand and contract at different rates. That is exactly what happens with the bi-metallic strip. Since one side of it expands and contracts at a different rate than the other, as the temperature changes the strip bends.

In your heater, when the bi-metallic strip gets cooler, it bends toward the stationary contact. When the bi-metallic strip touches the stationary contact, it completes the circuit. This allows current to pass to the heater coil—producing heat. When the strip gets warm again, it will bend away and separate from the stationary contact. This disconnects the circuit and turns off the heater. When the tank cools down a couple of degrees, the bi-metallic strip will expand and turn the heater on again. It is all automatic.

A couple of options to this process determine the quality of your heater. Better heaters will have a small magnet on the bi-metallic strip and the stationary contact. As the contacts get close together, the magnetic action takes over and snaps them together instantly. When the heater turns off and they separate, they separate quickly, too.

You may wonder what the big deal is about that. The big deal is that as the two contacts approach each other, a spark can occur as the circuit completes. If the circuit closes slowly, more sparking occurs, and this causes carbon to build up on the contacts. Eventually this insulates them too much to function. The other thing that happens is that the sparking may go on for several seconds, and it produces static that can interfere with your favorite radio program. So magnetic contacts are better than non-magnetic ones.

Electronic Heaters

Electronic heaters are even better. They eliminate the bi-metallic strip and stationary contacts completely. Instead, they have electronics inside that turn the circuit on or off.

Also, they usually have a thermostatic sensor that mounts in a separate tube, away from the heater coil. Or the thermostat may read the temperature from a special sensor mounted directly on the heater's glass tube (as opposed to the bi-metallic strip, which monitors the air inside the heater, not the water). Since glass conducts heat well, this method gets a more accurate measurement of true water temperature.

The other nice thing about an electronic heater is that it stays on until it reaches the desired temperature, then kicks off. It's all one step. Since bi-metallic-strip thermostats read air temperature inside the heater instead of true water temperature, heating becomes a staged operation. That is, the heater kicks on and the air inside gets very hot. So the heater turns off before the water is quite warm enough. The air inside cools a bit and the heater kicks on and heats some more. This process repeats a few times for each heating cycle. That is why you will often see the pilot light in some heaters flicking on and off a lot, rather than staying on for a couple of minutes and then staying off for a while.

Fish and Tips
An aquarium heater cannot function properly if there is no water circulating past it to distribute the heat. Your tank must have aeration or filtration for the heater to work. Without circulation, the water next to the heater will be heated, and the thermostat will sense this and shut off before the rest of the tank gets heat, too.

Preventing Breakage

Aquarium heaters are electrical parts sealed within a glass tube. As you know, water and electricity don't mix safely. It is always wise to take steps to be sure you don't break your aquarium heater. First, *never* take the heater out of the water or put it into water when it's plugged in. Heaters get red hot when they are on. You can get burned. You can start a fire. Also, if you take a hot heater and put it into cold water, you will crack the glass on the heater tube, getting water inside, and potentially causing a shock to you or your fish.

Fish and Tips
When you use suction cups to mount your aquarium heater, be sure not to position the cups over the heating coils. The suction cups are plastic, and will melt.

The other step you need to take will help prevent accidents based on some of the dumb things your fish might do. Many large fish are very good at abusing aquarium heaters. They can bang them against the glass. They can slap them with their tails. I've even known fish that got so severely ticked off at the heater's pilot light blinking at them that they decided to give it a good bite!

To help prevent your fish from breaking the heater, I highly recommend that you install it with suction cups. These will anchor it firmly to the side of the tank, so that it can't get smacked up against the glass. Submersible heaters normally come with suction cups, but the hang-on-the-tank heaters don't. You should buy optional suction cups for those.

Shopping for Thermometers

Every aquarium must have a thermometer. There are no exceptions. How else are you going to know the temperature of your tank? Even if you have a heater with a temperature control gauge, without a thermometer you will have no way to tell if the heater if functioning properly.

Your dealer sells several varieties of thermometers. All are quite inexpensive. Here are some typical types:

➤ *Floating thermometer.* This is a glass thermometer that floats. If you press it into a front corner of your tank, it will stay there for easy reading. Otherwise, the water current will carry it where it may, and you'll have trouble finding and reading it.

➤ *Standing thermometer.* This is like a floating thermometer, but with extra weight at one end. It sinks to the bottom. You could just drop it in the tank, but I prefer to wedge it in the gravel. Otherwise, the fish tend to knock it around, and it always seems to end up facing backwards in some far corner when you want to see it.

➤ *Stainless steel thermometer.* This is a glass thermometer attached to a metal bracket that hangs over the edge of your tank. I don't much like these, because the hanger interferes with the proper nesting of your glass canopy or full hood on top of the tank.

➤ *Liquid crystal thermometer.* You can find this in many shapes, styles, and temperature ranges. It is absolutely the most accurate and easiest to read. It is inexpensive, too. You may note that every liquid crystal thermometer on the peg hook gives the same reading, while the cheaper glass thermometers vary by several degrees. A liquid crystal thermometer mounts on the outside glass. The one disadvantage is that you really should not move it, once installed. So it isn't much use for testing the temperature of a bucket of water that you've drawn for your water change.

➤ *Thermometer-hydrometer combination.* A hydrometer measures the specific gravity of the water. It looks like an extra large floating glass thermometer, and may include a thermometer inside. It

Something's Fishy
Floating, standing, and stainless steel thermometers are often quite inaccurate. I've seen a 10-degree range in the temperature reading of thermometers hanging on the same peg hook. Also, check to be sure that the line of red indicator liquid inside has no bubbles. That will ruin the accuracy.

Fish and Tips
Liquid crystal thermometers are the most accurate and easiest to read. They come in various styles, but my favorite is the horizontal strip version. I like to mount it on the front of the tank, just below the gravel line. It gives a good, accurate reading there, without obstructing my view of the fish.

has a long thin neck that sticks out of the water. Where the waterline falls on the neck determines the reading. However, you really don't want this item. It is for mixing up seawater, and is of very little use to the typical freshwater aquarist. Since a hydrometer sticks several inches out of the water, it breaks easily when you close the top on it. So forget about buying a hydrometer.

The Least You Need to Know

➤ Choose the proper size heater. A typical rule is five watts per gallon for small tanks, and three watts per gallon for tanks over 50 gallons.

➤ Don't buy a heater that is too long to fit your tank.

➤ Use suction cups to anchor your heater to the side of the tank.

➤ Never install or remove a heater that is plugged in.

➤ Liquid crystal thermometers are the best choice.

Chapter 7

TAN-O-MATIC

SPF 15

Brilliant Choices in Lighting Systems

In This Chapter

➤ Determine your lighting needs

➤ Learn about incandescent and fluorescent lighting

➤ Explore the color spectrum

➤ Examine the relative advantages of glass canopies and full-hoods

➤ Find out how little electricity you will use

When my editor hired me for this job, she told me to be sure to include a "little light humor." Unfortunately, I can't think of a single joke about aquarium light bulbs! (Rest assured that I just gave myself 30 lashes with a wet eel for that pun.)

Light is very important to your aquarium. Obviously, the primary advantage of having a light on your tank is that it helps you to see the fish. It serves other functions, too. If you have live plants, they need light to sustain themselves. Fish need light, too. Light helps them see and find food. It also helps them to see you coming with the fish food can. It helps them find partners for spawning, or spot predators that are nearby.

Light has some less obvious purposes, too. Regulating circadian rhythm is a primary one—circadian rhythm is the day-night cycle that is regulated by an animal's inner biological clock. Lighting cycles help a fish decide when it is time to eat or rest, and when to breed. Some fish spawn at daybreak, some at night, and so forth. The length of the lighted day, the indoor equivalent of seasons, also affects breeding and other fish behavior.

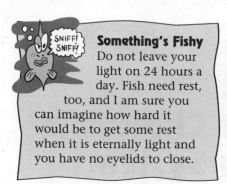

Something's Fishy
Do not leave your light on 24 hours a day. Fish need rest, too, and I am sure you can imagine how hard it would be to get some rest when it is eternally light and you have no eyelids to close.

Sometimes light has some unexpected effects. The typical silver angelfish is a silver fish with vertical black stripes. A dusky angelfish is a solid grayish silver, with no stripes at all. You may think these are two different varieties of fish, bred for their different appearance, but you'd be wrong. They are the same fish! The colors were determined after birth. The striped fish is one that was raised with a normal day-night cycle. The solid colored fish was raised in 24 hours of light. So you can see that light, or the lack of it, may have a substantial effect on the development of young fish.

How Much Light Is Right?

In earlier chapters, I told you some things that would help you decide what kind of tank you want. Particularly, you need to know whether you plan to keep live plants, you want to be limited to the hardier species, and your tank is going to be tall or shallow. All these things will be factors in deciding how much light you will need on your tank.

Obviously, a tank with plastic plants can prosper with a lot less light than a tank with live plants, because the plastic plants don't need light to live and grow. In fact, if you are going to use plastic plants only, you don't want strong light because it will tend to cause algae problems for you.

Some species of live plants, particularly the red ones, need a lot more light to prosper. If you want to get lush plant growth with all species and have more choices of species that you can successfully keep, then you need more light.

Fish Tales

A principle of science states that light decreases with the square of the distance. In layman's terms, this means that if one aquarium is twice as tall as the other, it will take four times as much light to illuminate its bottom equally. The taller the tank, the more light required to grow plants well.

So, how much light is right? Well, if you are not going the live plant route, then the typical full-hood or single strip light will provide enough lighting for you to see the fish and enjoy the tank. However, if you want lush plant growth, that will not be enough.

To do well with plants, a common recommendation is to have two to five watts of full spectrum lighting per gallon of aquarium water. Since I have devoted all of Chapter 22 to planted aquariums, I will save the detailed discussion of the lighting requirements of plants until then (I'll bet you can't wait!). For now, keep in mind that the typical full-hood or strip light is only going to provide about one watt of light per gallon. That is less than half what is necessary to achieve acceptable plant growth, and much less than what you need for lush growth.

Bright Choices in Light Bulbs

Before discussing the various types of lighting equipment your dealer may have available, I want to talk a bit about the bulbs themselves. The light unit that you purchase will house the bulbs, but the bulbs produce the light. It can be difficult choosing, because there is a large array of styles varying in color, intensity, and consumption of electricity.

> **Fish and Tips**
> You can buy inexpensive automatic timers to turn your aquarium's light on and off at the same time every day.

Incandescent Bulbs

These are the bulbs with a screw-in base that fit standard household sockets. The major difference in the aquarium version is the shape. They are elongated, rather than bulbous. Think banana, not pear. Showcase bulb is another name for this shape of incandescent lamp. Incandescent bulbs are falling out of style in aquarium setups, and are only available for the smaller tanks.

Incandescent bulbs work by passing current through a wire suspended in a vacuum. The wire glows, giving off light and heat. Most incandescent bulbs put out a white light, with a slightly yellowish cast. There are Gro-Lux style incandescent bulbs that are designed to be better for plant growth. The bulb looks bluish when turned off, but gives off white light with a pinkish cast when lit. I like these better than the standard clear incandescent bulbs, because they show the colors of the fish a bit better. Red fish look red under this bulb, whereas they look a bit more orange under the clear bulb. Do not buy colored bulbs (red, yellow, green, blue, pink). They are detrimental to the health of your tank.

> **Something's Fishy**
> Colored incandescent bulbs (red, blue, green, yellow, pink) are sometimes sold in pet stores. Do not buy these bulbs! White light is much better. Colored light has been shown to be harmful to fish and other organisms. Besides, why buy fish with beautiful colors and then put a bulb over them that will remove most of the colors?

Typical sizes for incandescent bulbs are 15-watt for 10-gallon tanks and smaller, and 25-watt for larger units. Occasionally, you will see 40-watt bulbs available, but be careful using them—the added heat output may melt the plastic housing of your light unit.

Fluorescent Bulbs

These bulbs are similar to ceiling lights that you see in commercial establishments. They are composed of a long tube with pins at each end.

When electricity is applied to fluorescent bulbs, internal coatings are excited by the electrons and fluoresce—giving the fluorescent bulb its name. Interestingly, since alternating current (AC) works by reversing the positive and negative poles 60 times a second, fluorescent lights don't actually put out steady light. Instead, they flash 60 times per second. This is too fast for your eye to catch, though, and so the output appears steady. The color output of the bulb will depend on the type of phosphor coatings used inside.

The high-frequency power needed to run a fluorescent bulb is generated inside a black box called a ballast. Usually you will be unaware of the ballast, because most manufacturers mount it inside the light unit, out of sight. However, some models have the ballast attached to the electrical cord.

Fluorescent bulbs come in standard lengths and wattages. The diameters of the bulbs do vary a bit, with 1-inch diameter and 1.5-inch diameter bulbs being the norm. Don't concern yourself with the diameter of the bulb, though. They are interchangeable. Just make sure you get the right length and wattage. Particularly, pay attention to the wattage, because all bulbs of the same wattage will be the same length.

However, not all bulbs of the same length will be of the same wattage. Here's why. There are three styles of fluorescent bulbs—SO, HO, and VHO—each using different types of ballasts and having output in different intensities. Normally, you will be dealing with standard output (SO) fluorescent bulbs. Strip lights and full-hoods normally have SO fluorescent bulbs in them.

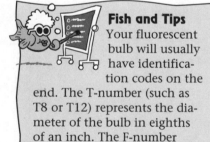

Fish and Tips
Your fluorescent bulb will usually have identification codes on the end. The T-number (such as T8 or T12) represents the diameter of the bulb in eighths of an inch. The F-number (such as F15 or F20) represents the wattage of the bulb.

Occasionally, especially in some high-end setups, you may run into some light units that have high output (HO) or very high output (VHO) fluorescent bulbs and ballasts. These bulbs put out two to three times the light of an SO fluorescent bulb. While SO, HO, and VHO bulbs all come in standard lengths of 12, 15, 18, 24, 36, 48, and 72 inches, the bulbs should not be interchanged. Do not try to put an SO bulb in a VHO fixture, for example. You will ruin your bulb.

Fluorescent lighting is a very cost-effective way to light your aquarium. It gives a bright, even flood of light, and uses little electricity. Fluorescent bulbs come in many spectra, but I'll discuss that shortly.

Compact Fluorescent Bulbs

These lights work on the same principle as the fluorescent tubes I just described. However, the bulb has a U-shape and higher output. You can fit more light into a smaller space with compact fluorescents, but they cost more than standard fluorescents. They put out light with an intensity similar to that of VHO tubes, but are cooler and more energy efficient. This style of lighting is becoming more popular in deluxe setups.

Metal Halide Bulbs

Shaped much like a household bulb, but larger and with a larger screw-in base, these bulbs are popular where high output is desired. Mostly used by saltwater enthusiasts for the corals in their reef tanks, these bulbs are also popular with those who want a lushly planted freshwater aquarium.

Metal halide bulbs usually come in 150w, 175w, 250w, and 400w sizes. They come in slightly different colors, rated on the Kelvin scale. The Kelvin scale is a method of describing color, based on the changes of color that occur "when an imaginary black body is heated." Anyway, degrees Kelvin is the rating system and you will typically see numbers such as 5500°K, 6500°K, 10,000°K, and 20,000°K. Bulbs on the lower end of that list tend to be more yellow, while those on the higher end are more blue. Consider all to be white light, though.

One interesting feature of metal halide lights is that, since they are a single point light source (as opposed to every point on a fluorescent tube generating light), they can produce an interesting ripple effect. You know how moving water scatters sunlight, making it dance all over the bottom? Metal halides will do that, too. That is, if the water surface is moving. It won't work in still water. Anyway, it is an interesting, relaxing, and more natural effect.

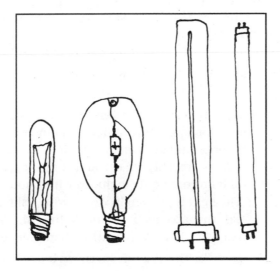

Common light bulbs (from the left): incandescent, metal halide, compact fluorescent, and fluorescent.

A Spectrum of Lighting Choices

Lights come in all colors, but your aquarium will look its best and your fish will stay healthiest under white light. You probably remember from science class that white light is composed of all the colors of the rainbow mixed together. White light is composed of the entire *visible* spectrum of light.

71

Sunlight is also composed of all the colors of the rainbow, but also thrown in are colors that are invisible to you and me—infrared (IR) and ultraviolet (UV) wavelengths. Infrared light is heat, and all light bulbs produce heat, but most don't produce ultraviolet wavelengths in any appreciable amounts. This is probably a good thing, because some types of UV light cause sunburns.

However, some ultraviolet light can be helpful. Many ani-mals require it to manufacture their own vitamin D. Humans are such animals. Anyway, light bulbs that give off the full spectrum of visible light, plus small amounts
of UV light, are called "full spectrum" lights. These cost a bit more, but generally produce lighting that is more plea-sing to the eye and more healthy for the fish and plants.

Something's Fishy
People sometimes request pure ultraviolet lights (black lights) for their aquariums, in an attempt to get Day-Glo colors. Don't do it! They won't give the effect you expect, and are unhealthy when not balanced with white light. *Worse*, the types of ultraviolet bulbs sold in aquarium stores are likely to be replacements for ultraviolet sterilization units. Incorrectly used, *these bulbs can permanently blind you!* Their purpose is to kill organisms.

Fish and Tips
Even though fluorescent bulbs from the hardware store will fit your aquarium's light fixtures, you should buy bulbs from a pet store. The bulbs sold in hardware stores will be of a different spectrum, and may cause algae problems for you.

Light bulbs are available in a wide array of spectra. By tweaking the mix of inner phosphors, the manufacturers are able to achieve varying effects in color output for special purposes. Though I've avoided using brand names in this book, I could not find an easy way to describe the spectra of various bulbs without making it so general as to become confusing. So, I am going to present you with a list of bulbs that are available from one popular manufacturer. There are many equivalent brands out there, but this one probably has the widest distribution. You probably won't have trouble finding these, but don't feel that I am recommending this brand above all others. And, don't worry—I wouldn't list them at all if they weren't good bulbs.

The following fluorescent light tubes, from Rolf C. Hagen Corp., are available in most pet stores:

➤ *Aqua-Glo.* This is the version of the Gro-Lux bulb sold for aquariums. When you buy inexpensive fluorescent lamps at an aquarium store, this type of bulb is probably what you will get. It is also the style of bulb commonly included with fluorescent hoods. The light is pleasingly white, with a slightly pinkish cast that accents the colors of the fish. Particularly, red fish will look red, rather than orange.

➤ *Sun-Glo.* This is a full-spectrum bulb. The light is white, but with a slight greenish tint that makes plants look superb. It's the color of sunlight on a warm day. Red fish look slightly orange under it, though.

➤ *Power-Glo.* This bulb has a higher intensity than most fluorescent bulbs, but it is not HO or VHO. Some extra blue is mixed into the spectrum, making it good for saltwater corals and freshwater plants. A nice, bright white light.

➤ *Life-Glo.* Similar to the Power-Glo bulb, but it has an internal reflector that directs the light downward, increasing the intensity of light delivered to your tank.

➤ *Marine-Glo.* A bluish, near-UV bulb, great for saltwater corals and helpful for some freshwater plants. However, this bulb should be used in combination with other bulbs for best results.

➤ *Flora-Glo.* A good bulb for many types of plants. I have had some cryptocorynes really take off under this bulb. It has an orangish cast to it, though, so you may want to mix it with other bulbs to make the light more pleasing to the eye.

Something's Fishy
Some stores sell colored plastic sleeves that fit over fluorescent tubes, altering the color. Avoid these! White light is much better for your fish. Also, the sleeves will make your tank much darker, because they work by reducing the light. For example, a red sleeve doesn't change all the light to red. Instead, it absorbs the yellow and blue light, letting only the remaining red pass through.

Got Your Tank Covered?

Now that I've talked about the bulbs, let's discuss the light fixtures themselves. Most light fixtures also act as covers for your tank. Covering the tank is important for several reasons:

➤ It reduces evaporation. Less refilling of the tank will be required. Replacing evaporation is not a substitute for making a partial water change, though!

➤ A cover keeps the fish from jumping out onto the floor. It also helps keep crabs and frogs from climbing out.

➤ Your aquarium's top will help keep the kids and the cats out of the tank.

If, for some reason, you don't feel the need for a light, or perhaps can't afford it now, you may buy a glass canopy or plastic cover alone to at least keep the fish from jumping out.

Let There Be Light

There are many ways to provide light for your aquarium. The range of light fixture styles and prices is quite wide, ranging from inexpensive full-hoods to metal-halide pendant lamps that may cost several hundred dollars. Typically, the lighting system will be the most expensive piece of equipment for your aquarium.

Full-Hoods

A full-hood is the most popular choice for covering and lighting your aquarium. It consists of a plastic chassis that has three basic sections:

1. A lid in front to access the tank

2. A glass section in the middle to protect the light strip from water damage

3. Either punch-outs or a soft plastic strip at the rear of the hood, to allow for custom openings for installing heaters, filters, and air lines

Fish and Tips
When you buy a fluorescent full-hood, the bulb is included in the price. With incandescent hoods, the bulbs are purchased separately.

A strip light is included, and fits on top of the full-hood's chassis. There are two types of chassis. In one type (often called *deluxe*), there are pegs on the underside that you snap off to make the hood nest perfectly on your brand of aquarium. There are also *recessed* versions of hoods. Rather than resting on top the frame, they nest down inside, on the inner lip. The one disadvantage to these is that not all aquarium frames have the same size inner lip, if any at all. So while the deluxe hoods should fit any brand of tank, the recessed hoods may not.

All sizes of full-hoods are available with fluorescent lights, with larger ones possibly having several rows of bulbs. Sizes under 30 inches, generally 29-gallon tanks and below, are also available in incandescent styles.

Personally, I think among the choices to cover and light your aquarium, full-hoods have the nicest appearance. However, they make it difficult or impossible to add additional lights for live plants.

A full-hood light. (Courtesy All-Glass Aquarium Company)

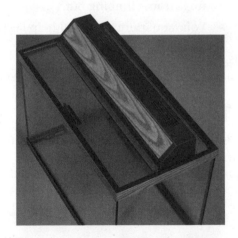

A glass canopy with a strip light. (Courtesy All-Glass Aquarium Company)

Strip Lights and Glass Canopies

The glass canopy functions similarly to the chassis on the full-hood. Except for the adjustable back plastic strip, the entire cover is glass, with a hinged glass panel creating a lid in front. Strip lights, which are the long plastic housing containing the light unit, sit on top of the glass canopy. If you thought strip lights were mood lights for exotic dancers, then I'm sorry I got your hopes up. Most strip lights are fluorescent models, but a few small sizes of incandescent strip lights are available.

While I believe the full-hood has a neater and more decorative appearance than the glass canopy-strip light combo, I've come to prefer the latter. Why? Because it is more versatile. My favorite style of aquarium is a heavily planted one. To do it right, you need lots of light. The glass canopy allows me to easily put multiple strip lights on top to provide extra light. Full-hoods greatly restrict the capability to add more light.

If you want to keep a heavily planted tank, or if you think you may eventually want to convert, it would behoove you to go with the glass canopy and strip light now. It will be cheaper to add light later. With the hood, you would have to scrap the chassis and replace it with a glass canopy before you could add more light strips. You would, of course, be able to keep and reuse the light strip from your hood.

> **Fish and Tips**
> Fluorescent full-hoods are a better choice. While they will cost a bit more than incandescent fixtures initially, fluorescent fixtures are more cost-efficient in the long run. Fluorescent lights give off a brighter, more even flood of light than incandescents. They use much less electricity, and the bulbs last longer.

Compact Fluorescents

With intense output and low energy consumption, these units do a very good job. Typically, bulbs are available in white (5000°K and 6500°K), and blue (7100°K). The blue bulbs are normally used for the corals in saltwater reef tanks, but some benefit may be obtained by mixing them with white lights for planted freshwater tanks.

Compact fluorescent fixtures come two ways. One way is as an upgrade kit. That is, you get the ballast and wiring along with a polished aluminum reflector with the bulbs mounted on it. You use small screws to mount the reflector and bulbs inside the decorative wooden canopy (purchased separately) that sits on top of your tank. Fluorescent compacts also may be purchased pre-installed in decorative wooden or metal canopies that you set on top of the tank or hang above it.

Enhancing the Light

If you want to increase the output of your existing fixtures, there are ways to do so without buying new ones. Many stores carry polished aluminum reflectors that fit behind the bulb in your light unit. These take light that normally comes out the sides and top of the bulb, and direct it down toward the tank. It is not as good as adding another light, but it is an improvement.

Also, some fluorescent bulbs come with either internal or external reflective coatings on the bulb's top half. This directs more light downward. You may want to consider replacing your bulb with one of these.

Electrical Consumption

Finally, all this talk of high wattage makes this a good place to dispel a myth. The typical aquarium will have no noticeable effect on your electric bill. In most areas of the country, a 10-gallon aquarium will increase your electric bill by less than $1 per month. Larger tanks aren't much different. Your heater probably will be the item to pull the most juice at any one time, but it will almost always be off.

Electrical Consumption of a 10-Gallon Tank With a Fluorescent Full-Hood

Equipment	Watts	× Hours Per Day	= Watts Per Day
Air pump and undergravel filter	2.5	24.0	60
Light bulb(s)	15.0	12.0	180
Heater	50.0	.5	25
		Total watts per day	265
		× Days per month	30
		Total watts per month	7,950
		÷ Watts per kilowatt hour	1,000
		Total kilowatt hours per month	7.95
		× Cost per kilowatt hour	$.10
		Total extra cost per month	**$0.79**

The Least You Need to Know

➤ Planted tanks and tall tanks require more light.

➤ Keep your tank covered to reduce evaporation, to keep the fish from jumping out, and to keep out small hands and paws.

➤ Full-hoods look a bit nicer, but glass canopies and strip lights are more versatile.

➤ Fluorescent bulbs give more light for the money than incandescent bulbs.

➤ Choose a bulb that provides the best color spectrum for the job.

➤ Turn off your light at night!

➤ Most aquariums will not drive up your electric bill.

Chapter 8

Interior Decoration for Aquariums

In This Chapter

➤ Choose your substrate

➤ Decide on a background

➤ Select rocks and driftwood

➤ Pick your plants

➤ Find fun ornaments

The fish for sale at your dealer's shop probably are kept in relatively bare aquariums. The dealer's tanks will be filled with fish, but may contain few, or no, plants or other decorations. Don't let this lead you into thinking that a bare aquarium is the way your tank should be. Your dealer may keep the tanks bare because it makes it easier for him to catch fish, and continuous netting of fish can damage the plants.

Your tank should be decorated. Your fish need places to hide and places to rest. Mainly though, you will find that a decorated tank is so much more pleasing to view. You can add natural plants, rocks, driftwood, and even some plastic or ceramic ornaments, if it suits your taste. This is your tank, so you get to be the interior decorator. Be creative and have fun with it.

Gravel: Let's Get to the Bottom of It

The first decoration to go into your tank will be the aquarium gravel. You will find that your dealer carries gravel in a wide array of colors, of varying pebble size. Your first impulse will be to pick your favorite color, or perhaps a color that you think best matches the room. However, that may not be the best way to go.

Fish School
Natural gravel is gravel without artificial coloring. Several stone colors are available. *Colored gravel* is natural gravel that has had colored coatings added, resulting in every color of the rainbow. *Clown vomit* is a term my friend Bob Lewis coined to describe those multicolored gravel mixes you find in the stores!

Once you install your plants and other decorations, the gravel may not be that noticeable. So the appeal of the color, or the way it matches your room, may not even be important. Before choosing a color that you like most, you also should consider how well your fish will like the colors. After all, they are the ones who will really be living with it.

One way that Mother Nature protects fish from predators is by darkening or fading their colors to better match their surroundings. A camouflaged fish is less likely to be spotted and eaten by another. So you will find that dark colored gravel and backgrounds will tend to bring out darker colors in your fish, while lighter colored gravel and backgrounds will cause your fish to fade.

Most fish will look better in tanks with dark gravel. I find that black, dark blue, dark green, and dark natural gravels tend to show fish pretty well. White, yellow, pink, and lighter natural gravels may cause the fishes' colors to fade. How much they fade will depend on the species and how many other decorations (plants, rocks, backgrounds, and so forth) are dark colored.

You also need to choose the size of the stones in your gravel mix. Particle sizes ranging from sand to two-inch pebbles can be found in stores. Most aquarium gravel, though, will be in the one-eighth inch to one-half inch diameter size.

One-eighth to one-quarter-inch stones are best. If the particles are too small, they can compact and make it difficult for plants to grow. Small sand-sized particles also can sift through the slots in an undergravel filter plate, if you have one, and clog it up. If the pebbles are too large, then the space between them also becomes larger. This means food can fall down between the stones, where it is out of reach of the fish, and can pollute the tank. If the spaces are large enough, small fish could even get stuck.

Fish and Tips
Small-size gravel is better than larger pebbles, but you can also mix them for pleasing effects. One thing you'll find is that, as the gravel settles, the smaller stones sink to the bottom and the larger ones rise to the top. When you use your gravel vacuum, they will be remixed.

Another reason not to pick pebbles of too large a size is that pebble size affects your biological filtration. Smaller stones have more surface area per pound, providing more space to grow helpful bacteria. To illustrate this, think of an apple as representing a large stone. You have a certain amount of surface area, as represented by the red skin of the apple. Now, if you take that apple and cut it in half, you will still have the original surface area *plus* the additional surface area of the two white faces that the cut created.

Gravel in Depth

How much gravel will you need? Well, that depends. You can get away with less gravel, if you just want to cover the bottom. However, if you want to have enough to root your plants, or allow the fish to dig a little without exposing the glass bottom, or to make an undergravel filter function properly, then you should create a layer of gravel that is one and a half to two inches deep. Serious aquatic plant enthusiasts go even deeper, putting of three to six inches of gravel in their tanks.

Gravel is usually sold in five-pound, 25-pound, or 50-pound bags. It can be difficult to determine how many pounds of gravel will be right for your tank. There are many general rules that you can follow to take a guess:

➤ One rule is that you should buy one pound of gravel per gallon. I don't like this guideline. You will find that this will give you enough gravel to cover the bottom of the tank, but not enough to make live plants really happy. It may not even give enough to hide the plastic shoe of plastic plants. It definitely is not enough to run an undergravel filter properly.

➤ Another similar rule would recommend one and a half pounds of gravel per gallon. I think this is a better guideline, but may provide a little more than you need—although, if you want to do any terracing in your tank it may work out quite nicely.

➤ An even better rule is to use at least 10 pounds per square foot of bottom. This is a better guideline, because it considers the actual space that you need to fill. There are three standard sizes of 20-gallon tanks on the market, and they have bottoms that are 2.0, 2.5, and 1.4 square feet, respectively. You can see that using a pounds-per-gallon rule to choose your gravel will give quite different results for each of these 20-gallon tanks.

The table on the next page shows how much gravel I recommend for typical sizes of aquariums to achieve a depth of one and a half to two inches. If I list a range, the first number fits the 10-pounds-per-square-foot rule, and the second number is the amount I prefer to recommend—because I feel that the higher number gives an effect more pleasing to the eye. (Some tanks have deeper frames, so the gravel appears to be more shallow. The higher amount of gravel counteracts that.)

Behind the Scenes With Backgrounds

Your aquarium will look best if you install some kind of background. Without a background, the wall behind the tank will show through. Since walls are commonly white or other light colors, they tend to make the fish fade. Many types of backgrounds can be found at your aquarium store, including presized ones and designs cut from a roll. Most are made to be attached outside the tank, but some are designed to go inside the tank.

Gravel Recommendations

Tank Size (in Gallons)	Tank Footprint (in Inches)	Gravel Needed (in Pounds)
5.5	16 × 8	10
10	20 × 10	15
15	24 × 12	20–25
20XH	20 × 10	15
20H	24 × 12	20–25
20L	30 × 12	25–30
29	30 × 12	25–30
30	36 × 12	30–40
40	48 × 13	45–60
50	36 × 18	45–60
55	48 × 13	45–60
70	48 × 18	60–75
75	48 × 18	60–75
90	48 × 18	60–75
100	72 × 18	100–150
125	72 × 18	100–150
135	72 × 18	100–150

Precut Scenes

These are presized backgrounds, designed to fit specific sizes of aquariums. You merely tape them on the back of your tank.

Scenes on a Roll

The most popular choices, scenes on a roll sell by the inch or the foot. Your dealer will help you pick a size that is wide enough to fit your tank, and he will cut off enough to fit the length of your tank. You may need to trim some off the top or bottom of the background to get an exact fit. To install, tape the background on the back of your aquarium. Many of these backgrounds on a roll come double-sided. That is, they may have a solid color or a second scene on the back, enabling you to flip the background over if you want a change in scenery.

3-D Backgrounds

There are several styles that fall into this category. The older styles have imprinted scenes on lightweight vacu-formed plastic sheets. They attach to the outside back of the tank.

There are also some fancier (and more pricey) styles of backgrounds made of solid plastic or other resins, and formed into three-dimensional shapes such as rockscapes or tree bark. These backgrounds go inside the tank. They may come with suction cups for mounting, or you may stick them on with some dabs of silicone aquarium cement. You can also just prop them against the back.

Mirrored Backgrounds

Some aquariums have a mirror built right into the back. This gives the illusion of added depth to a tank. If your tank has a mirror back, you will be limited to that choice because it is not removable. For everyone else, you can buy reflective mirror backgrounds that tape to the back of your tank. They come in standard silver and colors.

Self-Sticking Backgrounds

One popular background comes in solid colors, and you cut it to custom fit your tank. Since it is self-adhesive, you can peel the protective layer and apply it directly. However, it is very difficult to do so without trapping air and causing bubbles. A better way is to apply it like window film. To apply, first take a cup of water and put a couple of drops of dishwashing soap in it. **Do not** *get soap into your tank! It is deadly to fish.* Wet the *outside* back of the tank with this solution. Then, remove the protective backing from the self-sticking background and position it on the wetted back of the tank. Use a credit card or other flat object to squeegee out the bubbles. The resulting finish looks like it was painted on.

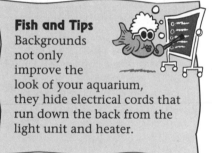

Fish and Tips
If you buy any kind of 3-D background, be sure to consider if it will interfere with the positioning of filter tubes, heaters, and other items. Many of these backgrounds are quite attractive, but the manufacturers didn't really stop to think about how they might co-exist with other objects in the tank.

Fish and Tips
Backgrounds not only improve the look of your aquarium, they hide electrical cords that run down the back from the light unit and heater.

Painted Backgrounds

Speaking of looking painted on, many people actually do paint the back of their tanks. Oil-based paint works best. Latex paints may peel if they get wet. A painted finish is very attractive, but less versatile. If you want to change to a different background, you must scrape off the old paint with razor blades or use a commercial paint-removing compound.

Diorama

A diorama is a 3-D display. Instead of mounting a background directly on the tank, you can build a little display *behind* the tank. Plastic plants, rocks, driftwood, and so forth are arranged behind the aquarium, with a background of some type behind that. It gives an added illusion of depth. You also can do some very novel things with this method. I have heard of people building glass cages and putting birds behind their tank, so that it looks like birds are flitting through the water!

Solid Information About Rocks

A large rock can make a great centerpiece for your tank. Rocks are super as stand-alone decorations, or you can use them to build ledges and terraces. African cichlid fanatics build huge rock piles in their tanks to provide lots of spaces for their fish to dart in and out. Be they large rough-hewn stones or smooth water-worn pebbles, rocks play an important part in most habitats.

The planned decor of your tank will influence what kind of rocks you want. If you want a river-bed look, scattering large, smooth pebbles and rocks can add to the effect. Narrow flat rocks, such as pieces of slate and shale, are great choices for building ledges, retaining walls, and caves. You can even buy rocks that have large holes drilled in them for the fish to swim through.

Some rocks may affect the pH and hardness of your tank water, so you do need to be careful what you pick. Any calcareous (limestone based) rock is going to have that kind of effect. So avoid limestone, marble, tufa, and others. That is, unless you want something to help raise your pH.

Your dealer probably will carry many varieties of decorative rocks from all over the world. You will find all colors of the rainbow, including one called rainbow rock that has red and white rainbow stripes running through it. You'll find red and black lava, green and pink quartz, red or gray slate, purple jasper, and chunks of colored glass. I wish I could give you a complete list of rocks that are suitable, but if you think that common names of fish are confusing, rocks are even worse! The ones that I've mentioned are typical, but many rocks go by several names.

You also can collect your own rocks. Be careful, though. Besides making sure that you don't pick rocks that will affect the hardness and pH of your water, local rocks also may be soaked with fertilizers and pesticides. They also may contain high concentrations of heavy metals or other compounds that are harmful to fish. So don't do this unless you know what you are doing. Various types of quartz and granite are normally safe. Make sure you thoroughly wash, rinse, and soak them before they go in your tank.

Fish and Tips
When stacking rocks, try to put the bottom rock directly on the bottom of the tank or on top of the undergravel filter plate. Do not put the bottom rock on top of the gravel. If you do, fish digging beneath the rock, or even simple settling of the gravel, can cause the rocks to shift, and fall against the glass and break it.

Fish and Tips
How many decorations do you need? Everyone has different taste, but I like to cover approximately two-thirds of the bottom with plants, rocks, and driftwood. The remaining open area allows plenty of room for swimming.

Picking Plants

Whether live or plastic, plants provide hiding places, shade, breeding spots, territories, and beauty. Live plants also may provide oxygen and a source of food. Live plants compete with algae, too. I much prefer live plants to plastic ones. Since you'll find the complete lowdown on popular species of plants and how to keep them in Chapter 22, I will limit my discussion of live plants in this section.

At this point, let me simply lament the fact that most dealers keep a very small selection of live plants, and some of those may not even be true aquatics. It's shameful. I hope you are lucky enough to have a dealer who recognizes the importance of live plants and offers a good assortment.

> **Fish and Tips**
> If you aren't sure if you want live or plastic plants, you may want to consider trying both. Pick out the hardiest species of live plants, and intermix them with plastic versions of the more delicate varieties. Once a touch of algae starts growing on the plastic plants, they will look fairly natural and blend right in.

Decorative Driftwood

The term driftwood best describes dead wood that has been soaking and rotting in water for a long time. Good-quality driftwood will have soaked long enough that it no longer floats. Several varieties can be found in pet stores and are suitable for both aquariums and terrariums. No two pieces are alike, so part of the fun is picking the ones that please your eye the most.

Mounted Driftwood

This wood does not sink on its own. It comes attached to a piece of slate that you wedge into the gravel to keep the wood from floating. You may even need to pile an extra rock or two on the base for a few weeks. Eventually, the wood will soak up enough water to stay down without the added rocks.

There are two styles of mounted driftwood. The first style is naturally shaped pieces. No two are alike. The second style is made from wood that has had holes drilled in it and been sandblasted to give it a weathered look. No two of these are exactly alike, but many are quite similar. Mounted driftwood usually discolors the water little, if at all.

> **Fish and Tips**
> If driftwood discolors your water, replacing or adding a good grade of activated carbon to your filter box should remove the color from the water.

Malaysian Driftwood

This dark-colored natural driftwood is heavy enough to sink on its own. I really love the look of it. The one downside is that when you first put it in your tank, it may release a fair amount of tannins. These turn your water yellow or brown, and may even acidify it a bit. There are some steps you can take to reduce this. Soaking the wood for a couple of weeks, with daily water changes, helps. If the pieces are small, boiling them could make a difference. Be aware that this is a natural process of the decay of the wood. It is generally harmless to the fish, even if the colored water is not as nice to look at.

Something's Fishy
Be careful using driftwood you've picked up from the beach, or any wood in the wild. You can never be sure you've cleaned out all the substances that can pose a danger to your fish.

African Driftwood

This unusual wood has a very knotty texture, giving it the common name of "rosewood." It is smooth and light colored on one side, and gnarled and dark on the other. Like the Malaysian wood, it sinks on its own. It can also discolor the water a bit—though it seems to do so to a lesser degree. Still, you may want to take steps to leach out extra tannins before putting it in your tank.

Artificial Driftwood

Many companies are using ceramics or resins to produce some very realistic-looking driftwood pieces. Some mimic hollow stumps or logs, and you can use them to hide heater tubes and filter stems.

Manzanita Wood

This is a very branchy type of hardwood that is usually sold for use in terrariums, or as perches for birds. Eye-catching pieces can be put in your aquarium, but be aware that you must wedge them in or find a way to weight them down. Manzanita wants to float.

Fish and Tips
Action aerating ornaments can be fun to watch, but be aware that they can sometimes be tricky to calibrate. You must use a control valve, and prepare to have to adjust them with some frequency.

Action Aerating Ornaments

In case you aren't familiar with them, there are a huge range of these items. They are usually plastic, but sometimes ceramic. When you hook an air line to them, most of these ornaments move. You will find treasure chests that open and close, a diver that battles an octopus, sunken ships with paddle wheels still turning, and even Goofy and Mickey Mouse in scuba gear. Kids especially like to have action aerating ornaments in the tank.

Popular action aerating ornaments.

Now, you have heard me say several times that I like my aquarium to be all natural. I want it to contain only what I would find in the wild. Still, I have to admit that there is a soft spot in my heart for the diving sea dog action aerating ornament. It is shaped like a dog with a scuba tank and diving helmet. When you attach an air line, he alternately bobs to the surface and then sinks to the bottom—his little legs kicking all the way. It really is kind of cute, but please don't tell anyone that I said so. It will ruin my image!

Ceramic and Resin Ornaments

Ceramic castles have been big sellers for ages. These days, manufacturers take them to a new level of sophistication. You can buy castle walls and cities that act as backgrounds in your tank. You can find Roman ruins that are single, double, and triple columns, and entire rows of Greek goddesses to stand in the middle of your tank.

Ceramic "No Fishing!" signs are an old standby, and frogs, turtles, and mermaids are still popular. Shipwrecks, sunken logs, you name it—somebody probably makes a ceramic version of it.

Resin ornaments are becoming quite popular, too. Many pieces have quite detailed design and color.

Artificial Rocks and Coral

Even rocks are being copied these days. Besides ceramic and resin versions, plastic rocks can be found in most pet stores. Some are designed quite well, I might add.

Something's Fishy

Seashells should not be put into a freshwater tank. They slowly dissolve, possibly affecting the pH and hardness of the water. Mainly, though, you will ruin your favorite shells this way. You will soon find that they have bleached white in the water.

Something's Fishy

Natural coral skeletons should not be put in a freshwater tank. Your fish may hurt themselves on the sharp edges. Also, coral slowly dissolves, possibly affecting the pH and hardness of your water.

Others come as a kit of pieces that lock together to build rock formations. There are plastic cliffs and caves, too.

Many brands of artificial coral have hit the market in the last few years. I don't like to recommend coral for freshwater tanks, though. Corals are colonies of saltwater animals. To anyone in the know, they look as out of place in a freshwater tank as an outhouse would look in the front yard of a mansion. However, some people like the looks of coral, so if you are set on putting it in your tank, at least get the artificial stuff. It won't affect your pH. Try to pick pieces that have few sharp edges.

The Least You Need to Know

➤ A decorated tank is more pleasing to the eye and more comfortable for the fish.

➤ Dark colors of gravel bring out the colors in your fish.

➤ Choose gravel with pebbles of one-eighth to one-quarter-inch in diameter.

➤ An aquarium background is attractive and hides unsightly air lines and electrical cords.

➤ Use plants, rocks, and driftwood for a natural decor, and add ceramic or action aerating ornaments for fun.

Chapter 9

Just a Few More Things

In This Chapter
➤ Other items you need to round out your complete setup
➤ Suggested optional gear for your tank

Previous chapters covered the major systems in your aquarium, including the tank, the stand, the filter system, and the heating and lighting systems—most of the items you need to properly set up your aquarium. But a few supplies remain. This chapter covers those items, and lists a few things that you can live without but may want to pick up anyway.

Go With the Flow

If you have purchased an air pump to run an undergravel filter or to power airstones or action aerating ornaments, you will need a way to connect the air pump to those items and to regulate the flow. Various kinds of tubes are available to make the connection.

➤ *Air line.* This flexible plastic tubing, about the diameter of a soda straw, sells by the foot and cuts easily with scissors. You cut pieces of the desired length and simply snug the ends over the valves and connections to hook everything up. Most air line tubing sold in stores is clear vinyl. You also may run across green silicone rubber air tubing. In most cases, it does not make any difference which you pick. The green tubing may be a bit easier to camouflage, though.

➤ *Mini-tubing.* The diameter of this air tubing is smaller than usual. It can be used to connect action aerating ornaments. The advantage is that the smaller diameter makes the tubing less buoyant and easier to conceal. Mini-tubing comes with end connectors that adapt it to fit regular size air tubing. You cannot connect mini-tubing directly to your air pump, valves, filter stems, or airstones. Nor would you want to. The small diameter puts more back-pressure on the diaphragm of your air pump. Use it only where you need to conceal tubing that runs to ornaments, and use regular air line tubing for all other applications.

➤ *Plant air tubing.* Perhaps even better for disguising air lines that run to ornaments is plant air tubing. Each package comes with several feet of green air line that you cut to length. Also included are several frilly sections that resemble aquatic plant leaves. You thread the leaves over the green tubing, and the result is a plastic plant with a hollow stem that allows air to pass through. Plant air tubing can be in plain view without sticking out like a sore thumb.

Fish and Tips
Remember that gang-valves divide the power of your air pump—they do not multiply it. So if you use gang-valves to run more outlets, first be sure your pump is able to put out enough air to do so.

Fish and Tips
Do not confuse *two-way* and *three-way* valves with *gang-valves*. A two-way valve inserts into a single line to control its output. A three-way valve adds another outlet to a gang-valve, or inserts into a single line to split off a controllable outlet.

Air to Spare

Sometimes you will be able to use air line to connect directly to the items that it will be running. However, if you need to connect to extra outlets, combine into fewer outlets, control flow, or vent excess pressure, you will need air valves to do so.

The easiest type of valve to use is a gang-valve. A gang-valve is several valves connected and mounted on a plastic or metal hanger. You can buy two-gang, three-gang, four-gang, and five-gang-valves, which can run two to five outlets, respectively. You hang the assembly on the back of your tank, attach the air line from your air pump to the side input connectors of the gang-valve. Then, you connect air lines to the valves and run the output to your filters or ornaments.

Ideally, you should put a check-valve on each outlet of your air pump (the outlets on the pump, not the outlets on the valve). The check-valve is a device that allows air to flow only one way. By placing one on each outlet, the check-valve prevents water from back-siphoning through the airlines, should a power outage occur.

Chapter 10 will have diagrams showing the proper way to connect air pumps, check-valves, and gang-valves with air lines.

Hauling in Your Catch

It helps to have a fish net. Normally, the only time you will ever want to net a fish is when it is dead. However, you never know when you may need to catch a fish to move it to another tank to breed, to recover from a fight, or to be medicated. Or maybe the fish has just outgrown the tank and you want to give it to a friend.

Fine Nets

These nets usually have a white mesh. They have a fine weave with very small holes in the mesh. Fine nets may be a bit easier on your fish, as the smaller holes make it more difficult for fins to get snagged. Some catfish are best caught with this style of net. The downside is that the tighter weave creates more drag, slowing the net down in the water. So they are less maneuverable than coarse nets.

Coarse Nets

Green in color, coarse nets have a looser weave with larger holes in the mesh. This is my favorite type of net. There is less drag, so it is much quicker and more maneuverable in the water, making it easier to catch fish. Also, I find that the plant-like green color is a bit less intimidating to fish. I once had to catch and move all of the neon tetras in a tank. I dipped the net in and got called away. When I came back, every single neon was hiding in the net, making it an easy catch! Some catfish may be easily snagged in this mesh, though.

Aquarium fish nets typically come in sizes varying from two inches to 10 inches wide. Two things need to be considered when selecting the size of your net:

1. What size fish will you be catching?
2. How big is your tank?

Obviously, you need to know what size the fish will be so you can pick a net that is big enough for them to fit into. The reason you need to consider the size of your tank is that you must be able to maneuver the net when you stick it in there. If the net is too big, you will have trouble getting it into the tank and trouble moving it about without snagging every plant, rock, driftwood log, and ornament. If the net is too small, you will have a hard time catching fish. A 2-inch net is a poor choice for a 55-gallon tank, and a 10-incher is equally useless in a 5.5-gallon tank.

Something's Fishy
Do not confuse *brine shrimp nets* with fine nets. Like fine nets, brine shrimp nets also have a white mesh, but they have an even finer weave that is necessary for catching microscopic baby brine shrimp. The weave is so tight on a brine shrimp net that you can barely drag them through the water. Only the slowest of fish can be caught with these.

Fish and Tips
Sometimes the easiest way to catch fish is with two nets. Hold one in place and use the other to herd the fish into the first. You may want to buy one fine net and one coarse net. That way, you will have the right size mesh for the job and two nets when you need them.

Also, some nets come with extra long handles. I usually recommend against these. While you may think a net with a longer handle will make it easier to reach the bottom of the tank, it's more often the case that the long handle makes the net too difficult to maneuver. Remember that you will most likely be netting through a small lid at the front of the tank, and you will not just be netting fish at the front, but also the top rear corners. A long-handled net makes this difficult or impossible.

Water Conditioners

Most aquarists need to treat their tap water to make it safe for fish. Your needs will depend on the condition of your local tap water. In Chapter 17, I'll tell you what factors to consider when you decide which water conditioner you will need. But right now let's look at some typical water conditioners.

> **Fish and Tips**
> Even if you don't have city water, but draw water from a well, you may still want to use a water conditioner. You won't have chlorine to remove, but you may need the other features provided by the water conditioner.

Dechlorinators

If you have city water, you will have to remove the chlorine. Your aquarium store will carry several water conditioners whose main purpose is to dechlorinate tap water. Many brands also offer other benefits. For example, some will remove chloramines and heavy metals or buffer the pH a bit. Some brands even provide a "liquid bandage" factor. That is, they will produce a temporary slime coat on fish that have been damaged by being netted.

Aquarium Salt

Many hobbyists and dealers recommend that you add one teaspoon of aquarium salt per gallon of water. It helps reduce disease, and is perfectly harmless to all species of fish. If you go this route, be sure to pick up some aquarium salt at the pet store.

Water Softener Pillows

If hard water is a problem in your area, you may need these. Ask your dealer about local conditions. If you do use water softener pillows, be sure to purchase a general hardness test kit. You need to be able to tell when you've softened enough.

pH Adjusters

You may not need to mess with your pH at all. It depends on your local tap water and the types of fish you want to keep. Usually, your water pH will be fine as is. It is probably the same water used by your dealer, anyway.

Specialty Conditioners

You can find "black water" extracts to soften and acidify water for discus or other fish that love those conditions. Also, there are many brands of cichlid salts designed to increase the hardness and pH of the water for those rift lake fish. Most of you will not need these products.

Tests You Don't Want to Pass

I highly recommend that you don't pass by the test kit aisle when shopping for your supplies. When problems develop, the proper test kit can often determine exactly where the problem is and what needs to be done. You can't tell the condition of your tap water by looking at it.

pH Kit

Always purchase a pH kit. There are many inexpensive and easy-to-use brands on the market. Besides measuring the pH of the water in your new tank, your pH kit can be used to monitor trends. A declining pH is usually a sign of insufficient water changes.

Ammonia and Nitrite Kits

I highly recommend these kits, as well—particularly in new tanks. In fact, the brand new setup is the one where ammonia is most likely to be a problem. Nitrite kits are also highly recommended for new tanks.

Kits You May Not Need

Most of you won't need to bother with general hardness or carbonate hardness kits, except maybe for curiosity's sake. Your local water conditions will determine whether you need to test these parameters. Ask your dealer for a recommendation.

Most of you also won't need dissolved oxygen and carbon dioxide kits. If you are going to set up a heavily planted aquarium, you may want them, though.

Don't Forget the Munchies

I recommend that you offer your fish a variety of foods. Minimally, you will want to offer a "staple" flake, which is a basic diet for most fish, but you also should buy at least one other food, just to make things interesting for the fish. Frozen brine shrimp is a good choice for a second food. It makes a great treat for most fish.

For more ideas, be sure to check out Chapter 19 on foods and feeding. The foods you need to purchase will be partially determined by the species of fish you choose to keep. So you may want to wait until you buy your first batch of fish before you buy fish food. Be sure to ask your dealer to let you know if you are picking species that have special dietary requirements.

Fishy First-Aid Kit

Usually, it is not a good idea to buy medications until you need them. Medications should not be used as preventives and they have limited shelf lives. So if you purchase them long before you need them, they may become useless or even toxic. Besides, there's a chance you will never have to medicate your fish. So why spend the money?

However, there is one type of medication that is cheap, has a long shelf life, and wouldn't hurt to have hanging around. That medication is a malachite green or formalin-malachite green ich remedy. I will tell you a lot more about this medication in Chapter 24 on stress and disease. For now, suffice it to say that ich (pronounced *ick*) is probably the most common fish disease experienced by new hobbyists, and is quite easy to treat—if you catch it in time.

Quarantine Tank

A quarantine tank is the other item that I would recommend, although I realize that few people go to the trouble. A quarantine tank doesn't have to be fancy. A simple 5.5- or 10-gallon aquarium with a sponge filter, heater, and a couple of plastic plants for cover is all you need. You can use a quarantine tank to medicate a single sick fish, rather than treating the whole tank (sometimes). A quarantine tank is also a good place to allow an injured fish to heal. And using it to quarantine new arrivals before they ever go into your main tank can help keep disease from getting there in the first place.

A net breeder can be used to isolate bullied fish.

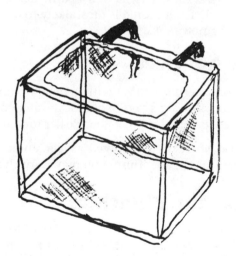

You also may want to have an isolation basket on hand. There are several styles of these, usually sold as net breeders, breeding baskets, breeding traps, or isolation containers. Some are clear plastic containers with perforations to allow water to flow through. They hang inside your tank, and you put the fish that needs protection inside. The best types are the ones made of a simple plastic frame with a net mesh all around. They allow water to flow through easily.

There are coarse mesh and fine mesh models, but the coarse mesh is usually best. It allows droppings and uneaten food to fall out of the net more easily. Of course, if you want to use the basket to protect baby fish, the fine mesh may be required.

Cleaning Supplies

There are a few items you will need for the routine maintenance of your aquarium. These items will make partial water changes and glass cleaning a snap.

> **Something's Fishy**
> *Never* use soap to clean your aquarium or any items in it! Soap is extremely toxic to fish.
>
> SNIFF! SNIFF!

Gravel Vacuum

If there is one item that will make your life easy, this is it. Gravel vacuums are quick, easy, and cheap to use. A gravel vacuum is a very simple device. It consists of a large tube attached to a siphon hose. There are no motors or moving parts. Use the gravel vacuum to siphon out water to make your partial water changes. As you do so, you poke the large tube into your gravel. The flow is strong enough to draw all the debris up out of the gravel, but not strong enough to siphon out the gravel, too. With a gravel vacuum, your partial water change gets rid of both dissolved waste and solid debris.

A gravel vacuum makes life easy for you and your fish. (Courtesy of Tetra-Second Nature, makers of Hydro-Clean)

There is a fancier "clean-and-fill" version of this device. Instead of having a short hose to siphon into a bucket, it comes with a longer hose and a valve that attaches to your sink. You can buy models with 25, 50, 75, and even 100 feet of hose. Water pressure from your sink powers the device. When you set the valve one way, the water pressure forms a vacuum that draws water out of your tank. A gravel vacuum tube on the other end cleans your gravel. When you're done, flip the valve and water flows the other way. So, you can refill your tank right from the faucet. Of course, you need to be sure that the new water is the right temperature, and don't forget to add a dechlorinator.

Algae Scrubber

Most hobbyists keep one or more algae-eating fish, and they are very helpful, but you still may need to clean the inside glass occasionally. Some types of algae aren't edible, or perhaps there is just too much for the algae eaters.

Something's Fishy
Do not use razor-blade-style algae scrapers on acrylic tanks. You may scratch the finish.

Anyway, there are several styles of algae scrubbers and scrapers on the market. My favorite is a plain scrubber pad. You can buy coarse ones for glass tanks, or softer ones for acrylic tanks. You can buy algae scrubbers on a stick, but they are much harder to maneuver than the hand-held pads. There are also razor blade scrapers for the really tough types of algae.

If you don't like to dip your hand in the water much, then 1) you are a little weird, 2) you may be in the wrong hobby, and 3) you should consider buying a magnetic algae scraper. This consists of two magnetic parts. One part, which has either embedded blades or scrubber pads, goes inside the tank. The other part goes outside the tank. The magnetic attraction keeps them together. When you move the outer piece, the inner scraper portion slides around, too. These are kind of fun, and most do a fair job, but they don't get into corners or tight spots very well.

Something's Fishy
Don't use your household cleaning bucket for water changes on your aquarium. Soap residue may cause problems. Instead, keep a separate bucket for aquarium use only, and make sure everyone in the house knows not to use it for other tasks.

A Bucket to Lug It

A fish bucket comes in very handy. You will need one to siphon water into when you make your partial water changes—unless you purchased one of the clean-and-fill systems. You also can use a bucket to carry replacement water back to the tank. Fish can be transported in a bucket. Plus, you can use one to hold dripping filters or filter media that you want to take to the sink for cleaning. If you ever break your tank, you may need a bucket to hold the fish while you go buy a new one. Get at least a five-gallon bucket.

Replacement Filter Materials

You won't need to have spares of these immediately, but it doesn't hurt to have your replacement filter media ready to go when you need it. Naturally, what you need will depend on the type of filter you buy. Be sure to ask your dealer if the initial set of filter media comes with the filter. Sometimes the media is included; sometimes you must purchase it separately. Your filter won't work without the proper media.

Buy a Book!

A good beginner's text will greatly increase your chances of success in the hobby. Naturally, I recommend that you buy *this* book. In fact, I'm pretty sure that the law requires it! Besides, when you're not busy reading it, the book is great for propping up the leg on that wobbly chair.

The Least You Need to Know

➤ If you purchased air-operated filters, be sure you also bought an air pump and the proper valves and air line to connect them all together.

➤ A gravel vacuum is something you won't want to live without.

➤ Don't forget food, net, and water conditioner for your new tank. A "fish only" bucket and algae scrubber pad are also recommended.

➤ You may want to set up a small quarantine tank.

➤ Buy a good beginner's book. I recommend this one, because I know the author personally.

Some Assembly Required

Okay, you've just gotten back from the aquarium store, where you shelled out as many hard-earned dollars as you could afford (maybe more). You proudly carried your new aquarium in from the car without dropping it or chipping it. You also dragged home a jumble of bags and boxes that represent all the equipment needed to set up the tank.

As you stand there with visions of colorful fish swimming in your head, you realize two things: 1) the fish should be swimming in your aquarium, not in your head, and 2) you haven't the slightest idea how to put all these expensive gizmos together into a functioning aquarium!

Don't worry, that's why I am here. That's why they pay me the big buck. In this chapter I'll go over some simple steps for putting everything together properly. I know this is your first time, so I'll be gentle. I even drew some diagrams to guide you along.

Something's Fishy
Besides following the steps in this book, be sure to take time to read all instructions and warranties that come with each piece of equipment. Do this *before* you try to assemble the equipment.

Fish and Tips
Try to set up your electrical outlets so there is enough slack to form "drip loops" with the electrical cords. That is, the cord should dangle lower than the electrical outlet, and then curve back up to be plugged in. That way, if any water runs down the electrical cord it won't go into the electrical socket. It will drop off the loop of cord at the bottom.

Choose a location near electricity and away from windows.

Step 1: Choose a Location

Hopefully, you did this before you bought your aquarium and stand. It would be pretty embarrassing to find out now that the tank won't fit where you want to put it, wouldn't it? It is usually best not to put your aquarium in front of a window. Direct sunlight may cause algae problems. It may also overheat your tank.

Be sure you have access to electricity. Most hobbyists need at least three electrical outlets—one each for the heater, light, and filter. You may need more.

It is also a good idea to install a *ground-fault (circuit) interrupter* (GFI or GFCI) in the electrical outlet where you intend to place the tank. In case this sounds like gobbledygook to you, a GFI is a special electrical outlet commonly used in bathrooms and other areas where water is going to be nearby. The GFI is able to detect current leakage (sometimes caused by spilled or splashed water) and shut down the circuit to prevent shock. After you fix the problem, you press a reset button to allow the GFI outlet to work again. It's kind of like having an extra sensitive fuse or circuit breaker built right into the wall outlet.

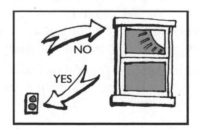

Step 2: Position the Aquarium Stand

Don't forget to allow enough room behind for electrical cords, filter hoses, or any hang-on-the-back filters that you plan to install. Be sure the stand is flat and level. If necessary, use shims under the bottom corners to make it that way. A crooked, wobbly stand can crack your tank.

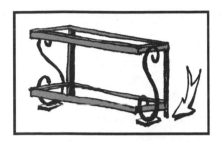

If necessary, use wedges to level the stand.

Step 3: Clean the Aquarium Glass

When you get your aquarium, it may be a bit dusty or grimy from sitting on your dealer's shelf or in his distributor's warehouse. Take some paper towels and plain water to clean the glass inside and out. Never use soap on your aquarium or any items that go into it. Soap kills fish.

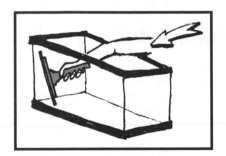

Clean the glass with plain water.

Step 4: Test the Tank for Leaks

The odds of getting a leaky tank are very low, perhaps one in several hundred, so this step in optional. However, if you happen to be unlucky enough to get that one, it is better to find out *before* you install the decorations and equipment.

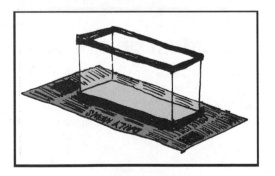

You may want to test for leaks before adding decorations.

Anyway, if you don't want to live dangerously, here is an easy way to leak test a tank. Lay out some dry newspaper on a flat, level surface. It can be on the floor of the garage or on your aquarium stand—wherever is convenient. Place the tank on top of the newspaper and carefully fill the tank with water. Fill to the bottom of the top plastic frame on glass tanks, or within an inch of the top for acrylic tanks. *Be very careful not to spill a single drop of water on the newspaper or outside the tank.*

Something's Fishy
Never try to lift an aquarium that is full of water. The stresses on the tank could easily break it. Always drain the tank first.

After you fill the tank, watch for water welling up inside the bottom plastic frame, leaking from any seam, or soaking the newspaper and making it dark. If you do see water welling up in the bottom frame, are you positive that you didn't splash any water down in there? If you did, when the tank is full and settles, it may squeeze out some water that dripped there, making you think you have a leak when you don't. Give it a few hours, and if everything is still dry, it is safe to proceed. You will need to remove the water from the tank to get the newspaper out from underneath.

Step 5: Attach Your Aquarium Background

You will find it much easier to do this now than after the tank is installed and filled with water. Most aquariums do not have designated fronts or backs. You can face either side out. However, some brands have special cutouts (acrylic aquariums) or notches in the top frame (some glass tanks) that make it easier to clamp a heater on the back or hang a filter. If your tank is this way, make sure you put the background on the true back.

Use cellophane or plastic electrician's tape to attach your background.

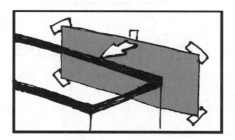

Step 6: Position the Aquarium on the Stand

Center your tank on the aquarium stand. Make sure it is sitting flat, with no wobble, and that no bits of gravel or other obstructions lodge between the tank and the stand. These objects could easily break a tank once the weight of the water is added. Check again to see that you left enough room for filters to hang on the back, or for electrical cords to snake behind.

Center the aquarium on the stand.

Step 7: Install the Filter(s)

An entire book could be written on the details of positioning and installing the many types of filters on the market. We don't have the space here to cover everything there is to know about installing all filter systems, so I'm going to stick with the basics on the more popular styles. Just because I list a style of filter doesn't necessarily mean that you should have purchased it. Your filter choices should be based on information in earlier chapters and advice from your dealer. Be sure you read the manufacturer's instructions that come with your brand of filter.

The main thing to note for now is that the instructions in this step only include directions for assembling and positioning the filter systems. We won't actually start the filters until later. *Do not plug in any electrical devices yet!* I will tell you when to plug them in. Doing so before that point could cause damage, injury, fire, shock, and perhaps plague.

Undergravel Filter

Basically, you are going to position the perforated undergravel filter plate inside your tank, on the bottom, and install the filter lift tubes. These days, most brands have one (or more) large outer tube (usually one inch in diameter) with an exhaust spout that goes on top. Inside the large outer tube goes the smaller rigid air line tube with an airstone attached at the bottom.

Fish and Tips
Always install the airstones for your undergravel filter in a position as low as possible, but above the filter plate. The lower the airstone, the better the water flow it will generate; but if you put it too low, air will go under the filter plate instead of up the lift tube. If bubbles burp out from under your filter plate, you have installed the airstones too low.

101

Install the undergravel filter system.

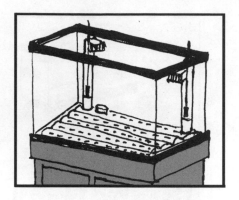

If you plan to use powerheads instead of an air pump to run your undergravel filter, you won't use the exhaust spouts, rigid air line tubes, or airstones. Instead, you will position the powerheads directly on top of the large-diameter lift tubes. Most powerheads come with brackets that clip over the tank frame. Some use suction cups to anchor the powerhead, instead.

Fish and Tips
Canister filters are more complicated to assemble than most filters. A common error is to reverse the input and output hoses. Most canister filters will have "in" and "out" clearly marked, but it may be unclear if "out" is out of the tank into the filter, or out of the filter into the tank. *"In" is into the filter*, from the tank. *"Out" is out of the filter*, and back into the tank.

You may need to trim the length of the lift-tubes on your undergravel filter to get a proper fit. A hacksaw will cut them, or you can cut them with a heavy razor blade. On air-operated models, the exhaust spout should be all or mostly submerged. With powerheads, make sure the exhaust spout is under water. If you mount the exhaust too high, you may get water shooting out of your tank.

Outside Power Filter

Hang the filter on the back of the tank. Many will have adjustable tabs at the bottom that you can use to make sure the filter hangs level. Make sure the impeller seats properly. Install the intake tubes and strainers. Go ahead and rinse the filter media and install it according to manufacturer's directions. If there is a lid to the unit, you can leave it off for the moment.

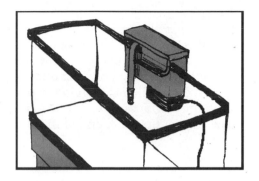

Install the outside power filter on the back of the tank.

Canister Filter

Rinse the appropriate filter media and fill the canister with it according to manufacturer's directions. Connect all filter hoses and valves. The candy cane-shaped intake tube, with the strainer on the bottom, should be connected to the hose that connects to the input side of the canister filter.

Now it's time to snap the top onto the unit. Be sure to follow the manufacturer's directions here. Some units require you to position a rubber O-ring or gasket, and may require you to lubricate it first with a bit of petroleum jelly. Some units must be filled with water before closing them up, or they won't start. Others will be difficult to start if you don't leave them empty. Remember, don't plug anything in until I say so.

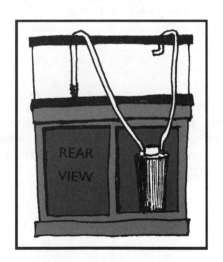

Install the canister filter.

Box, Bottom, and Corner Filters

These are the cheap filters that come with some starter kits. Inside the plastic box is a perforated platform with lift tubes in the middle. The platform goes on the bottom. On top of that, make an activated carbon sandwich, using polyester filter floss as the bread. (That's a half inch of floss on the bottom, one inch of carbon in the middle, and another half inch of floss on top.) Put the lid on the box, attach an air line to the top, and place the filter inside the aquarium. For now, just let the other end of the air line dangle outside the tank.

Install your box filter or sponge filter.

Sponge Filter

To attach the lift tube to the sponge, follow the directions on the package. Then attach the air line as directed. Some sponge filters sit on the bottom (and can be buried in the gravel, if you want), and others attach to the side glass with suction cups. For now, just let the air line hang out of the tank.

Trickle Filter

These are an excellent choice, but there are too many styles and options to describe here. Follow the manufacturer's directions, and ask your dealer for further assistance in assembling and positioning the filter. The basic steps involve installing the sump beneath the tank, installing the overflow system on the tank, installing the water pump, and connecting pumps, sumps, and overflows with the appropriate hoses.

Install your trickle filter.

Step 8: Add Aquarium Gravel

Before doing so, you probably should give the gravel a quick rinse to remove dust—especially with natural gravel. The colored gravels are usually prewashed by the manufacturer, but some abrasion occurs during shipping. A household colander usually works well, or simply put the gravel in a bucket, add water, and stir. Then, pour off the dirty water and repeat until the gravel rinses clean.

Usually, you will want to add enough gravel for a layer that is 1.5 to two inches deep. It can be helpful to slope the gravel so it is a bit higher in back. That way, debris collects at the front for easy removal. If you want to do any terracing, you can use rocks to build the walls.

Add gravel to the tank, sloping down toward the front.

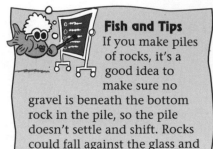

Fish and Tips
If you make piles of rocks, it's a good idea to make sure no gravel is beneath the bottom rock in the pile, so the pile doesn't settle and shift. Rocks could fall against the glass and break it.

Step 9: Add Decorations

Rocks, driftwood, and ceramics can be positioned now. Be very careful not to drop them and break the tank. If you have action aerating ornaments, you may want to position them now, and run the air lines under rocks and such to obscure them. Their buoyancy makes this more difficult once there is water in the tank. Be sure to leave room for your plants, which we will add shortly.

Position rocks, driftwood, and other ornaments.

Step 10: Install Your Thermometer

If you bought the stick-on liquid crystal-type thermometer, it goes on the outside glass at the place of your choosing. Try to put it somewhere innocuous, though. Other styles of thermometers go inside the tank.

Something's Fishy
If you fill your tank with a garden hose, run some water to rinse it out before use. The plasticizers that keep a hose flexible are toxic to fish. Water that has been sitting in the hose may be unsafe.

Step 11: Fill the Aquarium With Water

The preferred temperature is 75°F to 78°F (24°C to 26°C). Try to adjust your mix of hot and cold water to achieve that range, and later you will be able to calibrate your heater in one step. You can lay a saucer on the gravel and pour the water onto it to keep from disturbing the gravel. When the tank is full, remove the saucer.

Liquid crystal thermometers go outside the tank. Other thermometers go inside.

Fill the tank by pouring water onto a saucer so you won't disturb the gravel. Premix hot and cold to achieve correct temperature.

Fill glass aquariums to the bottom edge of the top frame. Fill acrylic tanks to within an inch or so of the top. As discussed in Step 4, be sure not to slop water on the outside of your tank, or you may have difficulty telling if you have a leak.

Step 12: Install the Aquarium Heater

If you bought a hang-on-the-tank model, the glass tube hangs in the water and the main body clamps to the back top frame of the tank. Turning the side screw knob tightens the clamp. If you bought optional suction cups to keep the heater from being bumped against the glass, slide them over the heater tube before placing the heater in the tank. Position the suction cups so that they aren't over the heater coils, or they will melt. *Do not plug in the heater yet.*

If you have a submersible heater, attach it inside the tank with the included suction cups. You can mount it horizontally or vertically, up high, or down low. It is

Something's Fishy
Never plug in any heater that is out of the water. You could get burned or cause a fire.

107

your choice. Sometimes it is convenient to mount the heater vertically with the control knob sticking out of the water for easier access. If you bought a model with a preset temperature scale, go ahead and dial up the desired temperature before installing the heater.

Install your heater, but don't plug it in yet.

Step 13: Add Your Plants

Some people recommend adding plants right before filling the tank. I prefer to add them after the water is in the tank. While it is a bit easier and less messy to root plants in a tank without water, the downside is that without the water to hold the plants up, you can't really judge how they will look. Besides, if you are afraid of getting your hands wet, you are in the wrong hobby.

Arrange your plants. The tallest plants look best at the back.

Be artistic. Arrange the plants to your taste. Try not to make the display look symmetrical and note that taller plants usually look best toward the back of the tank.

Step 14: Install the Light System

Before installing glass canopies or full-hoods, you probably will need to trim the rear plastic strip to allow your heater and outside filter to hang on the back of the tank. Follow the instructions for your brand. Also, with any light system, check the light bulbs to make sure they fit snugly in the fixture. Then, continue by choosing the directions for the appropriate lighting system below.

Full-Hood

Most of you will choose a full-hood. If so, follow the manufacturer's instructions for mounting it. Some brands have pins that snap off the bottom to get a custom fit for different brands of aquariums. Others may have plastic strips that snap off the edge. Still others sit recessed into the aquarium's top frame without modification.

Install your full-hood or other lighting system.

Glass Canopy–Strip-Light Combo

Glass canopies should sit inside the top aquarium frame, resting on the inner lip. Not every brand fits every tank, so if yours doesn't seem right you may have bought the wrong brand. The strip light should sit directly on top of the glass canopy.

Other Light Systems

For other styles of light systems—such as metal-halide units and power-compact fluorescents—follow the manufacturer's recommendations for installation.

Your light unit can now be plugged in.

Step 15: Start Up the Filter System

Choose the instructions that apply to the type of filter system(s) that you bought.

Undergravel Filter

Position the air pump *outside* the aquarium, preferably on a shelf above the water level. This will prevent the possibility of water siphoning back into the electrical portion of the pump during a power outage. If you are going to position the pump lower than the water surface, install check-valves in the main air lines for added safety.

To connect an undergravel filter system, first (A) connect air lines to the top of the filter stems or to an optional gang-valve. Then (B) use check-valves to prevent water from siphoning during a power outage.

Cut air line tubing to the appropriate lengths, and use it to connect the air pump outlets to the top of the undergravel filter stems. You will need to run the air lines through the holes in the back of your full-hood. Airflow should go from the air pump to the check-valves (if any), to the gang-valves (if any), and to the lift tubes of the undergravel filter. If you are using check-valves, be sure they face in the right direction—narrow end away from the pump. If you are using a gang-valve, hang it on the back of your aquarium and connect the air lines coming from the air pump to the *side* fittings of the gang-valve, and then connect the air line from the *top* fittings to the undergravel filter stems. Simply snug the tubing over the fittings. Leave enough slack to prevent kinks.

Fish and Tips
Remember, don't buy fish until after the tank is fully set up and has been running for 24 hours. You need to make sure all equipment is functioning, and that the temperature is stable. Besides, you want to be sure that you don't have a leaky tank. (It's rare, but it happens.)

Adjust your gang-valves, if any, so that they are all wide open. *Plug in the air pump.* Bubbles should now be flowing out all filter outlets. If the flow of air from all outlets is not equal, decreasing the flow to the stronger outlets will divert air to the weaker ones. Adjust as necessary to get strong equal flow from all outlets. If the flow is not equal, your filter may not function properly—even though it has a strong flow of bubbles. This is because the stronger flowing lift tubes can pull water down the weaker tubes, rather than pulling it through the gravel where the filtration takes place.

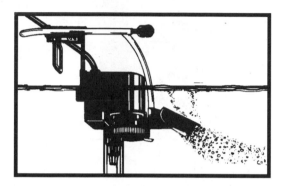

A powerhead can be used instead of an air pump. (Courtesy of Rolf C. Hagen Corp., makers of AquaClear powerheads)

If you use a powerhead instead of an air pump, you will not have to worry about connecting air lines and valves. You probably will have to close off extra ports in the filter plate with the special caps provided with the undergravel filter. *Go ahead and plug in the powerhead.* The powerhead has two adjustments to make: One controls the amount of water it puts out, and the other controls the amount of air it mixes into that water.

Fish and Tips
For best circulation, point the exhaust from your undergravel filter at the front center of the tank.

Outside Power Filter

Fill the filter box at least half full of water to prime it. *Plug in the filter.* The filter will now take a minute to expel any air remaining in the filter intake tube. It will then begin pumping and filtering the water. The filter will be a bit noisy during this process, but will quiet down once it expels the remaining air. If your filter has a lid, you can put it on now.

Canister Filter

There are so many brands of these that it is difficult to give directions in the space we have. So be sure to follow the manufacturer's directions. Some canister filters are easier to start than others, though. I usually find that I have the best luck by starting out with no water in the filter, and connecting all hoses. Then I disconnect the output hose near the top of the tank and suck on it to start water siphoning into the unit. Keep the hose disconnected until the canister fills with water and water starts coming up the output hose. Then reconnect the output hose.

Fill the outside power filter with water before plugging it in.

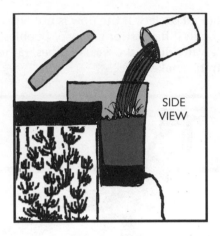

At this point, *plug in the filter* and hope for the best. Some brands will start right up. Some will spit and sputter for a minute as they expel trapped air (tilting the unit may help speed the process). Other times, the unit may stall if air gets trapped in the wrong place. Though some canister filters are a bit tricky to start, once operating they tend to be excellent filters.

Box, Bottom, Corner, and Sponge Filters

Something's Fishy

With any air-operated filter system or ornament, the air pump always goes outside the tank. Never allow an air pump to get wet.

At this point, connecting the main air line to the air pump and *plugging in the pump* should be all you need to do. Position the air pump *outside the tank* and above water level to prevent back-siphoning during a power outage, or insert a check-valve. If you are using a gang-valve to run other outlets from the same pump, connect everything with the air line before plugging in the pump. The air line should travel from the pump to the check-valve (if any), to the gang-valve (if any), to the filter and ornaments (if any).

You may need a gang-valve to connect a filter and ornament to the same air pump. (A) air in from pump; (B) air out to filters, etc.; (C) control knobs.

Trickle Filter

Tricky filter may be a more appropriate name for this one, because there are so many styles of connections for them that I can't give you anything but very general directions for activating the filter. If you set things up wrong, you can get a flood, a burned-out pump, or both. Here, though, are some general steps for getting a properly installed trickle filter running, assuming that you have already filled the aquarium to the desired water level:

1. Fill the sump to within one or two inches of the top.

2. If you have a hang-on-the-tank overflow, make sure there is water in the overflow box and that the siphon tube in the box is full of water, too. Also, adjust the depth of the slotted skimmer box so that water just starts to flow from the tank, through the slots in the box.

3. If you have through-the-glass plumbing, make sure the top of the overflow tube is right at water level.

4. Plug in the pump. As water pumps from the sump to the tank above, two things happen. First, the water level in the tank will slightly increase. Second, the water level in the sump will decrease. Water will begin to spill over the overflow and return to the sump.

5. Keep an eye on this process for a few minutes, and adjust accordingly. You want to make sure that the tank doesn't overfill, and that the sump doesn't run dry and burn out the pump. Properly done, your pump will not run dry, and in the event of a power outage the sump will have safe capacity to handle the small amount of water that backflows.

6. Once equilibrium is established and you are confident the tank or sump won't overflow and the pump won't run dry, mark a line at the water level of the sump. As evaporation occurs, you can safely refill to this line without worrying that the sump will overflow in a power outage.

Fish and Tips
Air pumps should be quiet. If yours hums too loudly or rattles, you may be restricting the output too much. Also, be sure the pump is not bumping against other objects, creating sympathetic vibrations. Finally, remember that water acts as the muffler for your air pump. So all pumps are noisy when disconnected from their air lines, valves, and outlets.

Step 16: Add Water Conditioner

Use your dechlorinator to remove chlorine from your tap water. The package will tell you the right dose, usually given in drops per gallon, or teaspoons per 10 gallons. If you are adding the teaspoon of aquarium salt per gallon, now is the time to do it, too.

Add water conditioner to remove chlorine from your tap water.

Step 17: Calibrate the Heater

Fish and Tips
Your aquarium will never be cooler than room temperature. So if your room is 80°F and you calibrate your heater for 75°F, the tank will still be 80°F and the heater won't turn on unless the temperature drops below 75°F.

Some of you will have selected a model of submersible heater that has a built-in temperature control scale. If so, you simply dial the temperature you want, *plug the heater in*, and then check in a while to make sure everything is functioning as expected.

Most of you, though, will need to calibrate your heaters by looking at the pilot light and coordinating with your thermometer. The process is a little complicated but straightforward, and once properly set, the heater should automatically maintain the proper temperature. Here's how to calibrate your heater:

Use the pilot light to help calibrate your heater.

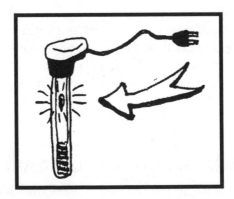

1. First, let your heater hang in the water for about 15 minutes (unplugged). That way, you can be sure the heater parts are the same temperature as the tank water.

2. After at least 15 minutes in the water, *plug in the heater* and look for the orange pilot light. If the light is off, the heater is off. If the light is on, the heater is on.

3. If the pilot light is on when you plug in the heater, turn the control knob down (usually counterclockwise) until the light just kicks off. If the light is off when you first plug in the heater, turn the control knob up (usually clockwise) until the light just kicks on. The point where the pilot light just kicks on or off is the point that calibrates the heater for the *current* water temperature.

4. Use your thermometer to read the current water temperature. If the desired temperature is higher or lower than the current temperature, you need to adjust the heater up or down slightly. Check the water temperature in an hour to see how you've done, and adjust further, if necessary. As an estimate, a one-eighth turn of the dial will usually give a two-degree change in temperature.

> **Fish and Tips**
> Some hang-on-the-tank heaters have a safety device that prevents the control knob from rotating more than one complete turn at a time. However, if you need to turn more than that, remove the control knob, turn the little stub of a knob underneath, and reinstall the control knob.

Step 18: Final Check

At this point, you should be able to clean up your mess. I know that you are excited, but give yourself 24 hours before buying fish. Patience. Meanwhile, check to make sure that there are no leaks, that the temperature is stable, and that all equipment seems to function normally. Don't be concerned if the water is a bit cloudy at first.

Wait 24 hours before buying fish.

The Least You Need to Know

➤ Always read and follow the manufacturer's instructions and warranties.

➤ Assemble all equipment and let it run 24 hours before buying fish.

➤ Do not plug in filters and heaters until they are fully immersed in water.

➤ Proper water temperature is 75°F to 78°F (24°C to 26°C).

Part 3
Look at All Those Cool Fish and Plants!

You're about a third of the way through this book, and it's about time I stopped talking about all that boring equipment and got into the exciting part—the livestock! It was the fish and plants that drew you to the hobby, not the heaters and filters, right?

Buying fish is not just a question of looking in all your dealer's tanks and picking the prettiest ones. Fish are not ornaments, they're living creatures. There are questions of size, habit, and personality to consider.

I'll start by giving you pointers on selecting compatible species. Then I'll talk about many popular varieties that make good, hardy starter fish.

Don't forget the plants! I'll recommend some good, hardy starter plants, too. Finally, you'll end Part 3 by learning how to transport your new fish and plants safely home. You also will learn how to acclimate the new arrivals to your aquarium.

Chapter 11

Picking Your First Fish

In This Chapter

➤ Considering compatibility

➤ Picking species to fit the environment

➤ Rules to prevent overcrowding

➤ Spotting a healthy fish

Time to get to the exciting part! So far we have spent lots of time discussing aquariums, filters, heaters, and a bunch of other pieces of equipment, but our only interest in those gadgets is the fact that we need them to keep the fish alive. Nobody gets into the hobby because they think filters and air pumps are cool. It is all those dazzling tropical fish that are the draw. Fish! Fish! Beautiful fish!

Picking out your first batch of fish is definitely fun. But guess what? Picking them out will be one of the hardest things you will ever do. It will be hard because your dealer is going to tempt you by offering so many varieties of fish for sale that you will not be able to make up your mind. Your tank can hold only so many fish, and I'm betting that your wallet holds only so many dollars. So deciding which fish to pick is going to be tough.

I've Got a Million of 'Em

There are thousands of species of tropical fish available in the aquarium trade. You are going to find yourself wanting at least one of everything. Probably, you will be wanting several of everything. Don't be surprised to find yourself wishing you had brought along more cash and credit cards to buy more tanks, so that you will have room to keep more fish.

Okay, now that you are feeling the need to get your first fishy fix, take a step back and take a few deep breaths. There are some things you need to consider before you buy that first batch of fish. After all, you want to do this right.

You cannot walk into a store and just pick out every cool fish you see, throw them in your tank, and expect success. Well, you *could* expect that, but you would have to be . . . ahem . . . a complete idiot. I can tell you horror stories about novices who found out the hard way that all fish don't mix. In fact, I think I will tell you one now.

A Horror Story

Recently, a woman came into my shop, disgusted with the service that she had gotten at another store. She was new to the hobby and had purchased a few fish from there. The clerk there had happily netted any fish she pointed to, without offering any advice. He wasn't a very good clerk. He was more of a dumb cluck, actually.

Anyway, if he had been a good clerk, he would have asked this woman several questions. Time would have been taken to find out what size tank she had, how long it had been set up, and if it already had other fish in it. It is important for a clerk to know stuff like that, because it helps prevent a customer from buying too many fish for the tank. Also, it helps the customer pick species that aren't going to beat each other's brains out—or eat them out, as the case may be.

So, the woman headed home and introduced 30 new specimens to her 10-gallon tank. The first day everything seemed fine. Some fish were active, some were hiding, but everyone seemed to be getting along. Of course, that was to be expected. In some ways, fish aren't much different from you and me. When we move into a new neighborhood, we don't start picking fights with the neighbors until we get to know them a little better.

Fish School
A *community tank* is an aquarium containing a mixture of small, peaceful fish.

The same is usually true with fish introduced to a new aquarium.

But tomorrow is another day, and when tomorrow came, this poor woman's community tank started filling with unexpected drama. Her angelfish and green terror decided they wanted to live next to the same rock. The green terror quickly showed Mr. Angelfish that he really would be better off living somewhere else, so poor scuffed-up Mr. Angelfish

120

fled to the opposite side of the tank for safety. Poor guy. How was he to know the jack dempsey had taken up residence there? Yes, jack dempseys are named after the famous fighter, and for very good reason.

The jack dempsey convinced Mr. Angelfish that he really didn't want to live in that aquarium at all, and so Mr. Angelfish's beaten body was found later, floating dead in the tank—its eyes eaten out by . . . well, by just about any fish with lips. I don't know why it is, but the eyeballs of a dead fish seem to be something of a delicacy to most live fish. Go figure.

Things were quiet in the woman's tank for a while. But soon it would be nighttime. *Webster's Dictionary* defines nighttime as the time when polka dot catfish discover that little neon tetras are even tastier than a dead fish's eyeballs. What? You doubt that is how Webster's defines nighttime? It's certainly accurate.

Anyway, the neon tetras were probably lucky, because 30 fish was way too many to put into a 10-gallon tank to begin with. The ammonia that all those fish excrete (we'll talk about ammonia in a later chapter) would have built up and killed them in a few days anyway, and it would have been a slower, more painful death.

Well, this woman soon lost most of the fish in her new tank because most of them shouldn't have been mixed in there in the first place. But enough of this horror tale. This story illustrates many possible problems that could result from picking incompatible tank mates. So how can you pick fish that will mix?

Big fish eat little fish. Even big peaceful fish eat little fish.

Be Prepared

For starters, do your homework. Get some books and read up on various species to find information about their quirks. In the next chapter, I will list many common, peaceful species that would make good starter fish in a community aquarium. With few exceptions, the fish listed there will readily mix and match with each other. Be sure to check out my recommended reading list in Appendix C, too.

Take Advantage of Your Dealer

Be sure to take full advantage of your dealer's expertise. If you follow the guidelines that I've presented, you should be able to avoid the worthless sales clerk who helped create the disaster described above. Before the salesperson nets each fish for you, be sure he takes a moment to describe its nature and considers if it will be compatible with its other tank mates. Also, don't forget to ask what diet is appropriate.

Be aware, though, that the best your dealer can do for you is to give an educated opinion based on the norm for that species. He cannot guarantee compatibility. Ultimately, it is up to the fish to decide if they are compatible or not. Even a peaceful species will have the occasional criminal individual.

Little Fish Equals Big Snack

Remember that big fish eat little fish. Even big *peaceful* fish eat little fish. Tank mates should always be of similar size, and when deciding this, don't just look at the overall size of the fish. Consider the size of the fish's mouth, too. There are many species that can eat a tank mate that is almost the same size as themselves.

Also, be sure to allow for growth. Very few of the fish sold in the local shop are adult size. For example, did you know that a full-grown goldfish can be over a foot long? I've even heard reports of them growing to over 18 inches. Try to pick species that will grow to similar size, and at similar rates. Although clown loaches and oscars grow to about 14 inches long, if you buy them both at a one-inch size the oscar will be large enough to eat the clown loach within a very few weeks.

Can't We All Just Get Along?

Unfortunately, no. We can't, and neither can fish. You can't just throw every fish that interests you into the same tank and expect them all to get along. You must pick compatible species.

Fish may fight for many reasons, but meanness is not one of them. When fish fight, they have good reason to do so. Perhaps they are protecting their home territory from squatters, or maybe they are driving off rivals who would steal their mates. They might be protecting their young from predators or reserving their favorite sleeping spot.

Fish and Tips
Often it will say right on the price tag if a fish is peaceful or aggressive.

Your dealer can steer you toward compatible species. Don't be afraid to ask for advice. Also, you can usually feel free to browse in fish books that are for sale in the store. Be careful not to bend them or get them wet, though, unless you plan to buy. In case you do end up with an ornery fish, check out Chapter 26 on aggression.

Dig That Crazy Fish

Sometimes another problem comes along with territoriality. Many territorial fish like to do their own interior decorating. That is, they like to dig pits and rearrange plants. Sometimes they do it to clear a spot for breeding. Sometimes it is to make a hiding place. Some fish seem to do it just for fun.

For whatever reason, you may find that your meticulously artful landscaping job gets destroyed by a fish with its own idea of what is good taste. I know of a large oscar that so hates the plastic plants its owner put in the tank, that every day it pushes open the lid on the tank and pushes all the plants out onto the floor.

When picking fish, this will be another consideration. The fish don't just need to be compatible with each other. They also need to be compatible with your decorations.

Fish School
Oscar is 1) the common name of the cichlid, *Astronotus ocellatus*; 2) a nickname for the Academy Award; 3) my baloney's first name.

Smart Fish Stay in Schools

Not all fish are territorial. Some are fin-loose and fancy free. They go where the currents take them and home is where they hang their . . . uh . . . well, not their hats, that's for sure—fish don't have hats. Except maybe for red cap orandas.

Anyway, not all fish are territorial. Some of them like to hang out in gangs. This is not a bad thing. They aren't going to spray paint graffiti on the aquarium walls, and they won't be spending weekends at the tattoo parlor. Rather, they'll be in schools. You will find that a school of fish is a relaxing thing to watch.

Fish that are in schools are almost always on the go. Schools of fish—some call them shoals—will add action to your tank. However, it doesn't always work that way. Schooling fish behave very differently, depending on how many of them there are. Next time you visit your dealer, watch him net some fish. Neon tetras (or other tetras) are a good choice, because they like to school. Notice how easy it is for the dealer to catch neons when there is a tank full of them? Now, watch him try to net one out of a tank where there are only half dozen left.

Big difference, huh? You're probably thinking it's easier to catch neons out of a tank that is full of them, because there are so many that it's hard *not* to catch one. Well, partly, you are right. But in reality, it is easier to catch them because the fish behave differently.

Safety in Numbers

When fish school, they depend on the school for protection. They know that there are so many fish that it's hard for a predator to single one out. They have a better chance of going unnoticed as an individual by blending into the school. So when there is a tank full of neons, they cling together and it is easy to net several at once.

However, when most of the fish have sold from that tank and only a few remain, things change dramatically. Try to net a neon now and you will find it frantically trying to escape from you. It will try to hide. It may even poke its tiny little body down between the bits of gravel. In general, it will give you a much more difficult time.

Even when you are not trying to net that neon, it probably will not be boldly patrolling the tank, the way the school of neons did. Instead, it will hang back and be a bit more shy. It does not feel safe, so it behaves cautiously. When you buy fish that prefer to live in schools, it is best to buy enough so that they want to behave as schooling fish. They will feel better, and put on a much more interesting show for you.

The Best Schools Are Crowded

How many fish make up a school? Good question. If we look at nature, schools of fish may have thousands of individuals in them. Certainly, schools of fewer than 25 fish would be uncommon in the wild. I would say that if you *really* want to see schooling behavior, you probably need a minimum of 50 fish per species. Unfortunately, our aquariums are going to prevent that in almost all cases. We just don't have enough room to put that many fish in most tanks.

So here is what I recommend. In large tanks, try to put at least a dozen fish in a school. In medium tanks, keep at least six per schooling species. In small tanks, it is going to take at least three fish to make a group. Even then, the chances are good that they won't stick together all that much. Still, keeping three of a schooling species is better than keeping onesies and twosies, because they will hide less and show less submissive color patterns.

Fish Tales

Tiger barbs like to school. They like to chase each other. But, when there are not enough tiger barbs to chase, they tend to chase and nip at other fish instead. If you keep them, keep at least six or damage may result to their tank mates.

Day Shift and Night Shift

Okay, I've just spent time discussing ways to pick fish that get along with each other. What else must you consider to select fish that get along in the perfect aquarium?

You can have a tank full of peaceful, beautiful fish, but if they are never out when you are around, how much fun would that be? The answer is not much, unless you are *really* easily entertained. When choosing species, consider whether they are diurnal or nocturnal.

Clown loaches are lovely, peaceful fish. They have an attractive pattern of bright orange and dark black stripes, with red fins and whimsical whiskered faces. But, dang it, they are nocturnal and will usually want to hide all day. Luckily, they often learn to come out at feeding time, so you will at least get to see them sometimes.

There is nothing wrong with keeping clown loaches or other night-active fish in your tank. In fact, some of the coolest, most unusual species are nocturnal. (Yes, like humans, the weirdos tend to come out at night.) Just don't fill your whole tank with them, or you will be spending lots of time watching your diving sea dog aerating ornament.

Fish School
For *diurnal* fish, lights out means time to zonk out. *Nocturnal* fish party all night and sleep all day.

I Want to Be on Top

When I discussed fish that like to stake out territories, I mainly referred to fish that like to claim space on the bottom of the tank. But wouldn't it be nice to have some fish swimming in the middle of the tank and at the top, too? An aquarium is art. It is much like a picture frame for living fish. Choose species that will balance the composition.

Many species will prefer to inhabit particular strata of the tank. Most of the schooling fishes will prefer mid-water. Most scavengers will want to hang out near the bottom. Most territorial fish will want to stake out a piece of ground, too.

However, there are exceptions. For example, the various species of gouramies are territorial, and they prefer to stay near the top of the tank. Silver hatchetfish and zebra danios like to school, but they also prefer the upper reaches of the tank.

Anyway, a good mix of top, middle, and bottom dwellers will help balance the aquatic picture. There will be fewer fights, and more enjoyment for you.

Please, Sir, May I Have Some More?

Some of your fishy pets will have specialized diets, and it is up to you to see that they get their fair share. For example, a tiretrack eel will need live blackworms in its diet, if it is to prosper. Any good aquarium store will sell them. You need to be willing to provide these to keep a tiretrack eel.

Also, if you are feeding during the day but have some fish that only eat at night, can you see what may happen? When the nocturnal fish come out looking for food, there is none left. They will starve, even though you feed the fish every day. Make sure your feeding regimen allows for this. I'll talk about that more in Chapter 19.

How Many Pesos for That Pisces?

You also may want to consider the price of the fish you buy for your first batch. Believe it or not, a brand new, sparkling clean tank is rougher on fish than an established, dirty aquarium. Check out Chapter 16 on cycling your aquarium to see why. Since your first fish are at the most risk, it is advisable to choose cheaper, hardier, species. You can add the more delicate or pricier fish a bit later.

Get Out Your Ruler

How many fish will fit in your tank? You'll get many answers to this question. Some are right. Some are wrong. And some answers are sometimes right and sometimes wrong. Let's look at a couple of popular rules:

1. You need 12 square inches of water surface for each one-inch length of fish.

2. Don't keep more than one inch of fish per gallon of water.

Let's talk about that first rule. An aquarium that is 12 inches wide by 24 inches long by 16 inches high would give you 288 square inches of water surface (length times width).

Fish and Tips
There are two ways to measure fish length: *Standard length* is the length from tip of nose to base of tail. *Total length* is measured from tip of nose to tip of tail. Use standard length to determine how many fish will fit in your tank.

Take 288 and divide by 12 inches of water surface per fish, and you can see that you could keep 24 one-inch fish in that tank—or, say, 12 two-inch fish. Either way, it's a total of 24 inches of fish.

Now let's look at the second rule—which, by the way, is the one that is most popular and you are most likely to be told by your dealer. I tend to use that rule with my customers, too. It just so happens that the dimensions for the aquarium I used to discuss the first rule are the dimensions for a typical 20-gallon aquarium. According to the one-inch-per-gallon rule, a 20-gallon aquarium will hold 20 inches of fish. That is, 20 one-inch fish, or 10 two-inch fish.

Fish Tales
Your dealer's tanks probably will be a lot more crowded than the rules above allow. Most dealers can do this safely because they have central filtration systems on their tanks. These systems connect each tank to a larger volume of water that is out of sight. This water circulates, via plumbing to each tank, 24 hours a day. Also, the central system allows the dealer to do *daily* partial water changes on every tank. In other words, *your dealer is a skilled professional. Don't try to crowd fish like this at home.*

It's Not So Much a Rule as a Guideline

You can see that both rules give similar results. The numbers are not that far off. However, *both rules only work for small fish up to three inches in length.* If you apply the same rules to larger fish, you will fail very quickly. One 20-inch fish would not live in either of those tanks, for example.

Here is why. Those rules only consider the length of the fish. The problem is that, when a fish grows, its height and breadth change, too. In fact, when a fish doubles its length, it is increasing its mass and volume about eight times. Technically, any change in length will cube the change in mass, or volume, of the fish. Below is a conversion chart to illustrate this for you. Notice how rapidly the change occurs.

Fish Mass

Fish Length	Equivalent in One-Inch Fish	How Many Gallons Per Fish This Size?
1 inch	1	1
2 inches	8	1
3 inches	27	1
4 inches	64	2
5 inches	125	4
6 inches	216	8*
7 inches	343	10*
8 inches	512	15*
9 inches	729	18*
10 inches	1,000	20*
11 inches	1,331	20*
12 inches	1,728	25*
24 inches	13,824	125*

These figures assume that you will make weekly partial water changes. Otherwise, waste will build up too quickly.

Notice how much difference there is between the mass of 24 one-inch fish (24) and one 24-inch fish (13,824). It is the same number of total inches in length, but the difference in fish mass units is 13,800. Yikes!

Anyway, the rules above are guidelines. If you only keep fish on the small end of the scale and don't bend the rules, you should have absolutely no problems.

By the way, don't forget to allow for growth. A fish that is one inch long today may be four inches long in a month, or a foot long in a year.

What I Just Said Is Not Quite True

Well, actually, it *is* true—but not quite yet. You see, while your tank *will* hold one inch of fish per gallon, it won't hold that much when you first set it up. In fact, *you should not put more than one-half-inch of fish per gallon in a new tank.* That is because the tank is not yet cycled. The helpful bacteria that break down ammonia and other fish waste are not yet present. See Chapter 16 on cycling your new tank for full details. *It's very important.*

Don't overcrowd. One inch of fish per gallon is a full load. (Stock only half that many fish while you cycle your new tank.)

You know that your tank is too crowded when . . .

. . . you toss in just one more fish, and it bounces.

. . . you toss in just one more fish, and they toss it back.

. . . you toss in just one more fish, and the floor sags.

. . . you can turn the lights on and the bottom of the tank is still dark.

. . . you remove all of the fish, and the water level drops 75 percent.

. . . sardine cans begin to look roomy.

. . . you can't do a 25 percent water change without the fish on top getting dry.

. . . all of the fish swim to one side, and the other side rises an inch.

. . . the only air pump that is big enough is made by Boeing.

. . . the algae eaters have to cling to the *outside* glass.

. . . you can do a 50 percent water change with a thimble.

. . . your ammonia-eating bacteria have grown to five pounds each.

. . . your fish *beg* you to flush them down the toilet.

. . . the cat walks across the top of the aquarium and you have no lid on it.

That's Sick!

It won't do you much good to be able to pick compatible interesting fish, if you can't tell a healthy one from a sick one. It only takes one sick fish to infect a whole tank and mess up your day. So let's talk about ways to spot a healthy fish. Be sure to read Chapter 25 on stress and disease for detailed descriptions of warning signs that signal a sick fish.

When you go fish shopping, look for fish with clear eyes and skin. The color should be bright and even, and there should be no unusual discoloration or bloody patches. Be sure the fish has good body weight. Avoid fish with hollow bellies and bent spines.

Watch the way they hold their fins. Healthy fish usually keep their fins fairly erect. They'll spread them even more when courting a mate or displaying to mark territory. Clamped fins (fins held folded against the body) are signs of a fish that is sick, tired, and droopy.

A healthy fish has fins with smooth edges and no splits. Ragged edges may be a sign of disease, or a sign that the fish has been bullied. Split fins are generally the results of fights, too. A split fin or two is not usually a big deal. Split fins heal quickly. But a ragged-looking fish has been through too much already.

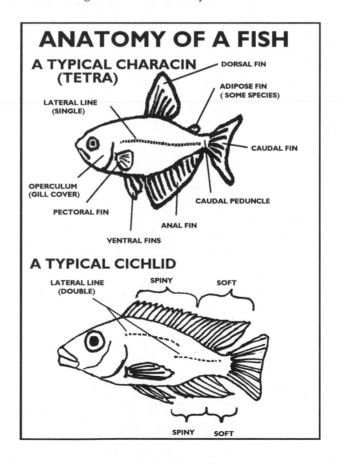

Look for fish that exhibit behavior and coloration that is normal for the species. For example, if a species likes to school, avoid the fish hanging around in the corner away from the rest of the group.

Note the activity level of the fish. Does it show an interest in life? Avoid lethargic specimens of normally active species, but be aware that it is normal behavior for many fish to sit there and do nothing most of the time.

Avoid purchasing from tanks that contain fish showing signs of stress or illness. Particularly avoid tanks that contain dead fish. Note the color of the water in the tank. Discolored water probably means the fish are sick and the tank is under medication.

Okay, that's enough about how to pick fish. Let's move on to which fish to pick, in the next chapter.

The Least You Need to Know

➤ Big fish eat little fish. Even big *peaceful* fish eat little fish.

➤ Be sure you know if a species is compatible with your tank before you buy it. Ask your dealer for advice. Don't forget to ask if the fish needs a special diet.

➤ Consider whether the species is a top dweller or bottom dweller. Also, some fish are active at night and hide during the day.

➤ If you like fish that school, always buy a small group, not just one fish.

➤ One inch of fish per gallon of water is a full load, but don't go more than half that in a new tank.

Popular Fish for Beginners

There are thousands of species of tropical fish available in the aquarium trade, and it is not within the scope of this book to talk about all of them. Instead, I want to focus on species that are readily available, easy to keep, and generally compatible. After all, it won't do much good to talk about fish that you probably can't find in your local store, are too delicate for a beginner, or can't be kept together.

Name That Fish

Before I tell you about some good choices of species for your new tank, I want to fill you in on the difference between common names and scientific names.

The scientific name is the standardized Latin name for a species. It is a name that has been agreed upon by the scientific community and is universal. In every country and every language, educated people will know what species you mean, because the name is standardized. For example, the guppy's scientific name is *Poecilia reticulata*. Normally, the scientific name will never change, but as science progresses sometimes fish get reclassified. The guppy, for example, used to be *Lebistes reticulatus*, and many books will still list it that way.

The common name or trade name of a fish is the name it will go by in the local stores. It is the name you are more likely to know the fish by and the name most people will use. Here in North America, the common name will be in English.

The thing about common names is that they are not standardized. Take the guppy as an example. Most of us call it a guppy, but in some places, they call it the mosquito fish (several other species go by that name, too) or thousand-color fish. Common names vary by country, region, dealer, and local custom.

Common names usually will be all you need to know, but if you get to a point where you want your dealer to find something exotic for you, it may help to know the scientific name. To make things even more, or maybe less, confusing, you also will run into many species where the scientific name *is* the common name. For example, the common name of *Melanochromis auratus* is melanochromis auratus. Sheesh!

Anyway, in the descriptions of individual species, I will list both the scientific name and as many common names as I've seen and can remember. I'll even be nice and give you the pronunciations of the more difficult common names. If you want to learn proper pronunciation of the scientific names, though, I suggest you take a Latin course.

Algae-Eaters

Fish and Tips
It may not be wise to add algae-eating fish to a brand new aquarium. There won't yet be enough algae to keep them fed and happy. Add them later.

Every tank probably should have some sort of algae-eating fish. Algae-eating fish help keep the glass clean—yes, they do windows—and they help keep algae off the plants, rocks, and decorations. They'll also scavenge for uneaten foods.

The algae-eating species that I'm about to list are egglayers, not commonly bred in the aquarium. They are all peaceful toward fish of other species, though they may fight a bit among themselves. They need a fair amount of vegetation to stay at peak health, so consider offering some Spirulina algae tablets in addition to the foods you offer the other fish. Plecostomus will munch away at the driftwood in your tank, too.

Chinese Algae-Eater

(*Gyrinocheilus aymonieri*) Talk about a misnamed fish! It is not from China, but from Thailand. This fish is common in stores, and the name would have you believe that it is an excellent choice. *It is not.* As the fish grows, it eats less algae and tends to attack other fish to feed off their body slime. Consequently, it often ends up being the last survivor in an aquarium. I recommend that you avoid this fish, and frankly, I wish dealers would stop carrying them. There are many better choices. It also sells as the Siamese or Thai algae-eater.

Otocinclus

(*Otocinclus spp.*) Pronounced *oh-toh-SINK-lus*. Usually, this fish will be listed as otocinclus, but you also may find it listed as pygmy sucker cat, pygmy algae-eater, or otto cat. It is a great little algae-eater. It stays small (under two inches) and is very peaceful. Since it stays small, it takes more of them to do the same job as some larger species, but they have the added advantage of being able to get into some tight spots, such as between plant leaves, where the others can't reach. Don't confuse this fish with the aggressive Chinese algae-eater. They look similar, but the otocinclus has a horizontal line down the side, while the Chinese algae-eater has a checkerboard pattern.

Plecostomus

(*Hypostomus plecostomus, Ancistrus spp., Xenocara spp.,* and others) Pronounced *pleh-COST-oh-mus*. Plecostomus has become a catch-all name for many types of bony suckermouth catfish. Pleco and suckermouth cat are other common names. There are many species available, and almost all are excellent algae-eaters. The most common varieties are a dull mottled brown, but there are species with bright yellow fins, red fins, blue eyes, and even black and white zebra stripes. Some species can get quite large—up to two feet in length. If you want varieties that stay small (under five inches), try asking for clown plecostomus, bushy-nose plecostomus, or wide-mouth plecostomus. Plecostomus are nocturnal.

Plecos do windows. They are great algae eaters.

133

Fish Tales

The black and white striped zebra pleco is the only pleco that is a lousy algae eater. When you see how beautiful it is, you may want it anyway. By the way, do you know what you call a $100 suckermouth cat? A plecostoomuch.

Whiptail Cat

(*Loricaria spp.*) This fish is very similar to plecostomus, but has a thinner, more delicate appearance. It is nocturnal.

Stick Cat

(*Farlowella spp.*) Also called twig cat. The name is very appropriate for this nocturnal fish. It really does look like a stick. It also acts like a stick. You don't even need a net to catch one. Just reach in and pick it up. I find it interesting the way they will hang inside the leaves of amazon sword plants, looking very much like a twig that should be there.

Siamese Flying Fox

(*Epalzeorhynchus siamensis*) This fish is also called the Siamese algae-eater, but that name is sometimes confused for the Chinese algae-eater. The Siamese flying fox is particularly popular because it is one of the few species that eats brush algae. None of the other algae-eating species listed here will do that. Unfortunately, there is much confusion about this fish. At least three species are sold under the same name. The true Siamese flying fox—the one you want—has a black stripe from the tip of the nose through the center of the tail. It also does not have a sucker mouth like most other algae eaters. A couple of other species, the false Siamese flying fox and the stone-lapping fish, are sometimes confused for it. Also, don't confuse it with the regular flying fox, *Epalzeorhynchus kalopterus*.

Borneo Sucker

(*Pseudogastromyzon myersi*) This fish is also sold as the Hong Kong pleco, Myer's hillstream loach, butterfly pleco, and who knows what else? Can you see why common names aren't always the best? Anyway, it's a nice little algae-eater, but it requires very high oxygen levels. So don't keep it in crowded conditions or water with low circulation.

Barbs

This fish has small whiskers, called barbels (*BAR-buls*), at the corners of its mouth, which is where it gets its name. Barbs are generally peaceful and most of the varieties that are available stay small enough to keep in a typical community tank. Barbs are egglayers, active during the day, and they prefer to live in schools. The males are usually more colorful and the females are usually heavier bodied. Barbs are great choices if you are looking for mid-water swimmers.

Tiger Barb

(*Capoeta tetrazona*) This is one of my favorites. It normally has a pattern of bold vertical stripes, though there are some albino and solid green-black varieties available. Tiger barbs grow to about two inches in length, and are generally peaceful. Note, however, that is best to keep at least six. Sometimes, when the school is smaller than that, they get a little nippy. It is also a bit risky to mix them with anything that has long fins.

Keep tiger barbs in groups to reduce nipping.

Gold Barb

(*Puntius sachsi*) This is an attractive little fish. It is a pastel yellow color, with some green or black speckled highlights. The adults develop a little red coloration, too. They grow to about three inches in length.

Checkerboard Barb

(*Capoeta oligolepsis*) Another small fish. It is mostly silver with black edges on each scale that give a checkerboard appearance. Males get a little reddish.

Cherry Barb

(*Capoeta titteya*) The female is pinkish, but the adult male turns cherry red. If the light hits them just right, you may see reflective blue highlights.

Black Ruby Barb

(*Puntius nigrofasciatus*) When young, it looks much like a tiger barb, but with heavier stripes. Adult males will lose most of the stripe pattern, turning more solid black with a ruby head and highlights.

Rosy Barb

(*Puntius conchonius*) The female is a flashy silver and the male turns bright pink to red. Long-finned and gold varieties are now also available. Rosy barbs grow to about six inches and also can stand cooler water than the other barbs.

Tinfoil Barb

(*Barbodes schwanenfeldii*) Here is a fish that gets larger than the rest in this group—up to 16 inches. However, it is quite peaceful and can be kept with smaller fish until it grows. This fish is metallic silver with black and red highlights on the fins. Tinfoil barbs also have a tendency to munch plants.

> **Fish and Tips**
> Usually, catfish with small mouths and short whiskers will be peaceful scavengers, active during the day. Those with large mouths and long flowing whiskers are usually predatory, and are more likely to be nocturnal.

Catfish

There are many species of catfish available for the aquarium. Some are peaceful scavengers. Some are vicious predators. You want the former, unless you are planning to mix it with other fish of similar size and aggression. Another benefit of the peaceful scavenger varieties of catfish is that they are more likely to be active during the day. So they are more fun to watch.

Corydoras Cat

(*Corydoras spp.*) Pronounced *kor-ee-DOR-us*. You can't find a better scavenger than the various species of cory cat. These fish generally stay under two inches in length, are hardy and peaceful. They're active during the day, eat just about any food, do a good job of rooting in the gravel, and have a very comical way of occasionally winking at you. Like most bony catfish, they'll often pop to the surface to grab a bubble of air, which they swallow. The oxygen is absorbed as it passes through the gastrointestinal tract. Cory cats are happiest in schools. I like to keep one per five gallons of tank water. The bronze cat (*C. aeneus*), leopard cat (*C. julii*), and skunk cat (*C. arcuatus*) are some popular subspecies. There are also some albino cory cats available.

Cory cats are unbeatable scavengers.

Armored Cat

(*Callichthys spp., Hoplosternum spp., Dianema spp.*) I've lumped several similar fish into this group. They are all peaceful scavengers, rarely growing over four inches in the aquarium. Porthole cat and hoplo cat are a couple of common names for them.

Raphael Cat

I'm going to lump many genera and species with similar body shape into this group. The striped raphael cat (*Platydoras costatus*), the spotted raphael cat (*Agamyxis pectinifrons*), and the talking cat (*Amblydoras hancocki*) are some popular varieties. The first two cats have chocolate color with cream stripes or spots. The last is mottled brown. All these cats can rub body parts together to make a slight squeaking sound, which is where the "talking" comes in. This group of cats is more active at night.

Upside-Down Cat

(*Synodontis nigriventris*) Yes, this fish really does spend most of its time swimming upside down. Mottled brown in coloration, it likes to hang underneath logs and driftwood, and grows to four inches. There are several species of *Synodontis* catfish available. Some are quite attractively marked. They'll all swim upside down at times. Beware, though—some species grow to over a foot in length.

Glass Catfish

(*Kryptopterus bicirrhis*) This species is just too cool. Except for a silvery sac where the internal organs are, it's completely transparent. You can see the skeleton and you can actually see objects that are behind the fish. Glass cats are not scavengers like most cats. They like to hang mid water, near the plants, darting out for food as it drifts by. Glass cats do best when kept in groups.

Polka Dot Cat

(*Pimelodus pictus*) Also called pictus cat, or angel cat. This is a very attractive fish. It is silvery white with black dots. However, it is *not* a good choice for most community tanks, because it is a predator. It will eat any fish that fits in its mouth, and often takes nips at those that won't yet fit. If you get this fish, be sure to pick fish that will grow along with it. It gets to be 10 inches long.

Fish Tales

Scavengers are very important in your aquarium. They help keep your tank clean by finding and eating leftover food that would otherwise spoil in the tank. Still, it is *food* that they eat, not fish waste. Only filtration and regular maintenance will remove fish feces from your tank. In other words, only you can keep your tank clean.

Cichlids

Pronounced *SICK-lids*. This group of fish includes a large array of species. Almost all are territorial and therefore aggressive to at least some degree. Most fish that get big and mean are members of this group, but there are species that are suitable for the typical community tank.

Angelfish

(*Pterophyllum scalare*) The unusual, graceful shape of the angelfish makes it quite popular. The scientific name translates to "winged leaf; like a flight of stairs," and is based on the unique shape of the fins. Angels will generally mix in a community tank, but be aware that they can grow to over six inches in length and may not mix well with fish that stay much smaller. Also, their long fins make them easy targets for fin-nipping species.

Angelfish are one of the most popular species. They grow to around six inches, though—so they may not be the best choice for your tank.

Kribensis

(*Pelvicachromis pulcher*) Kribensis, pronounced *krih-BEN-sis*, is a delightful little fish. The species' true namesake, *P. kribensis*, is rare in the hobby, though. These colorful fish have horizontal stripes, bright pink bellies, and yellow-edged fins. The fins have peacock spots on them, particularly those of the male. If you get a pair of kribs, they will spawn quite freely in the community tank, residing near a rock or piece of driftwood. Like other cichlids, the parents will guard the young, and it is entertaining to watch them herd a school of fry. Adult males may grow to four inches; females grow to maybe three inches.

Ram

(*Microgeophagus ramirezi*) The blue ram is the version of this fish with natural coloration. There are also gold and long-finned varieties that have been developed through selective breeding. Rams are beautiful, with spots of iridescent blue and yellow. Females tend to have pink bellies. This fish is a bit more delicate than most cichlids, though, and not at all aggressive. Rams are truly a dwarf cichlid, rarely growing over two inches.

Danios

Pronounced *DAN-ee-o*, this group of fishes is one of the most popular. They are bred in huge quantities on commercial farms, so the price is very low. Danios are also among the hardiest of fishes and, being highly active, they will add action to any tank. To best enjoy them, keep them in schools.

Zebra Danio

(*Brachydanio rerio*) The zebra danio is a fish that rarely sits still. It has horizontal stripes of navy blue. Like all danios, the female is heavier bodied than the male. Adult size is around two inches. Long-finned and gold varieties of this fish are also available.

Zebra danios never slow down.

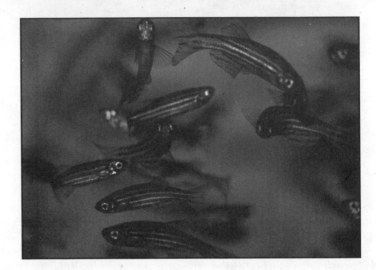

Pearl Danio

(*Brachydanio albolineatus*) The general color of this fish is pink with a light blue sheen. It grows to two inches.

Leopard Danio

(*Brachydanio frankei*) There is some question whether this fish is a true species or a hybrid of the pearl danio and the zebra danio.

Giant Danio

(*Danio malabaricus*) This fish gets quite a bit larger than the other danios—up to four inches. Couple that with its high level of activity and it may not be the best choice for all community tanks. However, it will mix with most fish.

White Cloud Mountain Minnow

(*Tanichthys albonubes*) People often have trouble identifying this fish in the dealer's tanks, because it is commonly labeled simply as white cloud. If you look for a white fish, you won't find this one. A man named Tan discovered it in China, at White Cloud Mountain. This fish is not a tropical fish at all. It comes from cold mountain water. However, it has adapted quite nicely to the aquarium. It is quite hardy and peaceful. When small, it has a horizontal stripe that is so iridescent that poor man's neon was once a common name for it. As the fish matures, the stripe fades but the fins get bright red with a bit of yellow. It is interesting that this fish won't eat its own eggs and young—but of course, every other fish in the tank will.

Eels

Some fish labeled as eels are not eels at all. In fact, some are not even fish. Additionally, most true eels are very poor choices for the aquarium because they are highly predatory, prefer saltwater, and present other problems. However, there are some eels suitable for freshwater aquariums.

Spiny Eels

(*Mastacembelus spp.* and *Macrognathus spp.*) The spiny eels are quite interesting and can do well in a community aquarium, if you offer live and frozen foods. They will not survive on flake food. Most won't even touch it. Live blackworms and brine shrimp are great for them. These fish like to dig, and will spend much of their time buried with only their heads sticking out. Peacock eels, zig-zag eels, and yellow spiny eels will all generally stay under six inches in length. Fire eels and tiretrack eels can grow to over two feet, though, so keep that in mind if you buy small specimens.

Gouramies

Pronounced *go-RAH-mee*. There are quite a few unique things about this group of fish. For starters, they have a special chamber in their gills, called the labyrinth. It allows these fish to grab a bubble of air from the surface and breathe from it, thereby surviving in places where other fish would suffocate due to low levels of dissolved oxygen in the water. Because of the labyrinth, gouramies can often survive quite well in fish bowls.

These fish usually live in shallow, weedy water, such as ditches. Since they live where there are many weeds but not much water, they tend to be protective of their space. All gouramies are territorial to some extent, and particularly toward their own species. Another interesting thing about this group of fish is that most build bubble nests when they spawn. We'll talk more about that in Chapter 21 on breeding. The feeler-like pectoral fins are another interesting feature.

Dwarf Gourami

(*Colisa lalia*) As far as gouramies go, this fish is quite peaceful. It normally will not harass other species. The male is spectacularly striped in iridescent red and blue, while the female is mostly silver. Adult size is about 2.5 inches. Due to its territorial nature, it is best to keep only one or two of these per tank. A pair will usually mix nicely with other fish. There are some strains of this fish that are nearly pure red or pure blue. They sell under names such as fire, flame, neon blue, and royal blue gourami.

Male dwarf gouramies have spectacular red and blue stripes.

Honey Dwarf Gourami

(*Colisa sota*, formerly *C. chuna*) This fish is very similar to the dwarf gourami, but the male has a chocolate brown color with a black to blue underside and yellow edging on the dorsal fin. The female is light brown with a central horizontal stripe.

Giant Gourami

(*Colisa fasciata*) The name of this fish is a bit confusing, because it isn't a giant at all. Unlike the true giant gouramy (*Osphronemus gouramy*), which grows to two feet in length, this giant gourami is a giant only in the family of dwarf gouramies, and grows to around four inches. The pattern is similar to the dwarf gourami, but the stripes are bolder and the colors are less iridescent.

Kissing Gourami

(*Helostoma temmincki*) Probably every hobbyist keeps this fish at one time or another. They really do kiss! Kissers are generally quite peaceful to other fish. They can grow to over a foot, though, so you may need to move them to a bigger tank at some point. The pink kisser is most popular, but there is a metallic green kisser on the market, too.

Fish Tales

The best way to enjoy kissing gouramies is to buy two of them. In short order, they will stake off opposite sides of the tank. Whenever one of them gets too near the imaginary territorial border between, the other will rush over and start kissing it on the lips. Kissing is how the fish mark their territorial boundaries, and it is very comical to watch.

Pearl Gourami

(*Trichogaster leeri*) The pattern on this fish is like a lace doily. The male develops long, lacy fins and a warm orange and blue coloration at maturity. Five inches is adult size.

Blue Gourami

(*Trichogaster trichopterus*) Three-spot gourami is a less-used common name for this fish. There are also other varieties, sold as gold, platinum, lavender, and opaline gourami. I am a bit reticent about including this fish in my list of popular beginner species. It is quite hardy and can sometimes mix well in community tanks. However, this fish is more aggressive than most of the other gouramies, and it also grows to six inches, so it really only works well in larger aquariums—I don't recommend it for 10-gallon tanks.

Siamese Fighting Fish

(*Betta splendens*) Also known as the betta—that's *BET-uh*—this fish is often well known even to non-hobbyists. The males fight with each other, the females fight with each other, and the males may kill a female that is unwilling to mate. So it is best not to keep more than one of this species in any tank. They will mix with most other fish, though. The popular belief that they will fight to the death is incorrect. However, the resulting injuries often lead to infections that lead to death.

Males are more popular because they develop long, flowing fins and come in several bright colors. Be careful what you mix them with, though, because this is a slow-moving fish and the long fins are easy targets for any species that likes to nip. Also, bettas will sometimes attack other species that have similar colors.

Fish and Tips
If you really want to see male bettas in full display, put a mirror up to the glass. When they see their own reflections, they put on quite a show for their "rival."

Paradise Fish

(*Macropodus opercularis*) This fish is red and blue striped, with a red tail. It is attractive, but more aggressive than most in the gourami family, so I don't recommend it for small tanks. However, it is an excellent choice to keep alone in a fish bowl, much the way male bettas are often kept. Paradise fish will fare much better in a bowl than a goldfish will, because goldfish don't have the labyrinth in their gills.

Guppies

The good old guppy was one of the very first fish kept in aquariums. It stays small, it is very hardy, and the males are sprinkled with many colors. Additionally, no two seem to be exactly alike. Even better, this fish is a livebearer, so it is very easy to breed. The anal fin of mature males changes into a tube, called the gonopodium, that is able to internally fertilize the females. Males will spend much of their day courting the ladies. It is best to keep at least two females for each male, so that the females will get some occasional rest.

Common Guppy

(*Poecilia reticulata*) Usually sold as feeder guppies (that is, food for other fish), this is the short-finned strain of guppy. It retains the shape and color of wild fish.

Compare the wild-type common guppy (left) to this selectively bred strain of fancy guppy.

Fancy Guppy

(*Poecilia reticulata*) Selective breeding of the common guppy has resulted in hundreds of strains of this fish. They come in all colors, with long fins, short fins, huge delta-shaped tails, pintails, lyretails, and veiltails. The males are quite impressive, but it should be noted that the selective breeding has resulted not only in better colors and larger fins, but also in genetic weakness. Fancy guppies are much more prone to disease than their short-finned common counterparts. This is because the large fins are easy targets for fin-nippers, and wounds are easy target for disease organisms. Some popular varieties are blue delta, red tuxedo, and green cobraskin guppies.

Loaches

The various species of loaches come in different body shapes. Some look like worms and some are more torpedo shaped. What they have in common is a spine beneath each eye, which can be erected to use as a weapon. It's a good idea to be careful handling this fish when you net it, particularly larger specimens, or you could get jabbed. Many fishes in this family are called botias, pronounced *boh-TEE-ya*. The ones labeled as loaches are usually peaceful, while the species with the word botia in the common name have a tendency to get nippy with other fish.

Coolie Loach

(*Acanthophthalmus kuhlii, A. semicinctus*) The oddity of this fish makes it quite appealing. It has an elongated body, much like an eel or worm, and the body is banded in pink and black. It is cute little devil, but likes to hide during the day. Mostly, you'll see it in the evening. However, like other loaches, it will learn to come out at feeding time, too. Maximum size is four inches.

A tank full of coolie loaches is always an attraction.

Dojo Loach

(*Misgurnus anguillicaudatus*) It is also called the weather loach because of its tendency to become very active when the barometric pressure changes. This fish is another with a worm-shaped body. The color is mostly mottled brown, though there may be a yellowish tinge. There is also a pure yellow commercial variety that has been developed. That one is sold as the gold dojo loach. It grows to about 10 inches.

Clown Loach

(*Botia macracantha*) The clown loach is a truly beautiful fish. The body is orange with a couple of bold black vertical stripes, and red fins. It is rare to see specimens above six inches in length, though I have seen 14-inchers. Generally, they are available in one-inch to three-inch sizes. This fish can be a little pricey. The price increases with the size of the fish, and at different times of the year.

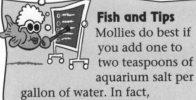

Fish and Tips
Clown loaches will commonly lie down when resting. People often see the fish on its side and mistakenly think it is sick.

You see, these fish are all wild caught. They spawn once a year, so the collectors catch millions of them—enough to last a year. They then care for and feed them until the next breeding season. Since it costs time and money to do this, the price increases until next year's crop comes around. Then it drops again. Clown loaches can live 25 years, so don't let the price scare you off. January or February is the cheapest time to buy them.

Yo-Yo Loach

(*Botia lohachata*) This fish has the same body shape as the clown loach. It has dark markings against a cream background that seem to spell the word Y-O-Y-O. Hence the common name. Adult size is around four inches.

Horseface Loach

(*Acanthopsis choirorhynchus*) This unusual fish has a slender body and a head shaped like a horse. They commonly burrow in the gravel, with only the comical face sticking out. Long-nose loach is a synonym. Horseface loaches are quite peaceful and grow to eight inches.

Fish and Tips
Mollies do best if you add one to two teaspoons of aquarium salt per gallon of water. In fact, mollies can even tolerate pure seawater. They also prefer temperatures around 80°F (27°C) and extra vegetation in the diet.

Mollies

This livebearing fish (*Poecilia latipinna, P. sphenops, P. velifera*) is available in several varieties. There are silver, black, gold, and marble colorations. One black-spotted silver version has appropriately earned the name dalmatian molly. The males of some species have a large sailfin that they splay during courtship or territorial display. In the wild, mollies are found in coastal areas. As with all livebearers, you should keep at least two females for each male. Sphenops mollies grow to around two inches; the others grow to six inches.

Platies

Pronounced *PLAT-ee* (*Xiphophorus maculatus*), they are sometimes also called moons. The blue moon is the closest thing to the wild coloration of this fish. Humans have selectively bred many other varieties, though, including gold ones and bright red ones. The red wag platy, with its solid red body and black fins, is one of my favorites. Platies are livebearers, growing to a bit over two inches in length.

Common Color Patterns of Platies, Variatus, and Swordtails

Fish	Pattern
Wag	Solid-color body, black fins
Crescent	Black crescent at base of tail
Tuxedo	Large black wedge-shaped patch on side of body
Sunburst	Front half yellow, back half red
Mickey Mouse	Crescent with two additional spots (turn your head sideways to see Mickey's shape)

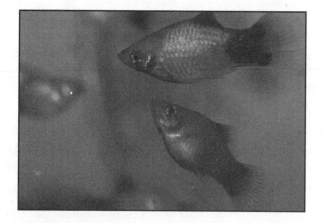

Wild platies are mostly gray, but tank-raised strains like these Mickey Mouse platies are full of color.

Rainbowfish

Rainbows are a group of fish from Australia and New Guinea. They are hardy and active, and most prefer a little aquarium salt in the water.

Australian Rainbow

(*Melanotaenia splendida*) This fish gives a good example of where we get the name rainbowfish. Practically every color of the rainbow is represented, depending on how the light hits the fish.

Banded Rainbow

(*Melanotaenia trifasciata*) Several varieties of this fish, including the goyder river rainbow, are available in stores. Color patterns vary, depending on river of origin.

Blue & Yellow Rainbow

(*Melanotaenia boesemani*) Usually sold as the boesemani rainbow, the male is navy blue on the front half and yellow-orange on the rear half. Adult size is around four inches.

Turquoise Rainbow

(*Melanotaenia lacustris*) Sometimes sold as the Lake Kutubu rainbow, this fish has a gentle turquoise color, and the male has more color and darker fins.

Red Irian Rainbow

(*Glossolepis incisus*) The red irian rainbow—that's irian, not Iranian—is a favorite rainbow species. The male turns solid red-orange in color, while the female is an olive-silver. Adult size is six inches.

Threadfin Rainbow

(*Iriatherina werneri*) This species stays much smaller than most other rainbows, growing to only two inches. The male has spectacularly long, thread-like fins. I've also seen thread-fins sold under the name featherfin rainbow.

Rasboras

Raz-BOR-uh is the correct pronunciation. There are several quite different body shapes in this group. All like to school and tend to stay in the middle or top zones of the tank.

Harlequin Rasbora

(*Rasbora heteromorpha*) This fish is one of my favorites. The body is pink with a large black triangle, edged in blue. The fins are red. The colors intensify as the fish grows. Adult size is over two inches.

Brilliant Rasbora

(*Rasbora borapetensis*) A silver fish with ablack horizontal line edged in yellow, and red at the base of the tail, this fish looks best in schools. Adult size is under three inches.

Scissortail Rasbora

(*Rasbora trilineata*) Scissortails are silver fish with a large black spot at the end of each lobe of the tail. When the fish swims, it makes a scissoring motion with its tail, which is how it got its name. They grow to four inches. Occasionally, you'll see the red scissortail rasbora, which has more red in the tail and grows to six inches.

Sharks

There are many species that fall into this group. None of them are true sharks. True sharks live only in saltwater. These fish have gotten the name "shark" for a couple of reasons. First, the shape of the dorsal fin is like that of a shark, but mostly I suspect that the name just helps them sell better. It would be more accurate to call most of them carp, but that is not so enticing.

Red-Tail Shark

(*Labeo bicolor*) This striking fish is black with a red tail. It is a good scavenger and may even eat a bit of algae—though I wouldn't count on it to control algae. Red-tail sharks get along with most fish, but they don't like others of their own, or similar, species. So just keep one per tank. Adult size is under six inches.

Rainbow Shark

(*Labeo erythrurus*) Rainbow sharks are very similar to red-tail sharks, except that all of the fins are red. The care and adult size is the same.

Rainbow sharks fight with each other. Only keep one per tank.

Tricolor Shark

(*Balantiocheilos melanopterus*) Also called the bala shark or silver shark, this fish develops more striking color as it grows. It is flashy silver, and the fins are red at the base and black on the edges. These sharks like to school. The fish are very peaceful; but adult size is 12 inches or so, so they are not a good choice for small aquariums unless you plan to move them to a bigger tank later.

Something's Fishy

The black shark (*Morulius chrysophekadion)* is very similar to the red-tail and rainbow sharks, though without any red fins. Avoid this fish. They grow to 18 inches in length and are quite a bit more aggressive.

Iridescent Shark

(*Pangasius sutchi*) This fish also sells under the names barracuda shark and pangasius cat. Iridescent sharks are very peaceful, but grow to over 12 inches. Plus, they are only happy in schools, so don't buy just one. One note about this species: When your dealer bags them, it is common for them to faint. They roll about in the bag as if dead. They aren't. The fish will recover when it gets home.

Swordtails

There are several strains of these *Xiphophorus helleri* available, including red velvet, red wag, gold, black, pineapple, green, and marigold swordtails. The male has a large, pointed extension on his tail that gives the fish its name. They're quite similar to platies, but with more elongated bodies. These are livebearers, so keep at least two females for each male.

Swordtails are excellent jumpers. Keep your tank well-covered.

Tetras

Pronounced *TEH-truh*, some of the most popular fish fall into this group, also known as the characins (*KARE-uh-sin*). If you want to see the best color and most peaceful behavior from these fish, be sure to keep them in schools.

Neon Tetra

(*Paracheirodon innesi*) Without a doubt, the aptly named neon tetra is the most popular aquarium fish in the world. The bright red and iridescent neon green stripes must be seen to be believed. The fish is peaceful, grows to only two inches long, and likes to school.

Fish Tales

Many fish will fade at night. Neon tetras and cardinal tetras probably illustrate this better than any other fish. After the lights have been out for a while, if you look at these fish you'll see that not only have their spectacular iridescent colors disappeared, but the fish will have become nearly transparent.

Cardinal Tetra

(*Paracheirdon axelrodi*) This is my absolute favorite fish. They are similar to neon tetras, but are even more colorful. The red stripe goes from head to tail—it only goes half way on the neon—and the other stripe is an iridescent neon blue. A tank full of cardinal tetras is spectacular. Adult size is about two and a half inches. These fish will school, but they prefer to hang out in the shade along the edge of the plants.

Black Tetra

(*Gymnocorymbus ternetzi*) Its coin-like shape and black markings make this a popular fish. Occasionally, it is reported to be nippy, but that is generally only when not kept in a school. Two inches is the size limit.

Serpae Tetra

(*Hyphessobrycon serpae*) *SER-pee* is the correct pronunciation of this red tetra. The fins are black with bluish white tips. The serpae tetra is another fish that is occasionally known to be nippy. It usually works out well, though. Two inches is adult size.

Serpae tetras are a popular choice, but keep them in groups.

Glowlight Tetra

(*Hemigrammis erythrozonus*) Glowlights have an iridescent pink horizontal line. They are peaceful, like to school, and grow to under two inches.

151

Head-n-Tail Light

(*Hemigrammis ocellifer*) This fish gets itsname from reflective copper spots on its eyes and at the base of the tail. It grows to a bit over two inches in length.

Black Neon Tetra

(*Hyphessobrycon herbertaxelrodi*) This fish has a black horizontal line nicely edged with a slightly iridescent white line.

Bloodfin Tetra

(*Aphyocharaz anisitsi*) The name comes from the red fins, of course. The body is silver.

Red-Eye Tetra

(*Moenkhausia sanctaefilomenae*) A silver fish with red eyes and black at the base of the tail, red-eyes look great in groups.

Hatchetfish

The marble hatchet (*Carnegiella strigata*), the black-lined silver hatchet (*Gasteropelecus sternicla*), and the silver hatchet (*Thoracocharax securis*) are all commonly available. These fish, with their unusual shape, are definitely surface dwellers. They're a great choice for filling in the top zone of an aquarium. Keep the tank covered, because they're excellent jumpers.

Silver Dollar

(*Metynnis spp.*) Several species sell under this name. They all are silver and coin-shaped. Some species grow to eight inches, so they are not the best choice for all aquariums. Also, they like to eat live plants. It is good to provide some algae flakes in addition to the usual diet, if you keep these fish.

Piranha

(*Serrasalmus spp.*) What can I say? Piranhas are tetras, too. However, you should *never* mix them with other fish. Keep piranhas *only* in dedicated piranha tanks. Piranhas are eating machines. The truth is that they are not very aggressive—in fact, you will usually find them to be quite shy in the aquarium. Many species are plenty tough enough to beat them up. However, piranhas have teeth that can bite through flesh as easily as any razor blade. So they can easily dismantle fish that are larger than themselves.

Fish Tales

It is usually quite safe to reach into a tank of piranhas. They will normally swim away from you. I like to say that they are vicious to humans only in the movies. However, it pays to play it safe and keep an eye on them when working in their tank. Piranhas can easily bite through fish nets, so be very careful if you have to catch them. I've never known anyone to get bitten by a piranha, *except* when handling them in a net. *Be careful.*

Variatus

These livebearers (*Xiphophorus variatus*) are very similar to platies and swordtails, with a body shape about halfway between the two.

Goldfish

This fish has been bred for ponds, bowls, and aquaria for hundreds of years. It is the first fish that was ever kept for decorative purposes. Personally, I don't recommend keeping goldfish with the other tropical fish listed in this chapter. Goldfish prefer cooler water, a slightly different diet, and tend to outgrow most of the species listed here. Also, most varieties are slow moving and long-finned, which makes them easy targets for other faster, slightly nippy fish.

There are too many varieties of goldfish to list them all. Though the varieties may look quite different, they are all of the same species, *Carassius auratus*. You will find that price varies according to size, variety, and origin. The cheapest fish will be raised in the U.S. The fish from China will have better color and body shape (and cost more), and Japanese stock will be even better and more expensive.

Common Goldfish and Comet Goldfish

The common goldfish is the standard single-tailed goldfish. The comet is the same fish, but with a longer tail. It is probably safe to say that every aquarium store will carry both, but they will most likely label them as feeder goldfish. Millions of goldfish are raised in this country, but almost all sell as food for other larger fish. Did you know that these fish can grow to over a foot in length? The available colors are orange, white, brown, or combinations of those three.

Fish Tales

All goldfish are brown when young. Any that have brown or black markings on them may change to orange later. In fact, it is common for goldfish to change color or markings as they age. I've seen them change to various combinations of orange, white, red, brown, and black.

Shubunkin

Also a single-tailed goldfish, this fish (pronounced *shuh-BUN-kin*) has a white background, with orange, blue, and black speckles and patches.

American Fantail

This variety is the double-tailed version of the comet goldfish. The colors are the same, but the body is more egg-shaped.

Calico Fantail

This is the double-tailed, fat-bodied version of a shubunkin.

Black Moor

Take a pure black fantail, give it bulging eyes, and you have a black moor.

Celestial Eye

Goldfish were originally bred to keep in garden ponds. That is why so many fat-bodied varieties have been bred—there is more to see when viewing from above. The celestial eye has taken this to a new level. Besides the fat body, the fish has been selectively bred to have bulging eyes that look straight up. A pond of these fish staring up at you is a humorous sight. Celestial eyes have a smooth back, lacking a dorsal fin.

Bubble Eye

Take a celestial eye and put a large liquid-filled, jiggling, balloon-like sac under each eye and you get a bubble eye goldfish. They are quite unusual. For some reason, I think of Dolly Parton when I see their eyes. This fish should have no dorsal fin.

Isn't this celestial eye goldfish the cutest little thing? It's truly eye-popping.

Oranda

A fantail with a large raspberry growth on its head is the oranda (*oh-RAN-duh*) goldfish. The most popular is the red-cap oranda, which is a white fish with a bright red bumpy growth on top of its head. The red patch resembles a beret.

Fish Tales

The origin of the oranda's name is unusual. Dutch traders brought goldfish from China to Japan. Japanese have trouble pronouncing the consonants "r" and "l," and it is said that "oranda" is the Japanese pronunciation of the word "Hollander"—after the Dutch traders.

Lionhead or Ranchu

An oranda without a dorsal fin is a lionhead.

The Least You Need to Know

➤ A fish may have several common names, but will have only one scientific name.

➤ Plecostomus and otocinclus are algae-eaters, and do windows.

➤ Goldfish prefer cooler water than tropical fish.

➤ Choose only peaceful, hardy species that stay small for your community tank.

Chapter 13

More Creatures Great and Small

In This Chapter

➤ Amphibians for your community tank

➤ Shrimp, snails, and other invertebrates

➤ Jumbo fish for big tanks

➤ Ornery fish for the bloodthirsty

I had intended to limit my discussion of popular species to the previous chapter. The idea was to point you toward the most common, popular, and hardy choices. I quickly realized that there are just too many cool fish and aquatic animals to limit the discussion to a single chapter. Since it is the fish that draw us to this hobby, why limit ourselves to one chapter? Let's talk fish!

Besides, not everyone wants to set up a classic community tank of small peaceful fish. Some people want to keep *big* fish. Some want to keep *feisty* fish. But, before I talk about those, there are some pretty interesting non-fish aquatic animals that I haven't yet mentioned. Let's start with those, and then I'll list some hardy fish that won't fit in the classic community aquarium.

Fish School

A *terrarium* is an enclosure with a land mass in which live plants and animals are kept. A *vivarium* is an enclosure for live plants and animals that is divided into two sections—one for water and one for a land mass.

Amphibians: Wet Pets With Backbone

Amphibians are a group of air-breathing vertebrates, although some breathe through gills in their larval stage. These creatures must be kept wet, or they will die. Most amphibians are better suited for life in a terrarium or vivarium than in an aquarium. Amphibians are escape artists, so keep their aquariums well covered.

African Frogs

Most frogs are poor choices for the aquarium because they need access to land and they only eat live food. However, the African frogs are totally aquatic and will eat any foods offered—even flakes—so they mix well with fish.

➤ **Dwarf African Frogs** (*Hymenochirus curtipes*) are the most desired variety, because they grow to only an inch and a half long. That means they are safe to keep with most fish.

➤ **African Clawed Frogs** (*Xenopus laevis*) are very similar but grow to over eight inches long. As this critter grows, your fish may find themselves becoming a meal. There is also an albino version of this frog available. Be sure to cover your tank, as the frogs can easily get out.

Fish and Tips

If your newt is not getting its fair share of food, consider moving it to a fish bowl or other covered container for feeding. This will allow the slow moving newt to eat without having its food stolen by the fish.

Newts

There are several varieties of newts found for sale in aquarium stores. Personally, I do not recommend keeping them with fish. For starters, newts like to come out of the water, so a vivarium would be a better choice for keeping them. Also, they are not as aggressive at feeding as the fish, so the fish usually eat all of the food and the newt slowly starves.

Plan to offer some live blackworms, frozen krill, and other foods, if you decide to try newts, and monitor their body weight to be sure they get enough food. Keep the tank well covered, as they can easily climb out.

Caecilians

Pronounced *see-SIL-ee-uns*, this unusual critter looks like a worm or a snake, but it is an amphibian. In other words, it is more closely related to frogs and newts. Being weird, this animal has some unusual common names. Black rubber eel, caecilian worm, and even snake frog are some names that I've seen.

This animal is generally quite harmless to fish, though I suppose it is possible that it could catch some really slow-moving ones. Worms and shrimp will comprise the bulk of the diet. Oddly, they have live babies, which are about the size of a pencil when born. Keep the tank covered, as these are escape artists extraordinaire.

Tadpoles

The larval (tadpole) form of several frogs, including the American bullfrog, can be found for sale. They are sold mostly for garden ponds, where they nibble on algae, and later, as adults, eat flying insects. Tadpoles will thrive in the aquarium, providing there is some algae to nibble on, along with other foods. Adding algae flakes to the diet can be helpful.

Once they metamorphose into frogs, though, you should be prepared to move them to a vivarium where they can have access to both land and water, and where you will offer live insects and worms as food. Adult frogs will not eat any food that is not alive and moving.

Spineless Choices in Aquatic Animals

There are not many backbone-free animals offered for the aquarium, but there are definitely some interesting ones. If you provide them with a predator-free environment, these invertebrates will fare quite well in an aquarium.

Crabs

Only a couple of species of crabs fare well in the aquarium. Most crabs are either saltwater animals, prefer to live on land, or are too predatory. Here are two crabs that adapt well to living in a freshwater aquarium—and one that doesn't, but is sometimes seen in pet stores:

➤ **Black Fiddler Crab** (*Uca pugnax*). This freshwater crab is a choice that usually works quite well. The female has two small claws, but the male has one small claw and one large decorative pincer. Though he can give you a decent pinch with it, this rarely happens. The claw is more for signaling than defense. The male saws it back in forth in front of a female's face to attract her for mating. (This fiddling motion is where the crab gets its name.)

Fish Tales

The male fiddler crab marks his territory by waving his large claw about, signaling to other males to stay away. This action caused one young customer to declare, "Look! That crab is dancing the macarena." He may be right.

Three crabs: red claw (left), black fiddler (right), and Phil.

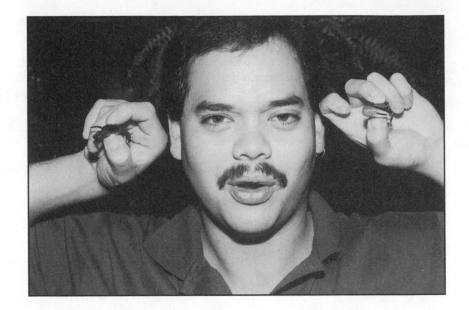

➤ **Siamese Red Claw Crab.** This small, attractive crab usually fares well in the aquarium. They are scavengers, but sometimes will damage plants. Particularly, they seem to like to eat the bulbous tubers of some plant species.

➤ **Calico Fiddler Crab** (*Uca pugilator*). Another species sometimes seen in pet stores, this pink and purple crab should be avoided because it is much more delicate and prefers saltier water.

Shrimp

Something's Fishy
SNIFF! SNIFF!
Crayfish are best left out of your aquarium. Although crayfish are interesting and quite hardy, they eat anything. That includes your fish and your plants. Also, they dig burrows, disturbing your decorating scheme.

If shrimp are your thing, you can choose from these:

➤ **Ghost Shrimp** are the most common species available. These transparent, inch-long shrimp are good scavengers and will even clean some hair-algae off plant leaves. On the downside, many fish like to take bites out of them, so they may get eaten.

➤ **Singapore Rainbow Shrimp.** Another desirable species, this one-inch shrimp will eat brush algae.

➤ **Wood Shrimp**, sometimes called rock shrimp, are especially interesting. Besides scavenging for food, they have four fan-like feeding apparatus that they unfurl in the water stream to filter out bits of food. Wood shrimp grow to three inches.

Snails

Here are some interesting species if you like snails:

➤ **Mystery Snail** (*Ampullaria cuprina*). This is the most popular snail, and the mystery is how they got that name. These snails grow to golf ball size, and have the unusual trait of laying their eggs in clusters above the water line of the tank. They are quite peaceful and don't bother plants, but sometimes the fish harass and eat them. Black, gold, albino, and other varieties are available.

➤ **Apple Snail** (*Ampullaria gigas*). A relative of the mystery snail, this critter grows to softball size. Unfortunately, this interesting species will eat just about every plant in your tank. They are highly herbivorous.

➤ **Japanese Trapdoor Snail.** Similar to the mystery snail, except that it bears single, live, pea-sized young.

➤ **Columbian Ramshorn Snail** (*Marisa rotula*). This large snail is also a plant eater.

➤ **Trumpet Snail.** A small, popular snail is the inch-long Malaysian needlepoint snail, also called the trumpet snail. These guys spend most of the day buried in the gravel, emerging at night. Their appeal is that they scavenge within the gravel and keep it from compacting. They bear live young.

➤ **Pond Snails** and most **Ramshorn Snails** (as in ram's horn) round out the list of available snails. Most hobbyists try to avoid these small snails because they can overpopulate. However, they really only overmultiply in tanks that have been overfed. No animal can grow and reproduce unless you offer it enough food to do so.

> **Fish and Tips**
> If you ever need to rid a tank of snails, adding a clown loach is the safest, easiest, most effective and attractive way to do so. Clown loaches love to eat snails.

Clams

You occasionally will see these available for sale, but you probably should avoid them—especially the large ones. No, they aren't going to eat your fish. They filter microscopic particles from the water for food. But that's why you shouldn't keep clams. Your water is going to be way too clean for them, and they will eventually starve. Besides, even if they did prosper, clam larvae are parasitic to fish.

Messin' With the Big Boys

Some of you are watching your platies, swordtails, and tetras. "I savor their beauty. They are a treat to watch," you think to yourself. Others of you will see those same small fish and think, "My piranha would savor their flavor as a treat for lunch." Yep, there are different strokes for different folks.

If you are a person who likes big fish, if you are a person who thinks that danios are baitfish, this section is for you. Following are some popular species that get large, but normally will mix with each other. Before you purchase any of these fish, be sure you have enough room. Remember that the one-inch-per-gallon rule *does not* apply to large fish. And don't forget to allow for growth. Make sure there isn't too much size difference between individuals, and don't just look at the size of the fish—be sure to look at the size of their mouths.

While we are on the topic of large fish, let's talk about fish growth. It is rare for large species to reach full adult size in an aquarium—except in large tanks at public aquaria. Crowding your fish will stunt their growth. You may hear it said that fish will grow only as large as the tank will allow. That's not quite true. The size of the tank has little to do with it.

The buildup of waste is what stunts the fish. Put a large species in a small tank with continuous water changes and it will grow huge. Put that same fish in a large tank with no water changes and, if it survives, it will be stunted.

Your fish will be happiest if you leave some room for growth. Be sure to keep up on those water changes, not just to limit stunting, but also to keep the fish healthy. Crowding initially stunts a fish, but eventually it kills the fish. That's why you don't see many 16-inch, 25-year-old goldfish.

Oscar

(*Astronotus ocellatus*) These personable fish are very popular. Many people buy them as cute inch-long youngsters, not realizing that they grow to 14 inches or so. Oscars are cichlids, which means they like to stake out a territory and can be aggressive. The natural coloration of an oscar is a marbled black and gray with a red ring at the base of the tail, but several strains have been developed. The red tiger oscar has red markings, the red oscar is nearly pure red, and there are also albino and long-finned forms of each. Some books list them as the velvet cichlid, but I don't know anyone who calls them that.

Fish and Tips
Think before you buy. When the fish in this section get too big for your tank, you probably will have a hard time getting rid of them. Not many aquarists have room for fish of that size, and most dealers don't want them, either.

Oscars are fish with personality. They will soon recognize you and can easily be taught to eat from your hand. Many people think of them as mean, but they really are a fairly gentle fish. However, they will protect their territory against other fishes, particularly other oscars or similar looking cichlids.

They are extremely hardy, too. I don't think I could name a fish that can stand more abuse. They survive in situations where the waste levels are high enough to kill most other fish, but they pay a price. It is common to see adult oscars with "hole in the head" disease. See Chapter 24 on disease and stress for more information on that.

Jack Dempsey

(*Heros octofasciatus*) Named after the famous fighter, you just know these fish like to kick butt. Mostly, though, it is each other that they don't like. They'll usually mix just fine with other large or aggressive fish. Juveniles are tan with dark markings. Adults are black with a field of blue dots, and grow to around 10 inches.

Severum

(*Heros severum*) These fish are more peaceful and vegetarian than other cichlids. The green severum is the normal coloration, but the lemon severum, a yellow strain, is probably more popular. Adult size is around eight inches.

Jaguar Cichlid

(*Heros managuensis*) These are highly predatory fish, growing to around 16 inches. The adults have red eyes and a field of small, dark blotches against a coppery background.

Red Terror

(*Heros festae*) The name says it all. Adults have red and black vertical stripes, and are ornery as heck. They can grow to 20 inches, but I've never seen them over a foot in length. Juveniles lack the red coloration.

Fish Tales

Never release unwanted fish into the wild. Exotic species can decimate native species by exposing them to new diseases, or eating them and outbreeding them. Oscars, tilapia, walking catfish, and other exotic species have overtaken many habitats in Florida and elsewhere. Unwanted fish should be given away or destroyed, not turned loose.

Red Devil

(*Heros labiatus*) At least one other species sometimes sells under this name, too. Like many cichlids, juveniles do not resemble the adults. Silver and gray banded youngsters turn into pure pink adults. They grow to around 10 inches.

Pacu

(*Colossoma spp.*) Pronounced *PAH-koo*, you can tell from the scientific name that this fish gets huge—up to three feet. Here is a fish that you can buy as small, medium, large, and

Fish and Tips
Can't find a home for a fish that has grown too large? Unless you've treated them with chemicals or medications that make them unfit, you could always eat them. Recycling is in.

egads! Pacus will eat anything that fits in their mouths, but they really are quite peaceful. They'll even eat fruits and nuts, along with live foods. Most hobbyists feed them pellets, though. Red pacus are most common, but black pacus are sometimes seen, too. Pacus are often confused with their toothy cousins, the piranhas.

Arowana

(*Osteoglossum spp.* and *Scleropages spp.*) There are at least three species in the trade: the silver, the black, and the golden Asian arowana. All are long slender silver fish, with large mouths. (The black arowana has black stripes as a juvenile.) They can be trained to eat pellets, but feeder fish, crickets, and other live foods are more typical fare. Arowanas grow to three feet and are extremely good jumpers. You may have seen documentary footage of them leaping from the water to grab insects from overhead branches. Keep your tank well covered.

Fish Tales

Male arowanas brood their eggs in their large mouths. Stores often offer three-inch babies, sometimes with yolk sacs still attached.

Snakehead

(*Chana spp.*) Red-line snakeheads are most popular. They have a wide red-orange stripe down the length of their bodies as juveniles. However, those three-inch youngsters turn into two-foot adults. Live foods are required.

Gar

(*Lepisosteus spp.*) Several species of gar appear in the trade, most from Florida. The adult fish can grow to five feet. However, they rarely grow bigger than two feet in the home aquarium. Live foods are required.

Freshwater Stingray

(*Potamogytron spp.*) Several species are available. The motoro stingray, with its large spots, is most attractive. These fish should be kept in an aquarium with a sandy bottom, so they don't get scratched and damaged. They like to bury themselves. Live and frozen foods are taken, including feeder fish, worms, and krill. They are a bit delicate, so don't mix with species that would pick at them.

Redtail Catfish

(*Phractocephalus hemiliopterus*) These lunkers grow to four feet. The fish is black with a white lateral stripe and red tail. It has a big mouth that will eat any fish that fits in it. They sometimes accidentally eat thermometers, aquarium heaters, castles, and other objects that get in the way of meals. (They'll eventually spit them back up, though.)

Shovelnose Cat

(*Sorubim lima*) These long, slender fish have a flat face that gives them their name. They are highly predatory and must have live foods. The fish is silver with a longitudinal black stripe. Adult size is around 18 inches.

The tiger shovelnose cat (*Pseudoplatystoma fasciatum*) is also common. It has variegated vertical strips and grows to three feet.

Clown Knifefish

(*Notopterus chitala*) Shaped like the blade of a knife, these unusual fish can swim forwards and backwards. Their base color is metallic gray with large peacock spots near the tail. Clown knives grow to three feet and eat live food. Some specimens also eat frozen and freeze-dried foods.

Tricolor Sharks

(*Balantiocheilos melanopterus*) Adults of this species are hardy and active, and mix with most species in this section, providing the sizes aren't too different. For more information on aquarium sharks, see Chapter 12.

Tinfoil Barb

(*Barbodes schwanenfeldii*) This barb species also gets large enough to mix with most of the fish in this section. It is described in detail in Chapter 12.

Something's Fishy
Stingrays can give a very serious sting with the barb on their tail. Though they are quite gentle by nature, be extremely careful when handling them.

SNIFF! SNIFF!

Fish School
Target fish are kept with aggressive fish to distract them from fighting. Always busy and active, they divert attention from territorial neighbors, reducing fights. They may also keep hormonally charged parents from beating on their mates.

Brackish Fish

Many fish inhabit coastal areas, where freshwater streams meet the ocean. Consequently, there are fish able to tolerate wide ranges of saltiness. Some sea-dwelling species spawn in coastal areas, so juveniles inhabit brackish water, but adults are really saltwater fish.

Fish School
Brackish means somewhat salty.

Hobbyists often set up brackish aquariums to keep these species. A brackish tank maintains salt levels somewhere between freshwater and seawater. Here are some common varieties of brackish fish. Take care, though, in your selection, because some brackish water juveniles become saltwater fish as adults.

Fish School
Dither fish are peaceful, active, mid-water schoolers that help to keep shy fish from hiding. Active mid-water fish act as an "all clear" sign to other fish, signaling that no predators are around and that it is safe to come out.

Scat

(*Scatophagus spp.*) The disc-shaped scats are attractively marked when young, but adults turn gray. The green scat (*S. argus*) has black spots on a green background. The red scat is the same, but with some red on the forehead. The silver scat is a different species that has fewer spots and a silver background. Juveniles live in coastal waters, but adults are saltwater fish. Adult size is around 10 inches.

Mono

(*Monodactylus spp.*) Pronounced *MAH-no*. Shaped much like freshwater angelfish, but with stubbier fins, the monos also sell as African angels (*M. sebae*) and Indian angels (*M. argenteus*). Again, adults are saltwater fish.

Archer

(*Toxotes jaculator*) The archer fish gets its name from its unusual ability to spit drops of water at insects well above the water line, knocking them into the water to be eaten. Archers grow to around six inches.

Shark Cat

(*Arius jordani*) Also sold as the black-finned shark, and silver shark, this silver catfish can live in freshwater or saltwater. It grows to around 12 inches.

Puffer

(*Tetraodon spp.*) The spotted puffer (*T. fluviatilis*) and the figure-eight puffer (*T. palembangensis*) are the two most common species offered. Sold as "freshwater puffers," they really do best in brackish tanks. Puffers need live and frozen foods. Plankton and krill are relished. They normally won't touch flakes. Puffers like to nip fins, so be careful.

Fish Tales

Puffers can inflate themselves with water or air to prevent a predator from swallowing them. They are also toxic. The Japanese dish *fugu* is made from marine puffers, and must be prepared properly or it is lethal.

The Fighting African Cichlids

That's *AF-rih-kun SICK-lid*—not "a frickin' Chicklette." African cichlids are an unusual and interesting bunch. While there are some river species available, including the kribensis, most African cichlids come from three large lakes in eastern Africa: Lake Malawi, Lake Tanganyika, and Lake Victoria.

Some say that the colors of African cichlids rival those of saltwater fish. I wouldn't go that far, but many of them are quite spectacular. Adult males of many species display the most iridescent blue you will ever see. Yellow, orange, and crimson are also common. Sexual dimorphism is common.

Even more interesting is that many species have several color morphs. The zebra cichlid (*Pseudotropheus zebra*) is a good example. Most males are powder blue, but there are blue and black banded varieties, pure orange fish, and even blotched varieties. Many of these fish were thought to be separate species when first discovered.

Fish School
Sexual *dimorphism* means that males and females have obvious physical differences in color, pattern, or shape. Often, juveniles of both sexes share the same characteristics as females, but adult males take on brilliant colors, as do many African cichlids, or even the male guppy.

Another interesting thing about these fish is that most are mouth brooders. The female carries the eggs in her mouth for protection, steadfastly refusing food for the duration. When you see one of these fish with its throat distended, it probably is incubating a mouth full of eggs.

Like other cichlids, these fish tend to fight with each other. They may protect territories or fight over mates. Hobbyists usually try to crowd African cichlids, which can make for a bit more peace. Crowding them makes it much more difficult for a fish to stake out a territory and defend it—there are just too many competitors to do so. So there is a tendency to accept the situation, and less fighting occurs. Don't forget that a crowded tank will need more frequent water changes to keep the water quality in good shape.

African cichlids should be kept in a dedicated aquarium. That is, don't try mixing them with New World cichlids or with your community fish. Massacres will result. Most African cichlids prefer different water quality than the fish in your other tanks, anyway. They come from lakes where the pH and water hardness are higher. Hobbyists often keep the pH around 7.8.

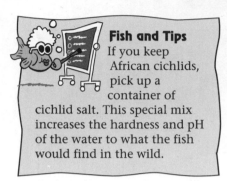

Fish and Tips

If you keep African cichlids, pick up a container of cichlid salt. This special mix increases the hardness and pH of the water to what the fish would find in the wild.

To truly appreciate African cichlids, be sure to look through some books with photos of them. Juveniles and females usually look alike, while adult males take on spectacular colors. The problem is that the fish your dealer sells are usually juveniles, and sexing juveniles can be difficult or impossible. Your dealer may have a "display only" tank set up, so that you can see how a tank of adult African cichlids can look.

Don't hold a grudge against a dealer who doesn't carry adult cichlids. Besides the fact that they may be much more expensive and harder for him to sell, keeping them is a problem for him, too. Adult fish fight more. You will have better luck mixing fish when they are young and letting them grow up together, anyway.

You may hear hobbyists referring to various African cichlid species as *mbuna*. Pronounced *um-BOO-nuh*, it is an African word meaning rock dweller. Mbuna are species that live among the rocks, and the best way to enjoy them is to build a big rock pile in your tank. Providing lot of nooks and crannies gives them plenty of places to hide and chase each other. Mbuna tanks are always active. Mbuna like to munch algae off the rocks, and are more vegetarian than most cichlids.

Another term you may hear is *utaka*, pronounced *oo-TAH-kuh*. These fish live out in the open areas of the lake. They stake out a territory along the bottom and feed on zooplankton (microscopic plants that live in the water).

Fish Tales

The shell dwellers are another interesting group of African cichlids. These dwarf *Lamprologus* species like to live and spawn in large, empty snail shells. An empty mystery snail shell is big enough for most.

Here are some popular species of African Cichlids.

Auratus and Chipokae

Juvenile auratus (*Melanochromis auratus*) are yellow with black horizontal stripes. The color pattern reverses on adult males to become black with blue stripes. It is best not to keep more than one male auratus (pronounced *uh-RAY-tus*) per tank, and don't mix similarly marked species. Chipokae (*Melanochromis chipokae*), pronounced *chih-POH-kee*, are very similar to auratus.

Rusty

(*Iodotropheus sprengerae*) These fish are blue, but with a rusty overtone. They are hardy and relatively peaceful.

Polystigma

(*Haplochromis polystigma*) These have an interesting brown and white camouflage pattern, with brick-hued dots mixed in.

Compressiceps

(*Haplochromis compressiceps*) Juvenile compressiceps are silver with black markings. Adult males turn metallic blue. This fish gets its name from its flattened shape. It looks like someone ran a rolling pin over it!

Peacock

(*Aulonacara spp.*) Hardy and relatively peaceful, these fish come in several peacock color morphs.

Red Empress

(*Haplochromis similis*) Red emperor would have been a better name, as it is the adult males that display a scarlet crosshatch pattern. Juveniles and females are silver with black markings.

Quad

(*Haplochromis quadrimaculatus*) The scientific name references the fact that juveniles have four spots. Adult males are mostly blue.

Zebra

(*Pseudotropheus zebra*) Probably the most popular African cichlid, several color morphs are available. Sometimes the color varieties are abbreviated: BB = blue blotches, OB = orange blotched, and RT = red top, for example.

Fish and Tips
One odd but common practice with African cichlids is to keep a tank of males only. Males are usually the most colorful, and many species fight viciously when females are present but get along much better when the ladies aren't around. Of course, because most males don't color until they're adults, the difficulty is choosing juvenile fish of the proper sex.

Kennyi

(*Pseudotropheus lombardoi*) Pronounced *KEN-ee-eye*, juveniles and females have vertical blue and black bars. Adult males become yellow and black.

Tropheus moorii

Don't confuse these with the less expensive *Haplochromis moorii* (pronounced *MOR-ee-eye*). There are many morphs of T. moorii available. The fish are mostly black, but come with yellow saddles, red blotches, and other interesting colors, depending on the morph.

Brichardi

(*Lamprologus brichardi*) Pronounced *brih-SHAR-die*, these gentle fish with their lacy fins stay relatively small and spawn readily.

Leluepi

(*Lamprologus leleupi*) *Leh-LOOP-eyes* are pure orange and in much demand.

Julies

(*Julidochromis spp.*) I'm going to take the liberty of lumping several species together here. Most have dark markings against a yellow background on a torpedo-shaped body.

The Least You Need to Know

➤ Dwarf African frogs are comical additions to your community tank.

➤ Snails and shrimp may help control a bit of algae.

➤ If you want to think big, a community of jumbo fish can be set up. Allow for growth, if you buy juveniles.

➤ A brackish tank contains coastal species that tolerate both freshwater and saltwater.

➤ African cichlids make a colorful, though aggressive, community.

Chapter 14

Popular Plant Picks

In This Chapter

➤ Hardy plants for beginners

➤ Species with special requirements

➤ Plants to avoid

Shopping for live aquarium plants can be almost as much fun as shopping for fish. There are over 100 species of plants available, in all shapes and colors. You can find plants with feathery leaves, ribbon-shaped leaves, heart-shaped leaves, leaves like pine needles, and more. Some plants grow tall and bushy, while others spread by sending out runners with new baby plants on them. Colors range from chartreuse and emerald green to brick red and brilliant scarlet. You can mix and match to build a spectacular landscape, with no two ever being alike.

Unfortunately, too many dealers carry a very small selection of live aquatic plants. I am not really sure why this is, as there are plenty of growers supplying plants to the aquarium trade. Possibly, they just don't know how to keep plants properly or don't have the interest. Or it may be that their distributor isn't set up to keep plants properly and their store is too small to order direct.

Fish School
Submersed means under water. *Emersed* means above water. Some plants grow in both conditions and produce leaves of two different shapes and textures.

Fish and Tips
Generally speaking, any plant that flops over lazily when removed from the water is probably a true aquatic. Any plant that can support its own weight out of the water is probably a terrestrial species, though it may be a species that thrives in both submersed and emersed conditions. Swordplants and cryptocorynes are two examples.

Don't Get Soaked

Worse, many plants that dealers carry are terrestrial, not aquatic. Don't be surprised to find common houseplants being mistakenly sold as aquatics. It is not uncommon to find bella palms and peace lilies (sold as Brazilian swords) drowning in aquariums at pet shops. Your dealer may not know better, so it will be up to you to do a little research before purchasing plants. Don't get soaked by buying non-aquatic plants!

A dealer should know better, but I think what happens is that many dealers don't provide enough light for plants to do well. So when they order plants, they don't live. As it happens, the soft-leafed aquatic plants die first, leaving the tough-leafed terrestrial plants still standing. This may give the dealer a mistaken impression that those species are hardier. In fact, I've heard many salespeople make just that claim. The terrestrial plants are doomed, too—they just take longer to die and rot than the softer aquatic plants. Given proper conditions, the aquatic plants would survive and thrive well after the terrestrials have died and rotted away.

In the next section, I will point you toward some plant species that are almost completely idiot proof. These are species that most people can successfully keep and grow. They tend to be more tolerant of water conditions, and more able to sustain themselves with lower light levels. However, don't let that be an incentive for you to reduce the amount of lights you buy. Even these hardy species will fare much better under stronger light.

Hardy Plants by the Bunch

Many of the hardiest and most readily available varieties are types of *bunch* plants. Most of these species are very fast growers, making them quite inexpensive. Most are grown on aquatic plant farms, but there are some species that are commercially harvested from wild stock in rivers in Florida and other locations.

Bunch plants may be true aquatics or species that can grow both in and out of the water. Usually dealers offer the aquatic form, but sometimes it is the terrestrial form that is sold. The tough terrestrial leaves probably will be shed after the plant is underwater for a time. By the time that happens, you will be ready to prune the old growth from the bottom and replant the top with its newer, softer submersed-form leaves.

Following are some of my favorite varieties of bunch plants.

Anacharis

Anacharis (*uh-NAK-uh-riss*) is the name in the aquarium trade, but if you are a school teacher, you probably know this plant by another name—elodea (*el-oh-DEE-uh*). *Elodea nutalli* is the scientific name. This attractive plant is dark green, with thick whorls of inch-long, ribbon-shaped leaves along the stem.

Anacharis is a very fast grower. I have seen stems actually put on six inches of growth per day in full sunlight! It is not likely to grow that fast in your aquarium, though.

> **Fish School**
> *Bunch plant* refers to seven or eight stems of a plant (clippings, actually) bound with a rubber band or strip of tape to form a bundle. The stems can be planted individually or in a group.

Give this plant intense light if you want it to keep its thick, full leaves. It will still grow in low light conditions, but it will get thin and spindly. The leaves will be smaller and much further apart, and it will become more of a light green color.

Like most bunch plants, anacharis will send out roots. So it looks best when planted in the gravel. Some people prefer to keep it as a floating plant. I don't much like to keep it that way, though, because it starts sending roots from various points along the length of the floating stem, reaching desperately for the gravel below. I think that looks a little weird.

> **Fish Tales**
>
> Anacharis (elodea) removes calcium salts from the water, softening it. *Egeria*, *hydrilla*, and *lagarosiphon* are similar genera that do the same, but you don't see these in the trade much. In fact, many states declare hydrilla to be a pest and forbid its sale.

Hornwort

This plant has soft, pine needle-like leaves. There are two species of hornwort seen in the trade. The most common is *Ceratophyllum demersum*, which has shorter needles and a bit darker green color. *Ceratophyllum submersum* is less commonly seen, but with its light green color and long graceful needles, I feel it is the more beautiful species.

Hornwort does not produce roots, and so is a true floating plant. However, most people tuck the stem bottoms into the gravel and let the plant grow toward and over the surface. This species provides great shelter for newborn baby fish, and is a fast grower.

Fish and Tips
You can improve the appearance of hygro by pruning it. If you pinch off the top of each stem, two shoots will grow from the pinch point. The part you pinched off can be pushed into the gravel, where it will root and grow into a new plant.

Hygro

Hygrophila polysperma (*hy-GROF-il-uh*) is a gorgeous plant, and one of my all-time favorites. The leaves are lanceolate (sword shaped), soft, and light green, growing as pairs on opposite sides of the stem. Hygro gets spindly if you don't give it enough light. With intense lighting, the leaves will be thicker and more compact.

Hygrophila rosanervis, or tropic sunset hygro, is another species sometimes seen. It is very similar to *H. polysperma*, but has pink veins in the leaves, especially the newer ones. Be sure to give strong light and iron supplementation for this plant to maintain its color.

Water Wisteria

Another of my favorites, this plant (*Hygrophila difformis*) has a much different appearance than the other hygros. In fact, you will find two completely different forms of this plant, depending on whether it grew emersed or submersed. The emersed leaves are large and solid, looking a bit like elm leaves. The submersed leaves are soft, with deep, finger-like serrations. Both types are beautiful, but emersed-grown leaves will drop off after submersion.

The more light you give this plant, the thicker and bushier it gets. Also, pinching off the tips of stems will cause two new stems to grow, filling out the plant beautifully.

Rotala Indica

Pronounced *roh-TAL-uh IN-dih-kuh*, this is the trade name for *Rotala rotundifolia*. This plant is similar to the hygros, but with smaller leaves. Older growth is light green, but newer growth has a pinkish cast. It is a hardy, attractive plant that can grow as tall as your tank.

Java Moss

Yes, *Vesicularia dubyana* is a moss, and it looks like a moss. The color is dark green. Once settled in, Java moss can be a very fast grower. You can let it drift as a good hiding place for baby fish; however, most hobbyists attach this plant to rocks and driftwood. Either wedge it into crevices, or use rubber bands to temporarily hold it in place. In very short order, it will grab onto the wood or stone and grow into a pleasant green carpet.

Willow moss (*Fontinalis antipyretica*) is also occasionally seen in the trade. It has a nearly identical appearance to Java moss, but prefers colder water (under 70°F).

Bunch plants are fast growing and inexpensive. The stems can be planted individually or in groups.

Delicate Choices

Following are some common aquatic plants that can do well in planted aquariums, if you meet their special requirements. Providing the proper amount of light and fertilization is even more important with these species.

Cabomba spp.

Even if you don't like the looks of this beautiful bunch plant, you'll have fun saying its name. Cabomba (*kuh-BOM-buh*)! It has fan-shaped, feathery leaves arranged around a stem. There are three species seen in the trade. One is light green, one dark green, and the third has some pink in it. This plant needs clean water and strong light to prosper. Otherwise, it gets spindly. It also prefers water on the cooler side. The leaves are quite soft, and are easily destroyed by herbivorous fish.

Ambulia

Ambulia (*am-BYU-lee-uh*) (*Limnophila spp.*) looks very similar to cabomba but is yellow-green in color, and the leaves form complete swirls around the stem. This is an extremely beautiful plant, but a bit on the delicate side. It likes strong light, but not too strong.

Foxtail

Here is a bunch plant (*Myriophyllum spp.*) sold under many names, including water milfoil, myrio, and foxtail. It has very fine thread-like leaves, giving the stem an appearance much like a fox's tail. There are green and reddish brown varieties. They all tend to prefer water on the cooler side.

You also may stumble across the emersed form of this plant under the name parrot's feather. The emersed leaves are the shape of serrated birds' feathers and you would think that they were a completely different species from foxtail.

Ludwigia

Ludwigia repens (lud-WIG-ee-uh) and *L. palustrus* are the most common species sold. This bunch plant has round leaves, often with a tinge of red. The amount of light and fertilization will affect the color. Needle-leaf ludwigia, *L. arcuata,* is also sometimes seen. Ludwigia prefers cooler water.

Majestic Crown Plants

Crown plants are species with all the leaves radiating from a central base, like the points on a crown. Usually dealers sell the plants individually, but you also can find potted versions that may have several plants in one pot.

Amazon Swordplant

Echinodorus bleheri is the most common of several species sometimes sold as Amazon swordplants. The Amazon sword is a very hardy plant and an all-time favorite. It can grow leaves over a foot long in strongly lit tanks. This plant makes a great centerpiece and stands out when surrounded by small-leafed plants.

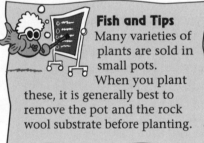

Fish and Tips
Many varieties of plants are sold in small pots. When you plant these, it is generally best to remove the pot and the rock wool substrate before planting.

Amazon swords can grow emersed or submersed. It is usually the emersed form that you will find in the stores. The leaves of the emersed form have a longer stem and broader, more compact leaf segments. Leaves grown under water have very short stems and much longer, narrower leaf segments. No matter. Even if you buy the emersed form, it will quickly sprout new submersed leaves—though it will tend to drop the older emersed-form leaves within a few weeks.

Pygmy Chain Sword

There are several species sold as pygmy chain sword, including *Echinodorus quadricostatus*, but *E. tenellus* is the smallest, usually growing to around four inches. It makes a great foreground plant. I've also seen it sold as narrow-leaf sword. Similar species grow to around six inches or so.

Ruby Swordplant

Echinodorus osirus var. rubra is a gorgeous swordplant that can grow up to three feet across! Depending on the light and choice of fertilizer, the color can vary from light green to reddish brown. Newer growth is the reddest.

Vallisneria spp.

Pronounced *val-iss-NEAR-ee-uh*—val for short. Eel grass is another common name, though it applies more to the saltwater species. These plants have long ribbon-like leaves and send out runners with baby plants. Another interesting feature is that the plants are either male or female. Females send a small flower to the surface on a long, thin stem. Males produce a pollen packet at their base that breaks loose and floats to the surface to release pollen.

Some common crown plants, left to right: amazon sword, vallisneria, anubias nana, banana plant, and cryptocorynes.

Corkscrew val (*V. americana*, AKA *V. spiralis*) is probably the most popular species. It grows a foot or so tall, with lightly spiraled leaves about a quarter inch in width. Other common species are: jungle val (*V. gigantea*), which grows up to six feet in length, with straight leaves up to an inch wide; and torta val (*V. tortissima*), which has highly twisted leaves up to three feet long. Vallisneria looks best when planted in groups.

Sagittaria spp.

The various species of sag (pronounced *saj-ih-TEHR-ee-uh* with a soft g) are quite similar to the vals. Several varieties of *S. subulata* are most common in stores, and *S. natans* and *S. pusilla* are synonyms for *S. subulata*. Pusilla stays small and works as a foreground plant.

Onion Bulb Plant

This unusual but hardy plant (*Crinum thaianum*) grows too large for some tanks. A large bulb-like base protrudes from the gravel, and ribbon-like leaves grow up to six feet long. Still, many hobbyists keep this plant, and give it the occasional haircut when it gets too long.

Anubias spp.

These tough-leaved African plants (pronounced *uh-NEW-bee-us*) grow in or out of the water. They are slow growers, but can stand low light conditions. *A. barteri* has sword-shaped leaves that can get over a foot in length. *A. nana* grows heart-shaped leaves about two inches in diameter. It also stays under four inches tall, making it a great foreground plant.

Java Fern

This undemanding plant (*Microsorium pterops*), with its dark green sword-shaped leaves, is happiest growing emersed at the water's edge. However, it does prosper in a submerged state. Most hobbyists attach it to a piece of driftwood (as they do with Java moss), where it will eventually anchor itself. A very hardy plant, the Java fern will survive with less light than many other species.

Aponogeton spp.

There are several species of aponogeton (*uh-pon-oh-JEE-tun*) available. *A. crispus*, *A. undulatus*, *A. ulvaceous*, and *A. elongatus* are the most common. They grow long, soft leaves from one to two feet in length, sometimes with a considerably long stem. Some species have flat leaves, others are ruffled. Some have round tips, others are pointy.

While you can buy these as full-blown growing plants, you will most often find aponogetons sold as dry bulbs. Instant bulbs is a common name for them, because they sprout so fast. You can have foot-long leaves within a week!

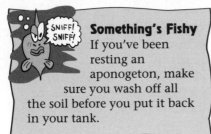

Something's Fishy
If you've been resting an aponogeton, make sure you wash off all the soil before you put it back in your tank.

These plants are extremely hardy, though fish nets can easily damage the long, soft leaves. One reason for the fast leaf growth is that, in the wild, these plants go through a seasonal resting stage. They grow fast and last a long time, but then they stop sending out new leaves. Most people end up pitching the dead bulbs after a year or two, but you can revive the plant by resting it. Place the bulb in a dish, cover it with some damp soil, and let it sit for three months in a room that is not brightly lit. When you replant, it should take off again.

Underwater Banana Plant

Nope, this is not the type of banana that you eat. Rather, *Nymphoides aquatica* is a dwarf water lily that stores energy reserves in small, green, banana-like tubers. The "bananas" should not be buried in the gravel. Let them rest on top, and the roots will penetrate the gravel. In low light conditions, the slow-growing plant will keep its leaves near the gravel. In strong light, they will reach for the surface like lily pads.

Cryptocoryne spp.

There are many species of cryptocoryne (*krip-toh-koh-RYE-nee*), or crypts, available to the hobbyist. Most will grow in or out of the water. They often do well in situations where there is too little light for other plants to prosper. Some species are green, some are reddish brown, and some are green on top and maroon underneath.

Fish Tales

The amazon leaf fish (*Monocirrhus polyacanthus*) has a body shaped like a leaf, right down to a chin protrusion that resembles a stem. This predatory fish sits perfectly still until prey swims by, and then its huge telescoping mouth vacuums up the unsuspecting victim.

Crypts grow like weeds for some hobbyists, while others have a tough time with them. Some say the plants are temperamental—responding poorly to big changes in lighting or to transplantation. They tend to be slow growing, and do best in well established tanks.

Some popular crypts are (and some of these are synonyms): *C. willisii*, *C. cordata*, *C. nevillii*, *C. petchii*, *C. affinis*, *C. ciliata*, and *C. balansae*.

Floating Above It All

Many species of plants have evolved to live at the water's surface. They spread their leaves across the top, with small roots dangling into the water. I find floating plants to be very beautiful, but they may not be the best choice for most aquariums. You see, floating at the surface, they block the light needed by the other plants. Also, they tend to be very fast spreading species. So if you keep them, be sure to thin them out regularly.

Water Sprite

There are several species of water sprite sold in stores, but *Ceratopteris pteroides* is the hardiest and the only true floater. The others should be rooted into the substrate. Water sprite resembles water wisteria, with its finger-like leaves. The plant is like a floating island, with a tangle of roots dangling below. Baby plants grow from the edges of the leaves on the adult plant. When I was a kid, this was my favorite plant. I used to love checking every week for new baby plants, and separating them for my other tanks.

Duckweed

This odd plant consists of a single BB-sized leaf and root. But don't let the diminutive size fool you. Duckweed is like the bacteria of the aquatic plant world! Each plant grows a second leaf, which splits away. Then they both grow another leaf and split, and so on, until your tank is covered with the little devils. Duckweed makes great food for koi, goldfish, and African cichlids, though.

Azolla and salvinia are very much like duckweed, but are larger and have fancier leaf shapes.

Weed These Out

Naturally, it would not be too smart to pick plants that are sick. Here are warning signs:

➤ Plants with rotting stems should be avoided. It is okay if the rot is only where the rubber band is holding bunch plants together. You can cut that part off.

➤ Shy away from specimens that are shedding leaves excessively. However, normal handling is going to break a few loose. That is not a problem.

➤ If the leaves have yellow spots, those leaves are dying. It may be due to damage, disease, or lack of fertilizer. A swordplant with six good leaves and one bad one isn't an issue, though. Simply remove the single bad leaf.

Giant Hygro

Giant hygro (*Hygrophila corymbosa*, sometimes listed as *Nomaphila stricta*) is very similar in appearance to *H. polysperma* (the hygro I described earlier), except that it has much larger leaves (three inches long) and a woodier stem. Giant hygro requires very strong light.

I have never had any luck keeping this plant, which is why I give it a special spot in the section about plants to avoid. Others claim to have had success with it, and it seems that almost every book about aquatic plants gives it high marks. However, if you look closely, the high marks usually refer to the appearance of the plant. When they talk about its durability, they always seem to show pictures of the plant with tough, emersed-form leaves!

The truth is that this plant grows into a large bush (over two feet tall) when grown emersed. When grown submersed, it suffers. The submersed-form leaves are quite beautiful, but their only purpose seems to be to photosynthesize long enough for the plant to grow to the surface. Submersed leaves survive a few weeks, then drop off, leaving a barren stem below.

Fish School

Bog plants are plants that grow in marshy areas and can survive above or below water. Some can survive underwater indefinitely and are good choices for the aquarium. Others will only survive a limited time underwater, and should be avoided.

If you want to enjoy the look of this plant, expect to trim off the dead bottoms regularly, replanting the top healthy part. Still, don't expect to get more than six inches of stem with live leaves on it. Some day I am going to put some giant hygro in a pot on my patio, just so I can see this plant in a truly happy state.

Anyway, many terrestrial houseplants are sold as aquarium plants. Those plants absolutely will not survive for long underwater. Do not buy the following species!

Mike's Top 15 List of Poor Plant Choices

15. Dracaena
14. Dragon's Flame
13. Red, Green, or Variegated Sanderiana
12. Red Crinkle
11. Purple Waffle
10. "Bella" Palms
9. Florida Beauty
8. Aluminum Plant
7. Mondo Grass
6. Dwarf Mondo Grass
5. Acorus Grass
4. Gold Dust Croton
3. Nephthytis (Syngonium) "Arrowhead"
2. Brazilian Sword (Peace Lily) (Spathiphyllum)

And the number one poor plant choice:

1. Princess Pine. It's hedge clippings, folks!

The Least You Need to Know

➤ Start with hardy species.
➤ Avoid damaged or diseased specimens.
➤ Buy only true aquatic plants.

Chapter 15

On the Road With Your Fish and Plants

In This Chapter

➤ How livestock is packaged for the trip home with you

➤ How to acclimate your fish and plants

➤ How to transport your fish, if you ever move

Wrapping Up Your Fish

When you buy fish from your dealer, you obviously need a way to get them home. Your dealer will provide everything you need. The dealer will place your selected fish in plastic bags that he will either seal with a rubber band or by tying the top in a knot. The bag should be fully inflated, so that it holds its shape and is less easily squashed. If the bag is flaccid, it is easier for fish to get trapped in the corners and squashed.

Some dealers will inflate the bag with pure oxygen, which will increase the amount of time that fish are safe in the bag. However, most dealers don't do this and use air only. In most cases, it really isn't necessary to use pure oxygen anyway. The trip to your house is much shorter than a trip from Asia.

Often customers ask if they can have extra water because they won't get home for a while. I have to explain to them that if they have a long trip, they don't *want* more water. You see, the water only keeps the fish wet. It is the air within the bag that keeps him alive. So the more air, the better. There is a lot more oxygen in air than in water. Typically, your dealer will fill the bag one-third with water, and this is usually what is best. However, if you are really going to be a while, say more than a couple of hours, then you may want to ask the dealer to use the next size larger bag. This will give you more water and more air. Better yet, make fish shopping your last stop, and go straight home after you buy them.

Fish Tales

Did you know that Siamese fighting fish are packed one per shot-glass-sized bag, and travel for two days that way without a problem? Your dealer's packaging will be quite roomy by comparison.

If the species is a spiny one, your dealer probably will double-bag it. The best way for him to do this is to tie off the first plastic bag and place it upside down within the second one. That way, when the second is tied off, it rounds off all the corners. This prevents the fish from lodging in and poking through the corners of the bag. Often, dealers will double-bag the tinier fish, too. That's because they can lodge in a corner, and as the bag shifts, it can roll over and squash the fish. Most fish only need single plastic bags, though.

Fish and Tips
If the weather is especially hot or cold, you may want to take the added precaution of bringing along a Styrofoam container or an empty cooler. This provides extra insulation for the fish on your trip home. Some dealers sell Styrofoam fish boxes.

Some dealers will use a separate plastic bag for each species. Some will mix species from different tanks in the same plastic bag. Either way is usually okay, as long as too many fish aren't put inside. You may want to ask if your dealer has central filtration systems. If he does, then the water in each tank is the same anyway, because it is flowing through from a central pump and filter. So there will be no shock in mixing species from different tanks. However, the water quality may be quite different in isolated tanks, and bagging fish separately from each tank would be preferable.

The procedure for packaging aquatic plants is similar, but generally they go into the plastic bags without water. Also, plain air is used to inflate the bag, not pure oxygen. Customers often worry that the plants won't survive the trip when packaged this way. Some request that we add water to the bag. The truth is that the plants will be fine without water. In fact, they arrive at the dealer wrapped only in wet newspaper, and they have been in transit for much longer. Also, adding the water is sometimes counterproductive. If the water sloshes a lot on the way home, it may bend and break up the plants.

When you ring up at the cash register, your plastic bags of fish and plants will be packaged into typical grocery bags for the trip home. In cooler weather, double folding the top of the grocery bag will help it retain heat.

Driving Miss Danio

Transporting your fish home is fairly straightforward. The main precaution you must take is to be sure the fish and plants are protected from temperature extremes. If you are comfortable, then the fish are probably comfortable, too.

In hot weather, be very careful about setting the fish anywhere where they might cook. Think of a sealed plastic bag as being much like a closed-up car. If the sun hits it directly, it will get very hot, very fast! Do not set your fish on the dashboard or leave them in the trunk. Try not to set them on a seat that is getting direct sunlight. Placing the fish on the floor in the shade is a better choice. Also, don't put the fish too near an air conditioning duct or they will get chilled.

Besides a sealed plastic bag being very much like a closed-up car, a closed-up car is very much like a closed up-car. Don't leave bags of fish and plants in an unattended vehicle. If you have to make a stop somewhere, take the fish in with you. Remember, if you are comfortable, the fish probably are, too.

In cold weather, the grocery bag probably will be ample protection from the cold for the short trip home—particularly if you turn on the car's heater. Be careful, though, not to set the fish too close to the heating ducts, or they may cook quite readily. Again, if you have other stops, take the fish inside rather than leaving them in an unattended car.

Try not to jostle the fish excessively during the trip home, but that doesn't mean you have to drive five miles per hour and have the kids try to balance the bag on the way. If you've ever seen fish in a stream or fish in the ocean, you will know that they can take quite a bit of jostling without a problem. In fact, a little jostling is helpful because it agitates and oxygenates the water in the bag.

> **Fish and Tips**
> When families buy fish, the kids often fight over who gets to carry them home. If necessary, let each child carry his own bag of fish. However, first put the plastic bag inside a grocery bag. Careless handling by little ones can pop the rubber bands off the neck of the fish bag. Better yet, teach your kids not to fight.

Acclimating New Arrivals

Ideally, all new specimens should be quarantined for two weeks before they are introduced into your tank. This helps prevent the introduction of diseases. If you want to learn how to set up a quarantine tank, see Chapter 24 on disease and stress. For now, though, we will assume that this is your very first batch of fish. So your main tank can act as a quarantine tank this one time.

You probably will be quite anxious to get your new fish into the tank, but you cannot just dump them right in. The temperature and water quality in the bag may be quite different from that in your aquarium. So you must acclimate the fish. Whether you choose to use a quarantine tank, or to put fish directly into your community tank, there are several popular methods for acclimating fish to their new home:

➤ Float and dump method

➤ Float and net method

➤ Float and mix method

➤ Float and drip method

You'll notice these all begin with *float*. You need to equalize the temperature in the fish bag with the temperature in your tank, to keep the fish from suffering temperature shock. To do this, merely float the plastic fish bag on top of the water in your tank for 20 minutes. This will allow the temperatures to equalize. There is no need to float longer than this. More is not better, because the temperature should be equalized by then, and there is a limited amount of oxygen in the fish bag.

The Float and Dump Method

This method is probably most popular. It involves floating the unopened fish bag as described above, and then dumping the contents into the aquarium. It's quick. It's easy. But there is a bit more risk of shock to your fish and transmission of disease. Your fish will be going from one type of water to another with no adjustment, and if the dealer's water is carrying parasites, you have just introduced them into your tank.

Float new arrivals, bag and all, for 20 minutes. It will equalize tempera-ture and prevent shock.

The Float and Net Method

Float and net is a little better. Again, float the unopened fish bag, but instead of dumping the bag into the tank, gently net each fish out of the bag and place it in the tank. It will still be instantaneous change from one type of water to another, but there will be a bit less chance of introducing disease to your tank. Discard the dealer's water.

The Float and Mix Method

Even better is the float and mix method. While the fish bag is floating, you open it up and pour a bit of water from your tank into the bag every few minutes. This will provide a more gradual change in water quality for your fish. After 20 minutes, you can either dump the contents into the tank, or better, gently net the fish from the bag, place the fish in the tank, and discard the water in the bag.

The Float and Drip Method

The best method of all, the drip method is merely a more methodical version of the float and mix method. The difference is, instead of adding water to the fish bag in stages, you place the fish and the water from the bag into a container on the floor. Then, using a piece of air line with a valve on it, you siphon water from your tank at a slow drip into the container on the floor. This makes the smoothest transition in water quality for the fish. When the container is full, or after 20 minutes (whichever comes first), net each fish and place it in the aquarium. Throw away the water in the container. *If you use the drip method, don't walk away and forget it, or you'll have a flood on your hands . . . er . . . floor.*

I usually take the quick float and dump route, partly because I'm in a hurry, and partly because I know the water quality of my tank and the fish store are the same. Once, though, I brought home an expensive zebra plecostomus. I figured I would take extra pains with it, and so I set it up for the drip method. That turned out to be a bad idea.

You see, I have had a pet monkey for over 20 years. Her name is Coco, but I call her Coco the Devil Monkey. She was out of her cage playing while the drip was going on, and I forgot she was out. When I went to check on my new zebra pleco, I found it on the floor, bitten in half! Apparently, Coco doesn't like plecos all that much.

Testing the Water

One thing you also may want to do is to run a full complement of tests on your dealer's water. You can take a sample from the fish bag (before mixing your tank water into it, of course), and check the pH, ammonia, and nitrite levels. It is always interesting to see what kind of water the new fish are coming from.

Ammonia and nitrite levels should be zero, but the pH is the one that concerns us most. If it is radically different from the pH of your tank, you may want to use some sodium bicarbonate or sodium biphosphate to adjust the pH of your aquarium before adding the new fish—to prevent shock. Again, I am talking about the very first batch of fish going into the tank. If you are adding fish to an existing tank, it would not be wise to change the pH of, say, 20 fish that are already in the tank so as to make it more comfortable for one new one. It would be better to stress one than 20!

If your tank's pH is well above 7.0, particularly if it is above 7.5, you may want to add a bit of sodium biphosphate to bring the pH level closer to neutral (7.0), anyway. We'll talk a lot more about water quality, water testing, pH, and other parameters in Chapter 17.

Fish and Tips
Crown plants should only be planted root deep. An easy way to do this is to first plant them deeper, and then tug lightly until the crown of the plant is at (or within one-quarter inch of) the gravel line.

By the way, while your fish are acclimating, feel free to plant any new plants you bought. There is no need to float them or adjust pH. You can position the plants wherever is pleasing to you. For the most natural appearance, do not plant them in straight rows and do not put all of one variety together. For many species, I like to make a large group, with a smaller group nearby that intermingles with another species. Also, taller plants look best in the rear of the tank.

When planting newly acquired plants, be sure to remove any lead weights or rubber bands that were put around the stalks. Bunch plants may be planted as a bunch or you can separate the strands. If you buy potted plants, I recommend that you remove the pot and rock-wool media before planting.

Monitoring New Inhabitants

Once you release the new fish into the tank, you probably will want to sit and watch them for a while. Don't expect them to display much interesting behavior at first,

Something's Fishy
Do not feed new arrivals until they have been in the tank for a few hours or more. New fish are under stress and are unlikely to eat, so most of the food will be wasted. You will just end up polluting the tank. Be patient!

though. New fish will be scared and tired. Many of them will want to rest and hide. Others, being in unfamiliar territory, go into a restless exploratory mode. No matter, the key thing is to observe everyone and keep your eye out for problems. Hopefully, you have picked compatible species.

Any problems that you encounter probably will not occur right away. There probably will be no aggression until everyone settles. Keep your eye out for serious fights. An occasional joust to jockey for territory or assert one's rights is not a big deal. If damage starts getting done, then corrective action may be necessary.

The New Guy in Town

If you are adding fish to an existing tank, it may be a bit tougher for the fish. The established fish will have their territories already staked out. The new arrival must fight its way into a territory. So keep an especially close eye when adding to an existing tank.

Fish and Tips
When introducing fish to an existing tank, it may help to feed the existing fish before introducing the new fish. Hungry fish are more likely to be aggressive.

Don't let me scare you too much, though. There is no need to remove a fish at the first bite. You have to give them time to work out their differences. Just don't let it progress to the point where someone gets seriously wounded or killed.

One thing you can do to help is to rearrange decorations in the tank when adding new fish. Moving the rocks and driftwood around, for example, will force existing inhabitants to find new territories, too. That way, the new guy won't be at such a disadvantage.

Keep an extra watch out for disease the first week. Fish are under the most stress when introduced to a new tank, and new fish may bring disease with them. Take time to notice changes and follow the advice in Chapter 24 (on disease and stress) if you need to.

Have Bucket, Will Travel

A time may come when you need to move your aquarium, or transport your fish. Perhaps you are moving to a new house and the whole setup needs to be relocated, or maybe you just have a fish that has grown too large and your dealer is willing to take it in trade. With a little planning, the chore shouldn't be too difficult.

Moving Your Tank

Moving your aquarium to a new location may be quite easy or more difficult. A few factors come into play:

➤ Size of the tank

➤ Distance of the move

➤ Stairs!

For short moves, be they across town or just across the room, smaller tanks are much easier to manage. The easiest way to move small tanks is to drain them down to where the water just covers the fish, and then pick the whole thing up and transfer it. Refill the tank at the destination. Plants and fish remain in place, though you may temporarily need to remove rocks or driftwood that might fall and crush the fish.

This method can work with bigger tanks, too, but the chances of you being able to safely lift the weight is in question. Some large aquariums may take six people to carry them *when empty*! Also, bigger tanks often have bigger fish, which means more water would be required to keep the fish covered. That is not good. You need the water to be very shallow if you plan to move the tank with fish and decor intact.

When moving a tank, don't forget to consider staircases that may be along the way—especially if you try moving the tank with decorations or fish intact. Will you be able to carry the tank up the stairs without tilting it? Tilting a tank with water in it is a very good way to break the seams of a tank, because you shift all the stress to one end or corner. Worse, if you are

Something's Fishy
The most important rule in moving aquariums is *never* move an aquarium that is full. Most tanks are too heavy for that, anyway, but even smaller tanks will twist and break more easily when full.

SNIFF! SNIFF!

already struggling to handle the weight, what do you think will happen when you tilt the tank and the water sloshes to one end, putting all the weight there? Disaster!

If you move an aquarium that is too large for one person to carry easily, it is probably best to empty it completely, and carry it that way. If necessary, use a hand-truck or appliance cart to move the tank up the stairs. (Stand the empty tank on its end on the hand-truck.) You can rent hand-trucks and appliance carts at any place that rents trucks and vans.

Move Your Bass!

For longer moves, or if you are moving large fish, it may be necessary to pack and transfer the fish and the aquarium separately. You can either package the fish in plastic bags—like your dealer does—or put them in your fish bucket for transfer. Be sure to put a lid on the bucket or line it with a plastic garbage bag that you can tie off. For really large fish, you might use a clean garbage can.

If your move is really long, say, across country rather than across town, things get more complicated. You may need to add pure oxygen to the fish bags to keep the fish safe for the trip, or you may need to place fewer fish in each bag—or both. You may need to go the full route of bagging and boxing the fish inside Styrofoam containers and shipping them via air freight. Your dealer may be able to help you with this—for a fee.

Fish and Tips
Oxygen isn't the only thing to worry about on long trips. Also make sure the fish won't be exposed to temperature extremes. A bucket of fish sitting in the sun on the back of a pickup truck may be cooked before they reach their destination.

Alternately, you may want to save yourself the hassle of moving fish long distances by selling, trading, or donating the fish to someone. Classified ads may bring in some cash, or your dealer may offer cash or trade. A "free to good home" ad may move the fish fast, you could donate them to a dealer or friend, or ask your kids if their teachers would like some free fish for the classroom aquarium. You could really be sweet and donate the tank, too!

The Least You Need to Know

➤ Protect fish from temperature extremes on the way home. Don't leave fish unattended in the car or place them too close to heating or cooling ducts.

➤ Quarantine new arrivals whenever possible. This helps prevent the introduction of disease to your tank.

➤ Float new arrivals for 20 minutes to equalize temperature. That is, float the fish bag with the fish in it on the surface of your tank.

➤ It is best not to add the dealer's water to your tank. It may harbor disease.

➤ Monitor new arrivals. Watch for aggression and shock.

➤ Cage all monkeys when acclimating fish!

Part 4
The Tank Is Running; Now What?

Read this part, or the fish die! Once you get your tank up and running, you can't just ignore it.

Healthy water is the basis for a healthy aquarium and healthy fish, so the first chapter in Part 4 deals with cycling your new aquarium. If you are setting up a new tank, that chapter may be the most important one for you to read. Don't skip it!

Afterward, I go into more depth about water chemistry in Chapter 17. This chapter is more technical than most of the others in this book, but don't let that scare you. I've put things into simple terms, and you don't have to remember anything from your high school chemistry class to get some use from it.

I know I said in Part 1 that aquariums are very low maintenance, but there are a few chores that you must do to keep things in good working order, and to keep your fish and plants alive. The most important duty is to give your aquarium regular partial water changes. I'll explain how in Chapter 18. Then, in the following chapters, you'll learn how to feed your fish properly and the few other chores that are necessary to keep the tank looking nice.

Still, it's not all work. I even threw in a couple of chapters on some fun stuff, such as breeding fish and propagating plants.

Chapter 16

Cycling Your New Aquarium

In This Chapter

➤ Why you need helpful bacteria

➤ The nitrogen cycle in detail

➤ The fastest, safest ways to cycle a new tank

➤ What to do if there is a problem

Please read this chapter very carefully. It could make the difference between getting your tank off to a good start or getting it off on the wrong foot. The environment that you set up in an aquarium is always a fragile thing, but it is especially fragile in a new tank. This is because a balance needs to be achieved between the waste your fish excrete and the helpful bacteria that live in the tank. Earlier in the book, I mentioned that you cannot add a full load of fish all at once. You are about to learn why that is and how cycling or breaking in a new tank can prevent problems.

Good-Guy Bacteria

The first thing you need to understand is that every healthy, established aquarium is heavily populated by helpful bacteria. These good-guy bacteria are essential to the proper functioning of your aquarium. They break down ammonia and other fish waste. Without them, fish waste quickly builds up to levels that are lethal to your fish. Eventually, all the solid surfaces in your aquarium—including the gravel, glass, rocks, plant leaves, and debris—will be coated with jillions of helpful bacteria.

The problem is, when you first set up your tank these helpful bacteria are not present in sufficient quantity. The bacteria won't develop until after you have added your first batch of fish. That is because the fish produce the ammonia that is the food for the bacteria. Without ammonia to feed them, the bacteria don't multiply.

That is why a new tank is a more fragile environment than an older, established aquarium. Until you add fish, the bacteria won't develop, but until the bacteria develop, the fish continue to excrete ammonia that won't all be broken down. So the time between the initial introduction of fish and the development of full colonies of helpful bacteria is a very dangerous one.

It may seem weird, but a fish is much more likely to die of high waste levels in a brand new, sparkling clean tank, than in an older, established, somewhat dirty tank. That's because there are enough helpful bacteria in the established tank. Now, don't take this to mean that you shouldn't keep a clean tank! On the contrary, performing the routine maintenance that keeps your tank clean is very important. Clean tanks are good, but sterile tanks are bad.

Fish Tales

The discus fish (*Symphysodon discus*) is a large, beautiful disc-shaped fish. However, this delicate species is not a good choice for beginners. It needs a lot of special care.

Over a period of weeks, your tank will develop plenty of helpful bacteria. The time lag between the introduction of fish and the final catch-up of waste-neutralizing bacteria is called the break-in period. We also say that we are cycling a new tank, as we progress through this period. The term derives from the nitrogen cycle, which is what is happening chemically during this process. I will tell you more about that in detail a bit later in the chapter.

It Depends on the Bioload

How long does it take to cycle a new tank? Well, every aquarium is different. There are many factors that influence how long it will take to break in a new tank, but it will probably come down to two things:

1. How big is the initial bioload of the tank?
2. Did you do anything to seed the filter bed with helpful bacteria?

The bioload of your tank refers to the waste-producing plants and animals, and is obviously going to be determined most by how many living things you put in there. Wastes from these plants and animals must be removed or neutralized to keep a system healthy. Plants probably won't add much to the bioload, because they don't typically produce waste products that we worry about. The exception to that is dead, decaying leaves. The fish, and any other critters, including snails, crabs, etc., will be the main bioload in the tank. These animals all eat, and they all excrete waste. Obviously, if you put more fish into the tank, more waste will be produced, and that will result in a higher bioload.

While we may use the number of fish to judge how large a bioload our system has, when it comes right down to it, the fish really aren't the problem. *You* are the problem. Now, before you get all defensive, stop and think for a moment. The fish can't excrete waste unless they first eat something, right? And who puts the food into the tank? That's right, *you* do. So when we get right down to it, you ultimately determine the bioload in your tank by how much you feed. Always remember that you are not just feeding the fish—you are feeding the tank.

Speeding the Process

Since you now know that cycling a tank is the process of developing enough helpful bacteria to handle the bioload of that aquarium, you have probably already figured out that there are ways to speed the process by introducing some extra bacteria to get the cycle moving. Let's look at how to do this.

The easiest, cheapest, and most effective way to speed the process is to seed your aquarium with some gravel from an established tank. Established tanks are fully colonized by helpful bacteria. Mix the cycled gravel in with your new gravel and your aquarium will quickly develop all the good-guy bacteria that it needs.

Where do you get some seeded gravel to add to your tank? If you have another aquarium you can take some from there, or maybe a friend will give you some from their tank. Some dealers will give you a free handful or two, and some will sell you some out of their tanks. I wish all dealers would make cycled gravel available to their customers. Ask your dealer to see if he offers it.

What if you have your heart set on setting up your tank with pure black gravel and the only used gravel you can find is shocking pink? Consider getting the used shocking pink gravel, anyway. You don't have to mix it in with your new stuff. Instead, make a bag out of an old pair of pantyhose (make sure they're clean and thoroughly rinsed!) and put the used gravel inside. You can then bury it or lay it on top of your new gravel to seed the tank. The helpful bacteria will still find their way to your new gravel, and in a couple of weeks you can remove the pantyhose and pink gravel from your tank.

Fish and Tips
If your dealer doesn't normally sell used gravel out of his tanks, offer to buy a new bag of gravel and trade it for some used gravel. This is good for both of you, because you get some gravel with bacteria to seed your tank, and he gets to freshen up the appearance of his tanks by trading some possibly worn looking gravel for some newer stuff.

Another way to speed the process is to add lots of live plants to your tank. They will be coated with well-established colonies of helpful bacteria. Now, I'm a skilled professional, so I stop just short of telling you to try this at home, but I have set up aquariums before where I put in lots of live plants and a heavy load of fish—way more fish than I would normally recommend to cycle a new tank. My test kits were never able to find detectable levels of ammonia or nitrite in those tanks. In other words, enough helpful bacteria came in on the plants so that the tank never went through a break-in period. It cycled instantly. Disclaimer: Your mileage may vary! When I talk about the nitrogen cycle in a moment, I'll also talk about the test kits needed to measure the progress.

You can also speed up your tank's cycle by using filter media from an existing aquarium. Filter media will be coated with lots of helpful bacteria. So swapping some media from an established filter into your new filter can be a big help.

There are some products on the market that claim to contain helpful bacteria in a dormant state. Adding these products to your tank is supposed to speed up the cycle. I must say, however, that I don't have much faith in these products. When I've tried them, I've seen little difference. Some contain enzymes that, while they will break down ammonia, don't actually seed your tank with the helpful bacteria you need. Others contain the wrong kind of bacteria. Additionally, there is the question of shelf life. My recommendation is to save your money and skip these products.

Safe Cycling

The most important quality needed for cycling a new tank is patience. You cannot rush this procedure, or you risk killing all your fish.

Okay, let's assume you have your new tank set up and running. You've given it 24 hours to make sure the temperature is stable, the tank doesn't leak, and all the equipment is functioning normally. You are ready to add your first batch of fish. To play it safe, we must assume there are no helpful bacteria in your tank, even if you've added plants or gravel from an existing tank.

Until we know the tank has sufficient good-guy bacteria, what steps do we take to ensure that ammonia won't build to toxic levels? The most important thing is not to get too excited and put too many fish in at once. An established aquarium can typically hold one inch of fish per gallon of water. When cycling a new tank, though, don't exceed one *half* inch per gallon. If you start with fewer fish, and feed only lightly, less ammonia will be produced. This will provide ammonia to grow the helpful bacteria without letting ammonia levels get so high that they poison the fish. Later, you will be able to add more fish to your community tank.

You are probably wondering how long this process will take. As I mentioned before, each tank is different. To know for sure, you must monitor the rise and fall of ammonia and nitrite levels with water test kits. I'll discuss them in more detail in a bit. For now, a general rule is: It will take two to three weeks to cycle most tanks. However, I have seen some tanks take over a month to cycle.

In any case, if you add a few fish and then let the tank develop enough helpful bacteria to handle them before adding more (up to the maximum of one inch per gallon, of course), things should go well. Adding fish in stages is a safe and easy way to cycle a tank, and chances are good that you won't lose a single fish during the process. But if you rush things and put too many fish in at once, you risk losing them all.

There is one method of cycling an aquarium that is totally safe, but it requires even more patience. Instead of letting your fish add the ammonia that the helpful bacteria need to develop in the tank, you can add the ammonia directly. Most aquarium stores will sell some products that contain ammonium chloride for seeding new tanks. You also can use ammonia from the grocery store, though you need to get the plain stuff, not lemon scented or whatever. However, I couldn't tell you how much of the household stuff to add. It's better to get the ammonium chloride from the pet store and carefully follow the instructions on the package.

Fish and Tips
Many dealers offer a water testing service that is either free or inexpensive. Feel free to make use of this service, but I still recommend that you buy your own test kits to keep at home. Even if you use your own kits, your dealer can help you interpret the results of the tests.

Something's Fishy
Never use ammonium chloride to cycle a tank while the fish are in it!

The way this process works is that you add the ammonium chloride and monitor your ammonia and nitrite levels. By monitoring those levels, you will be able to tell when the tank has cycled. At that point, you do a major water change and then add your fish. You can add them all at once, because your tank will be cycled.

Now, remember that I said this method requires patience? That is because you cannot add a single fish until *after* the entire process is complete, or you risk killing the fish. Let me say that again: This method involves cycling the tank—probably for around three weeks—*without* the fish.

Finally, it is not uncommon to lose fish while cycling a new tank. If it happens to you, don't feel too badly, because it happens to many people. However, if you follow the guidelines that I've presented, you have a very good chance of having every fish survive the process. If things go wrong, don't be afraid to seek help.

The Nitrogen Cycle—in Detail

I am going to get a bit more technical in this section and delve more deeply into the chemistry of cycling a tank. Don't let this scare you off. Even if you didn't do well in high school chemistry, you should be able to maneuver through this section. It is important that you read this part, even if you don't memorize all the details. When you emerge from the other side, you should have a better understanding of how the cycling process works, and therefore, a better understanding of why you don't want to rush it and what happens if you try to bend the rules.

When you first set up your tank, there will be no ammonia (NH_3) or nitrite (NO_2), in the water. (An exception would be if there is a pre-existing problem with your tap water.) Soon, though, this will change.

Just as we produce ammonia in our urine, fish produce ammonia, too. However, they excrete it to a much lesser extent in the urine. Instead, fish mostly excrete ammonia through respiration in the gills. No matter, the result is the same, which is that the ammonia ends up in the water. Ammonia also enters the water when heterotrophic bacteria break down uneaten food, dead plant leaves, feces, and other detritus in the tank. These bacteria are different from the nitrifying bacteria, which are the good-guy bacteria we've been discussing.

I don't think I have to tell you how toxic ammonia can be! *Nitrosomonas* are the helpful bacteria that break down ammonia. They convert the ammonia into nitrite, which is still toxic to your fish, though not as toxic as ammonia. In a new tank, the ammonia levels will typically rise for about seven days after you introduce the first batch of fish. By this time, the helpful *Nitrosomonas* bacteria will usually have increased their population to the point where they can break down the ammonia faster than it is produced. So a week after introducing fish, you usually will see ammonia levels drop back to zero.

Now, remember the ammonia is being converted to nitrite. So as the helpful bacteria get things under control and the ammonia levels drop, you will see a simultaneous increase in the nitrite levels of your tank. Nitrite levels will tend to rise for roughly another seven days, and then they, too, will drop. That's because by this time another group of helpful bacteria, the *Nitrobacter*, will have developed a big enough population to oxidize the nitrite faster than it is produced. The result is that nitrite levels will drop back to zero.

Still, as the nitrite levels decrease, you will see nitrate (NO_3) levels increase. Fortunately, nitrate is generally considered harmless to freshwater fish, except in very high quantities. Your regular partial water changes will keep nitrate from building up to toxic levels. Additionally, plants in your tank may use it as a nutrient.

Fish and Tips
The normal full load for a community tank is one inch of fish per gallon. However, when cycling a new tank, don't put in more than one-half inch of fish per gallon.

Anyway, once you've seen the ammonia level rise and fall back to zero, and then see the nitrite level rise and fall back to zero, your tank will be cycled. It should be safe to add the rest of your fish. Be aware that, when you do, you may see some temporary spikes in those ammonia and nitrite levels again, because you have increased the bioload in your tank and it takes the bacteria some time to increase their population to adjust to that.

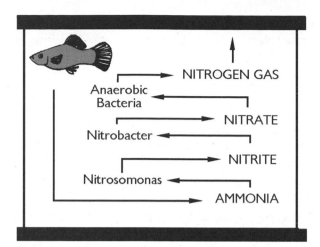

The Nitrogen Cycle

Disclaimer

The preceding information on the nitrogen cycle represents the way this subject has been taught for decades. However, I would like to note that my friend Tim Hovanec of Marineland Aquarium Products in Simi Valley, California, did some experiments that seem to show that *Nitrosomonas* and *Nitrobacter* bacteria are probably not the bacteria involved in breaking down ammonia and nitrite. Nevertheless, the process I described still holds. It is only the species of bacteria that is in question.

The Timetable

Again, every tank is different, so the timetable will be different, too. The numbers I use in the following list are typical for tanks that I set up, but your results may vary.

Let me stress that the timetable I'm giving you is only a guideline. Only the actual running of ammonia and nitrite tests can tell you what stage your tank is at in the cycle, and when it is safe to add more fish. Do not ignore your test results because you want something else to be true.

If you are careful, you probably will see the following:

➤ No ammonia or nitrite will be present until after you introduce the fish. (The clock doesn't start ticking until you add the fish.)

➤ Once fish are added, ammonia will climb for approximately seven days. Then it will fall back to zero over a day or two.

➤ As ammonia falls, nitrite will climb for approximately the next seven days. Then it, too, will fall back to undetectable levels.

➤ As nitrite falls, nitrate will increase. Note, however, that I normally consider it a waste of time to test nitrate levels, unless you are having problems and no other cause can be found.

Corrective Action

When cycling a new tank, it's a good idea to run your water tests for ammonia and nitrite every day until the cycle is complete. Then, you can drop back to testing every week or two. What should you do if you find that ammonia or nitrite levels are elevated?

The answer that is usually best may surprise you. That answer is: Do nothing. That's right, do nothing—but only if you aren't experiencing any problems with your fish. If they all appear healthy, if none are dying, then leave well enough alone. As the tank continues to cycle, Mother Nature will fix those ammonia and nitrite problems all by herself. On the other hand, if you are losing fish, or if the fish look overly stressed, corrective action may be necessary.

This graph shows ammonia, nitrite, and nitrate levels during the cycling of a typical aquarium. Your results may vary.

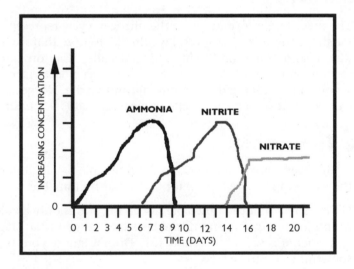

Moaning About Ammonia

So, what can you do if your ammonia level is high and the fish are having problems? Here are some possible solutions that you can mix or match:

➤ Add some ammonia-removing chips to your outside power filter. This stuff looks like white gravel, and is a naturally occurring substance called zeolite. It will remove some ammonia, and then you can throw it away.

➤ Add one of those dormant bacteria products to break down the ammonia quickly. Note that some may cloud the water temporarily.

➤ Lower the pH slightly, perhaps to 6.8. We will talk about this more in the next chapter, but for now be aware that ammonia is more toxic in alkaline water. Lowering the pH below 7.0 will make the water acidic. Do not lower it too far, though, or you will create other problems. The ammonia will become the less toxic ammonium in slightly acidic water, and so it may not bother the fish at all. Eventually, the cycle will remove it.

➤ Change some water. Partial water changes will remove some ammonia. Keep in mind, though, that tap water is alkaline in most areas of the country. So you need to monitor the pH to avoid making the remaining ammonia more toxic.

➤ Add Amquel. This is a product that neutralizes the toxicity of ammonia. There are also some lesser quality copies of it on the market. If it neutralizes ammonia, why did I save this option for last? Wouldn't it be the best choice? Well, the answer is probably a resounding yes. It works great, but I'm reluctant to recommend it because I've just seen too many people misuse it.

As a dealer, I find myself wasting lots of time helping people figure out that they really don't have an ammonia problem, all because they used Amquel and didn't read the directions! To use Amquel properly, you need a compatible ammonia test kit. Not all ammonia test kits can be used with it. The salicylate-based kits must be used with it, while the Nessler's Reagent-based kits cannot be, because they give false positive readings when used with Amquel. In other words, you will think you have ammonia when you don't. So you will add more Amquel, which will make you think your ammonia has gone up even more, which will make you panic.

Fish Tales

The spotted headstander (*Chilodus punctatus*) gets its name from its peculiar habit of swimming with its head down, at a 45-degree angle.

When Nitrite Isn't Right

What if the nitrite level is high and the fish are dying or looking stressed? What do you do, then?

➤ If you haven't done it already, add a teaspoon of aquarium salt per gallon of aquarium water. Salt doesn't remove the nitrite, but it makes it much less toxic to the fish. It also helps prevent some diseases. This probably is the only thing that you need to do if you're worried about high nitrite levels.

➤ Do a partial water change. This will dilute the nitrite.

➤ Try one of the dormant bacteria products. Some claim to reduce nitrites as well as ammonia, though I have serious doubts.

New Tank Syndrome

Here is a term that you will occasionally hear bandied about. Sometimes new tank syndrome refers to ammonia and nitrite levels and the cycling of new tanks. Sometimes it is used to describe cloudy water problems that often appear in newly set up tanks. Since we've already talked about ammonia and nitrite, let's just look at the cloudy water aspect of new tank syndrome. Basically, two things cause cloudy water: suspended particulates and suspended bacteria.

A brand new, sparkling clean aquarium filter is not as efficient as an established one. The established filter is apt to be partially clogged, thereby allowing it to filter even finer particles. It will also have stickier filter media—since a bacterial slime will inhabit it. So a new filter is apt to let more particulates get through.

Until your aquarium cycles, there will not be a biological balance of bacteria in the system. Sometimes other bacteria in the water column will supermultiply, feeding on available nutrients. There are so many of them that they can give a cloudy appearance to the water. Note, however, that these are not the desired nitrifying bacteria. Those good-guy bacteria live on solid surfaces, not in the water column. Time will usually fix the problem, so be patient!

Fish Tales

It is common fallacy that dissolved ammonia makes the water look cloudy. While ammonia may be present, it is not ammonia that is making your water cloudy. If there were enough ammonia in your tank to make the water cloudy, your fish would be long dead.

The Least You Need to Know

➤ Helpful bacteria break down toxic ammonia and nitrite in your tank.

➤ Don't cycle a new tank with more than one-half inch of fish per gallon.

➤ Most new tanks take two to three weeks to cycle.

➤ You can't tell the condition of your water by eye. You must run ammonia and nitrite tests to know when your tank has safely cycled.

Basic Water Chemistry

First off, let me state that I am not a chemist. I don't even play one on TV. I am a geek, though, so you know I won't be happy unless we talk about some technical stuff. That's what this chapter is all about. The topics are important, however, and I will do my best to keep them light.

Pondering pH

pH (always spelled with a lower case p and a capital H) is the measurement of acidity or alkalinity. According to *Webster's Dictionary*, the term pH comes from the French *pouvoir hydrogéne*, which means "hydrogen power." It is a measurement of hydrogen ions. We measure pH on a scale from zero to 14, with a pH of seven being neutral. A pH of less than seven is acid, and a pH above seven is alkaline (or basic). The lower the pH, the more acid. The higher the pH, the more alkaline (or basic) we consider a sample to be.

pH is measured on a scale of zero to 14, with seven being neutral. Low pH is acid. High pH is alkaline.

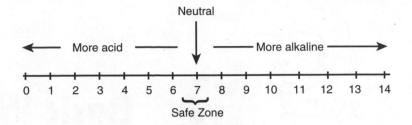

Additionally, pH is measured on a logarithmic scale, which means that each numerical change in pH actually represents a 10-fold change. That is, a pH of 7.0 is 10 times more alkaline than a pH of 6.0. And a pH of 6.0 is 100 times more acid than a pH of 8.0. Don't concern yourself too much with that detail. The main thing to remember is that a one-point change in pH is a pretty big change, and a two-point change is a huge change. It is dangerous to change the pH of your aquarium too rapidly—either up or down.

What should the pH of your tank be? That may depend on what species you plan to keep. Livebearers, for example, prefer water that is harder and with a slightly alkaline pH, say around 7.4. Most African cichlids also prefer hard, alkaline water, with a pH around 7.8. In the wild, many tetras come from areas where the pH is in the low sixes.

Most fish, no matter where they come from, can tolerate a pH between 6.5 and 7.5. In fact, if you keep your tank's pH around the neutral point of 7.0, there isn't a fish around that won't do well in it. 7.0 is as ideal as you can get for the broadest mix of species.

Assessing Acidity

How do you know what your pH is? Simple—you test it. There are many kits on the market that are cheap and easy to use. The basic procedure is to fill a vial with water from the aquarium, add a few drops of the reagent, and then compare the color to a color chart to get your numerical reading. Most kits use bromothymol blue as the reagent (the testing agent), which will turn yellow if the pH is acid, green if it is neutral, or blue if it is alkaline. Some kits use powdered reagents. You may still run across pH tape, which is a test kit that uses strips of litmus paper that change color when you dunk them in the tank. Litmus paper test kits are much less accurate.

Fish and Tips
Follow your test kit's directions carefully. Some kits require you to view through the side of the vial to determine the color, and some require you to view down through the top of the vial. Improper viewing will distort the reading.

It is a good idea to measure the pH of your tap water, so that you have a baseline. However, don't measure it directly out of the tap, as you probably won't get an accurate reading. Tap water has been stored under pressure in your water system, and will have extra gases dissolved in it. Coming from underground, tap water also may be devoid of some necessary gases. Some gases affect the pH. So aerate the sample—put it in a jar and shake it for a couple of minutes—before testing. This will drive out excess gases, allow regular atmospheric gases to be absorbed, and result in a more accurate reading. There is no need to aerate samples taken from the aquarium for testing. Your filter has already aerated the water for you.

My pH Has pHallen and It Can't Get Up

One thing you will find with regular testing is that the pH of your tank probably will not be stable over time. Instead, it will tend to drop. How fast this happens will depend on how many natural buffers are in your tap water. You may find that the pH drops within days or weeks, or it may not appear to drop at all—unless you go a really long time without a water change.

Why does the pH tend to drop? The answer is biological activity. You will remember that bacteria convert ammonia to nitrite, and nitrite to nitrate. Well, a by-product of that process is the release of acids into the water. If your tap water is low in natural buffers, these acids will cause the pH to drop. If your tap water is high in natural buffers, it may take a long time for the acids to deplete them all, so you may not see the pH drop until you've gone a long time without a water change.

Fish School
A *buffer* is combination of an acid or base with a salt that, when in solution, tends to stabilize the pH of the solution.

What else affects pH? Carbon dioxide forms carbonic acid when dissolved in water. So if your aeration is insufficient to drive off excess carbon dioxide, the CO_2 can build up and cause the pH to fall slightly.

Photosynthesis also affects pH. Plants use CO_2 when they photosynthesize. That means that during the day they will pull CO_2 from the water, resulting in less formation of carbonic acid. So the pH will rise slightly during the day. At night, plants respire and the pH will fall a bit.

Salt affects pH—sometimes. It depends on the kind of salt. When you buy aquarium salt, which is straight sodium chloride, it should have absolutely no effect on pH or hardness. Sea salt, however, is another story. It contains other minerals that will increase the hardness and pH of the water. African cichlid salts do the same.

Okay, I've talked about some things that affect pH. Now, let's talk about things that are affected *by* pH.

Ammonia and pH

The most important thing that pH affects is the toxicity of ammonia. Ammonia (NH_3), excreted by the fish, is much more toxic in alkaline water. In acid water, it ionizes into the less toxic ammonium (NH_4^+). So the higher the pH in your tank, the more dangerous will be any existing ammonia.

Interestingly, if your pH falls below 6.4 or so, the helpful bacteria that break down ammonia will start failing and the ammonium levels will climb. Fortunately, since the pH is low, the less toxic ammonium may not bother the fish much. However, do you see the danger here? What happens if something makes the pH go up? That's right. The ammonium becomes the very toxic ammonia.

Altering pH

In a moment, I'll tell you what to do if your pH is too high or too low. But first, I want to emphasize that it is usually best not to mess with your aquarium's pH. If your tank normally stays within that 6.5 to 7.5 range, it is probably best not to fiddle with the pH to try to make it "perfect." My recommendation is to only mess with the pH when you're having problems that seem attributed directly to it. Remember that a one-point change in pH is really a 10-fold change. So fiddling with the pH is sometimes much rougher on the fish than letting them adapt to what is normal for the local water conditions.

Something's Fishy
Calcareous (calcium containing) rocks will increase the pH and hardness of your water. So be careful when you select gravel and rocks for your tank. Your dealer can tell you which rocks will have this effect. Generally, you want to avoid calcareous stones. But if you live in an area where the natural buffering capacity of your tap water is very low, you may need them to help keep your pH stable.

Bumping the pH Up

It is usually fairly easy to increase the pH. Here are some ways to do it:

➤ Change some water. This is the best choice for most of you. Usually, when your pH is low it is because you are not changing enough water. Remember that pH tends to drop over time, due to biological activity in the tank. Water changes are usually the best way to bring the pH up, because tap water is usually alkaline. However, if you live in an area where it isn't, look at the next possibilities.

➤ Add a little sodium bicarbonate (baking soda) to the tank. This will bring up your pH, but be careful not to add too much at once. Test your pH to get a baseline, then add perhaps one-eighth of a teaspoon of sodium bicarbonate per 10 gallons and test the water again to see how much change it made. Proceed from there. It is best not to change the pH by more than one-half point per day, to prevent shock to the fish.

➤ Mix some dolomite or crushed coral (gravels normally sold for saltwater tanks) into your substrate. These calcareous gravels will increase the pH and water hardness in the tank. Unfortunately, I can't begin to tell you how much to add, because every tank is different. Perhaps you could try adding a pound or two per 10 gallons, and then give it a few days before you decide if you need more. Too much will raise your pH higher than you probably want it to go.

➤ Add a decorative calcareous rock or two. Most of the whitish or light-colored soft rocks available at the pet store will fit this category. Your dealer can point them out. The advantage of this method over the calcareous gravel is that the rocks are easier to remove if you decide they aren't working the way you want.

➤ Try one of the other chemicals sold. There are some tablets available that contain a mix of buffers designed to achieve a designated pH. They may be designed to achieve 6.5, 7.0, 7.2, and so on.

Knocking the pH Down

Lowering the pH is usually much more difficult. Depending on the amount of naturally occurring buffers in your water, the chemicals that you add to acidify a tank may be quickly neutralized. It is not uncommon to test the next day and see that the pH has returned to its original level. I'll talk about buffers more in a bit. Here are some ways to lower pH:

➤ Use sodium biphosphate powder, available at your aquarium store. Follow the directions I gave above for sodium bicarbonate.

➤ Try one of the other pH-reducing chemicals available for sale. There are liquids and also buffer tablets that target a designated pH, as mentioned previously.

➤ Add some peat to your filter box. Peat lowers both pH and hardness, but it can be tricky to use. I generally steer people away from this method. For starters, not all types of peat are safe—the stuff sold in aquarium stores should be, though. Also, there are different grades of it, so it's hard to say how much to use. Peat also releases some organic matter along with the acids, and that's not particularly good. Peat may turn your water an ugly brown.

A Salute to General Hardness

Your tap water may be either soft or hard. When we talk about water hardness, called *general hardness*, or GH, we are referring to the measurement of certain dissolved minerals—particularly calcium and magnesium.

Most aquarists don't measure the hardness of their water. Most fish can tolerate a broad range of water hardness. However, if you live in an area where the water is extremely soft or extremely hard, or if you want to breed some species that are extremely temperamental about it, you may need to track and possibly adjust the hardness of your tank water.

General hardness usually is measured on the German scale, as degrees of general hardness (dGH or DH).

Something's Fishy
The hardness of your aquarium water may affect the potency and toxicity of some medications, including Tetracycline and copper sulfate.

Sometimes you will see hardness listed in parts per million (ppm). Depending on the text you read, you may have to convert. The conversion chart below should help.

Scales for Measuring Water Hardness

Hardness	dH	ppm
Very soft	0–4	
Soft	4–8	0–75
Medium hard	8–12	75–150
Fairly hard	12–18	
Hard	18–30	150–300
Very hard	30+	300+

When you measure hardness, 3 to 10 dH and 30 to 120 ppm are generally okay in your aquarium. So what do you do if your water is really hard or soft? In most cases, do nothing. If the fish are surviving well, don't worry about it. Also, before you consider altering the hardness of your water, perhaps it would be better to consider altering the species you intend to keep. Some fish love hard water and some love soft water. So it may be simpler just to keep a different mix of fish.

Making It Harder

It's much easier to harden water than to soften it. Here are some ways to increase the hardness of your water:

➤ Add some calcareous gravel, such as dolomite or crushed coral, or add some large calcareous rocks or crushed oyster shells.

➤ If you are using one teaspoon of salt per gallon, as discussed elsewhere in the book, consider using sea salt instead of regular aquarium salt. Sea salt has some extra dissolved minerals that will help harden the water.

➤ Calcium chloride is often sold for reef tank enthusiasts to help grow the hard skeletons of their stony corals. This could be used as an additive.

➤ Add a bit of Epsom salts.

Making It Softer

Softening your water is much more difficult. Here are some ways to decrease the hardness of your water:

➤ Add water softening pillows to your filter box. These are special resinous beads in a net bag that you drop in the filter box. Most aquarium stores sell them, and this is probably the first method I would try.

➤ Add peat to the filter box to soften the water. But be aware that it can have the same negative side effects we discussed in the section on pH.

➤ Use a commercial water softener. If your water is that hard, you may already have one installed in your house. Be aware, though, that water softeners often work via ion exchange. That is, while they remove the ions that create hardness, they replace them with other ions. These ions may not be all that good for your fish, either.

➤ Dilute your tank water with water from a reverse osmosis (RO) purification unit. These are special filters that pump water through a semipermeable membrane. Water gets through the membrane, but most of the dissolved substances cannot. They are separated and rinsed away with waste water. By design, several gallons of water are wasted to produce one gallon of RO water. So this may not a good choice, ecologically speaking.

➤ Dilute your tank water with water from a deionization (DI) unit. Deionization filters contain two types of resinous beads. One type removes the positive ions (cations) and the other removes the negative ions (anions) from the water.

➤ Dilute your tank water with distilled water. This is a very expensive way to go, though.

➤ Try growing some anacharis in your tank. This plant removes some calcium salts from the water.

Fish and Tips
When adding chemicals to alter the pH or hardness, always start out with less than you think you'll need, and add from there. Once added, you can't remove the stuff without changing water. It may be helpful to put some aquarium water in a bucket, add a measured amount of adjusting chemical to it, and then test to see how much change it made. You can then prorate the measurement to dose the whole tank.

Something's Fishy
You should never use pure reverse-osmosis (RO), pure deionized (DI), or pure distilled water to set up your fish tank. These waters will not contain enough essential minerals to maintain life properly. In fact, using waters so pure may actually soak minerals out of your fish! Only use these pure waters to dilute water that is too hard.

Carbonate Hardness

Remember I said that hard water is usually alkaline and soft water is usually acid, but that pH and hardness are different? It gets even more confusing! There is more than one kind of hardness, and alkalinity doesn't always refer to pH.

The other type of hardness is *carbonate hardness*, or KH. Carbonate hardness is also called *alkalinity,* or *acid neutralizing capacity*. It is a measurement of ions that act as buffers and stabilize the pH in your tank. The more of these ions that are present (usually carbonates and bicarbonates), the more stable the pH in your tank. Carbonates tend not only to keep the pH stable, they tend to keep it high.

Depending on the test kit you use, the value of carbonate hardness may be stated in the German scale of degrees (dKH or KH), the metric milliequivalents per liter (meq/l), or the English parts per million (ppm CaCO3). Here's a conversion chart.

Carbonate Hardness Equivalents

dKH	meq/l	ppm CaCO$_3$
1	.36	17.8
2	.71	35.7
3	1.07	53.5
4	1.42	71.4
5	1.78	89.2
6	2.14	107.1
7	2.50	125.0
8	2.85	142.8
9	3.21	160.7
10	3.57	178.5

A measurement of 2 to 8 dKH is generally considered to be favorable. Anyway, most of you will not need to worry about the carbonate hardness of your tank, because regular partial water changes will usually keep it at a safe, stable level. However, if your water is naturally low in buffers and has trouble maintaining a stable pH, you may need to add chemicals to adjust the KH. Heavy plant growth also can have an effect, as the plants remove carbonates from the water. So you may need to adjust for that, as well.

Something's Fishy
SNIFF! SNIFF! There are many interactions between general hardness, carbonate hardness, pH, and other chemical processes in your aquarium. Often, messing with one parameter results in changes to another. Be careful when using chemicals to alter water quality. I also recommend that you seek out some texts that explain the reactions in more detail.

Changing Carbonate Hardness

Here are some methods that can be used to change your aquarium's carbonate hardness. Some are the same methods I described earlier to change hardness or pH, so I won't repeat the detailed descriptions:

➤ Adding calcareous gravel or rocks will increase dKH.
➤ Adding sodium bicarbonate will increase dKH.
➤ Adding sea salt or African cichlid salts will increase dKH.
➤ Adding peat will decrease the dKH.

➤ Boiling will drive off carbonates and soften water, but geez, you would need an awfully big pot!

➤ Diluting with reverse osmosis (RO), deionized (DI), or distilled waters will decrease carbonate hardness.

Dissolved Oxygen

Obviously, your fish need to breathe oxygen to live. Since most fish take their oxygen directly from the water via gills, you must be sure that there is enough dissolved oxygen in the water to sustain them. There are test kits that measure the level of dissolved oxygen (DO), but you normally don't need to concern yourself with them. Instead, merely note the behavior of your fish to be sure that they aren't gasping, and regularly verify that your aeration and filtration is adequately circulating the water.

Many of you may be thinking that photosynthesis plays a big role in the oxygenation of your aquarium. You learned in biology class about how plants take in carbon dioxide that the animals have excreted, and through photosynthesis, release oxygen (O_2) back into the environment. That does happen, but unless your aquarium has no aeration or filtration to circulate the water, photosynthesis has little effect on the tank.

While it is true that plants can convert carbon dioxide to oxygen, they only do it when the light is strong enough for them to photosynthesize. At night, plants respire. That is, they use oxygen—just like animals. So in a heavily planted tank with no circulation, the dissolved oxygen levels can dip drastically at night. The result is that you can't count on the plants to keep the oxygen levels sufficient.

The real exchange of CO_2 for oxygen takes place at the surface of your water. It is the circulation of the water that aerates your tank. Circulation takes the carbon dioxide-laden water from down below and carries it to the surface, where the CO_2 can escape and new oxygen can be absorbed. Without circulation, your tank becomes stagnant and has trouble making this gas exchange.

Fish and Tips
Many people mistakenly think that the bubbles from the aerators add oxygen. It is easy to see why they think so. However, experiments have shown that the bubbles add practically no oxygen to the water. Rather, their job is to circulate the water past the top surface, where the carbon dioxide can be exchanged for oxygen.

Carbon Dioxide

Carbon dioxide is excreted by your fish. This compound probably has the most extensive effect in your aquarium, because it affects so many things. Obviously, if the carbon dioxide level is too high or the oxygen level too low, your fish will suffocate. Carbon dioxide is a source of nutrition for plants, as well. It also plays many other roles.

Dissolved CO_2 is the key ingredient in the *carbonate system* of your aquarium. The carbonate system is a complex interaction of CO_2 that affects both the general hardness and carbonate hardness of the water in your aquarium. Let me say that this relationship is so complicated and dynamic that even I have trouble understanding it. So I'll just list a few key points that you may find interesting:

➤ In acid water (pH below 6.0), dissolved carbon dioxide exists mainly as free CO_2.

➤ In neutral or slightly alkaline water (pH 7.0 to 8.0), dissolved carbon dioxide is mostly found in the form of bicarbonates.

➤ In highly alkaline water (pH over 10), dissolved CO_2 exists largely in the form of carbonates.

➤ Carbonates and bicarbonates influence the carbonate hardness of the water.

➤ Carbonates can combine with calcium to fall out of solution as calcium carbonate, lowering both general and carbonate hardness.

➤ Additionally, carbon dioxide can lower the pH and the resulting acids redissolve calcium carbonates, increasing both general and carbonate hardness.

The result is that carbon dioxide has a relationship with the pH, the carbonate hardness, and even the general hardness. CO_2 is busy stuff! There are test kits available, if you are curious about your tank's CO_2 level. But generally, this stuff gets so complex that I wouldn't mess with it unless you suspect a problem.

Hydrogen Sulfide

Once you start your filter systems, you should never turn them off, except to do maintenance. The helpful bacteria in your tank need oxygen to do their job. They are aerobic bacteria. If you turn off the filters, especially with undergravel filters, the water won't circulate enough to get the oxygen where it needs to be. So the good-guy bacteria die off. In their place, anaerobic bacteria develop. They break down waste, too, but they do it in a manner that produces toxic hydrogen sulfide gas as a by-product. Hydrogen sulfide is the gas that makes rotten eggs smell.

The Least You Need to Know

➤ A neutral pH level (7.0) is ideal for most fish. A range of 6.5 to 7.5 is usually safe.

➤ Ammonia is more toxic in alkaline water.

➤ Depending on local conditions, or if you have a desire to breed delicate species, you may not need to concern yourself with water hardness.

➤ It is circulation, not bubbles, that oxygenates your water.

Chapter 18

Be Partial to Water Changes

In This Chapter

➤ The importance of water changes

➤ How to use a gravel vacuum

➤ Conditioning tap water

➤ Dealing with evaporation

Your fish are swimming in their own toilet. It is your job to flush it for them once in a while! Regular partial water changes are extremely important to your fish. They are so important that they get a whole chapter of their very own, apart from Chapter 20 that discusses other routine chores.

Partial water changes have two main purposes:

1. They remove dissolved waste. (If you use a gravel vacuum to perform this chore, you also will remove solid waste.)

2. They replace depleted trace elements.

Partial water changes have other incidental benefits, too. Your fish will show better colors. They will grow faster. They will be more disease resistant. If you want your fish to breed, you will also have better success.

Time for a Change

Water quality degrades as waste builds up in your tank. It would degrade even quicker if you didn't have a filter, but filters can do only so much. How fast the water quality degrades will depend on many factors, including how many fish are in the tank, how big they are, how much food you give them, how many plants you keep, what type of filter system you have, and how often you clean it.

Fish and Tips
Evaporation doesn't count! Your partial water changes should be made in addition to replacing any water that evaporates.

For most tanks though, a good rule to follow is to change 25 percent of the aquarium water every two weeks. That is enough to keep the typical aquarium in healthy condition. However, be sure to consider the bioload in your tank. If you are keeping large fish, or if your tank is crowded, you may need to change more water, more often, to keep the water quality in good condition.

Your test kits can help you judge if you are changing enough water. If you find that the pH is falling, for example, you may not be changing enough water. Test kits are very helpful for finding problems. They are also very helpful for monitoring trends.

While your test kits can tell you when you are *not* changing enough water, they cannot tell you when you *are* changing enough. In other words, don't let good readings fool you into thinking that you can skip regular partial water changes. We can test only a very limited number of water quality parameters. There are many other things that we cannot test, and regular partial water changes provide assurance that we are dealing with those things, too.

The Price of Procrastination

What happens if you don't keep up with your regular partial water changes? It depends. If you miss one occasionally, it is probably no big deal. If you miss them often, it gets more dangerous. How dangerous depends on the bioload in your tank and the natural buffering capacity of your local tap water. Perhaps the best way to illustrate the danger is to tell you a couple of horror stories that I see happen way too frequently.

You probably recall from Chapter 17 on water chemistry that as waste builds up and biological filtration occurs, acids are produced. Over time, the pH in the aquarium falls. You also may recall that if the pH falls low enough, the helpful bacteria in the tank will stop breaking down ammonia, so ammonia levels climb. Fortunately, ammonia is much less toxic in acid water. So the fish (being hardy creatures) may survive the acid pH and high ammonia for some time without obvious detrimental effects.

However, if the owner of this low pH-high ammonia aquarium decides it is time to make that long overdue partial water change, what do you think will happen? Remember that tap water is usually alkaline. Let's say the owner, realizing that a water change is overdue, changes 50 percent, instead of the usual 25. That means 50 percent of the ammonia will remain after he refills the tank. Since the tap water is alkaline, it is going to raise the pH in the aquarium.

Remember that ammonia toxicity increases with pH. So, while this hobbyist removed 50 percent of the ammonia with the partial water change, by increasing the pH he made the remaining 50 percent much more toxic. He stands a very good chance of seeing his fish suddenly go belly up.

Another problem I see with not changing enough water occurs when customers buy new fish. Perhaps their tank has run a long time without a water change, and all seems well. Maybe no fish have died or just an occasional fish over time. Anyway, the customer decides that it is time to add a few more fish. He does so, and tosses them into his tank— a tank where the pH is probably quite low and the ammonia may be quite high.

It's a big shock to the new fish. Unlike the fish already in the tank, the new fish haven't had a chance to adjust to the low pH as it gradually fell over weeks or months. To the new fish, pH shock is a definite possibility. Many kick off within hours. The customer is madder than a betta looking in a mirror! He thinks he bought sick fish, because all his old fish are still okay. But in fact, he's to blame.

Worse, adding those new fish will pull the water quality of the tank even lower—perhaps low enough to kill the old fish, too. Anyway, it all comes down to this: If you don't change your water regularly, the fish will pay and you will pay.

Suck Muck? Yuck!

A gravel vacuum is your best friend when it comes to aquarium maintenance. This inexpensive muck sucking device makes it very easy to clean gravel and change water, all at the same time. Some would even say that a gravel vacuum is fun to use. (I wouldn't say that, but some would.)

The gravel vacuum is a simple device, consisting of a large-diameter tube attached to the end of a siphon hose. You use it to siphon water from your tank. While siphoning, you poke the large tube into the gravel. The flow of water through the large tube is fast enough to tumble the gravel and rinse out the detritus, but not fast enough to siphon out the gravel, too.

With a little practice, you probably will be able to clean the entire gravel bed with your gravel vacuum during each 25 percent water change. If you can't cover the entire bottom while siphoning the allotted amount of water, don't worry. Just take up where you left off at the next water change. Or, if you like, change a bit more than 25 percent.

Fish and Tips
Don't waste money buying a siphon hose. Buy a gravel vacuum, instead. A regular siphon hose only removes the old, waste-laden water, but the gravel vacuum also removes solid waste from the gravel bed. You will never have to move your fish or tear down the tank to clean the gravel.

Starting a Siphon

Gravel vacuums work by siphoning water. That is, simple gravity causes water to run down through a hose to a lower level. There are no motors or moving parts. The hose acts a bit like the spout on a watering can.

Fish and Tips
When vacuuming aquarium gravel, work around the plants, rocks, and other decorations. It is not necessary to get 100 percent coverage of the bottom. If you want, you can move large rocks and driftwood every few months to vacuum underneath.

There are several easy ways to start a gravel vacuum:

➤ I use the quickest way. I place the large tube in the tank. I use my mouth to give a quick suck on the hose end of the device, and then quickly flick that end of the hose down into a bucket before water comes out. If you do it right, you can start the siphon without ever getting a drop of fish water in your mouth. However, fish water doesn't taste any different from regular water, if you ask me.

➤ Other methods of starting a siphon involve filling the hose with water by scooping with the large end, or by submerging the whole thing in your aquarium. Once the hose is full of water, put your thumb over the small end to keep the water from flowing out. Then, being certain to keep the vacuum end of the device underwater in your aquarium, point the hose down toward a bucket and remove your thumb to let the water flow.

➤ I suppose I should mention that some brands of siphon hose have a squeeze-bulb you can use to start them easily, but I don't believe I've ever seen a squeeze-bulb gravel vacuum. Bits of debris, such as plant leaves, would quickly lodge in the valve inside the squeeze-bulb. Keeping such a device in working order would be a major pain.

Cleaning the Gravel

Something's Fishy
Be careful not to suck up any fish while gravel vacuuming. Usually the fish are smart enough to stay away, but not always. Plus, they sometimes rush over thinking that the particles of tumbling gravel are bits of food. If a fish does enter the vacuum tube, simply place your thumb over the output hose to stop the flow until the fish swims back out.

Once you have the siphon started and water is flowing into the bucket, merely poke the large tube deep into your gravel, then lift. When you lift, the water flow will rinse up through the gravel in the tube, washing away any detritus. The gravel, being heavier, will tumble back down into the tank. Continue the poke and lift method until you've removed the amount of water intended for replacement.

The smaller your particles of gravel, the higher they will rise inside the tube of the gravel vacuum. If they start getting too close to the hose—close enough to where they might siphon out—just place your thumb over the end of the hose to reduce or pause the flow. With a little practice, you can master the technique of lightly pinching or releasing the end of the hose to increase or decrease the flow.

*A gravel vacuum
makes life easy.*

Once you finish, discard the dirty water that you collected in the bucket. You may be surprised at how much crud you pull out of a tank! Another great thing about gravel vacuums is that they remove all that crud without stirring up things in the tank. You can use the same bucket (after you've rinsed it) to draw water to refill your tank. Make sure the new water is within 2°F (1°C) of the existing water, so that there is no temperature shock to the fish.

Never Lug a Bucket Again

Personally, I don't mind lugging buckets of water. I figure the exercise never hurts, and besides, I have the strength of 10 men. (Ten really wimpy men.) Carrying buckets is also the quickest way to get the job done. Still, if you would rather not carry buckets of water—maybe you are afraid you will slop water on the floor, or maybe the bucket is too heavy for you (40 to 50 pounds for a full five-gallon bucket)—there is another way.

Consider buying a *clean-and-fill* unit. Often, these are called pythons, because the Python No-Spill is the most popular brand. A clean-and-fill unit consists of a gravel vacuum with an extra long hose (from 25 to 100 feet), and a special valve unit that fits on any faucet. Water powers the device.

To drain water from your tank, you attach the valve to your faucet and turn on the water. The water pressure from the tap forms a suction inside the valve that draws water through the gravel vacuum hose. Since pressure from the tap is powering the gravel vacuum, instead of gravity, a clean-and-fill device makes it possible to siphon uphill! The device will still function, even if the sink is higher than the aquarium.

The Python No-Spill clean-and-fill system.

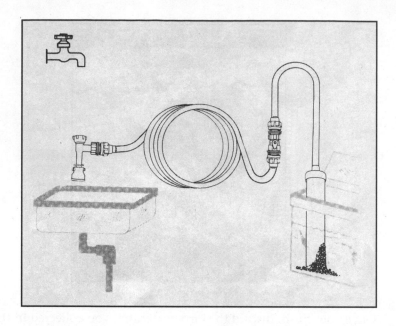

A disadvantage of the clean-and-fill unit is that several gallons of tap water will be wasted for each gallon drawn from your tank. If you live in an area where there is water rationing, this device may be a poor choice. Also, if you have low water pressure in your pipes, the device will function much more slowly.

Fish and Tips

If you buy a clean-and-fill gravel cleaning device, consider buying an optional brass faucet adapter. The plastic adapter that comes with the unit will wear out very quickly. The metal threads of your faucet will soon wear away and strip the threads on the soft plastic connector.

Clean-and-fill devices not only drain your tank, they also fill it. First, you make sure water of the correct temperature is flowing through the valve. Then you give the valve a twist, and it directs the water through the gravel vacuum hose to your aquarium. There is no need for buckets to drain or fill the aquarium. All water pumps directly to or from your sink.

Anyway, these devices do a nice job, and many people swear by them. However, they don't get me very excited because I'm too impatient. It takes time to drag out the hose and attach the valve to the faucet to get the thing running. Afterwards, you need time to drain water from the hose and time to roll up the hose and put it away. Also, clean-and-fills siphon slower than a gravity operated gravel vacuum. So, although they work great, they take longer to do the job.

Be a Quick-Change Artist

Many hobbyists put off changing their water because they think it is too much work. It shouldn't be. If you know the right way to make a partial water change, you can do it quickly. Of course, like anything else, practice makes perfect. So you may not be able to achieve maximum speed on your first try.

Oddly enough, it is water changes that got me into this hobby. Back in 1963, when I was in third grade, my best friend Kurt had a 10-gallon aquarium. One of his weekly Saturday chores was to completely strip down and clean his aquarium. Let me rephrase that: His chore was to strip down his aquarium completely and clean it.

Anyway, in order for him to be able to come out to play sooner, I would help him clean his aquarium. We would net out the fish, empty the tank completely with a scooper, put the gravel in a bucket and rinse it until it was clean. Then we'd set the tank back up. It took at least half an hour, and usually more. It was my first exposure to aquariums and it is what got me interested in fish. Of course, we now know that it is a *very bad* idea to strip down an aquarium. In those days, we didn't have ammonia test kits and stuff. The hobby was a lot less mature.

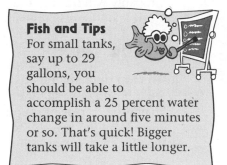

Fish and Tips
For small tanks, say up to 29 gallons, you should be able to accomplish a 25 percent water change in around five minutes or so. That's quick! Bigger tanks will take a little longer.

Change for a 20

In case you grew up with a friend like Kurt, let me describe how it only takes five minutes to make a partial water change in a typical 20-gallon aquarium. I picked this size tank because it is typical, and because a 25 percent water change fits nicely in a single five-gallon bucket.

Gather Your Supplies

You need the following items:

✔ Gravel vacuum

✔ Five-gallon fish bucket

✔ Dechlorinating water conditioner

✔ Optional: A teaspoon to measure out the water conditioner, if it is not a drops-per-gallon brand

✔ Thermometer

✔ Optional: Saucer (the thing you put under your coffee cup)

Remove the Old Water

Set the bucket on the floor beneath your tank. Use your gravel vacuum to siphon water into the bucket, removing as much debris from the gravel bed as possible. When the bucket is full, carry it somewhere to be dumped—perhaps to a sink or toilet.

Collect Fresh Water

Rinse the bucket and refill with water of the correct temperature. I have been doing this for so long that I can tell the temperature of the water merely by touching it, but you probably will need to use a thermometer. The new water should be within a couple of degrees of the existing tank water.

Refill the Tank

To refill the tank, I merely lift the bucket of new water and pour it slowly into the tank. I pour it onto a large rock or piece of driftwood to keep it from disturbing the gravel. You may need to place a saucer on the bottom of the tank and pour onto that, to keep from disturbing the gravel. Also, if the bucket is too heavy for you, you will either need a smaller container to dip water with, or perhaps you can use a small powerhead or water pump.

With a little practice, you can accomplish all the above in around five minutes or so. It's quick. It's easy. More important, you never have to move the fish or tear down your tank to clean it.

Conditioning Tap Water

One thing to remember as I talk about this topic is that we don't all live in the same place. (Thank goodness! My apartment is too crowded already.) Your local tap water may be very different from mine. It may be harder, softer, more acidic, or more alkaline. You may have lots of iron or none at all. You may buy your water from the city, or you may have your own well. Run-off from fertilizers on farms may give you high levels of nitrates, pesticides, and other nasty stuff in your water.

Conditions vary everywhere. Sometimes conditions are such that you will have trouble keeping certain species. Cardinal tetras are my favorite fish, but I couldn't keep them alive when I lived in southeastern Michigan. The water was so hard that they weren't happy at all. In Maine, where the water is soft, cardinals may feel like they are in heaven.

Anyway, it is important to keep in mind that there is a lot of variation in local tap water, so it is impossible for me to put in this book a simple recipe for conditioning tap water that will work for everyone. Besides running your own water tests, you may want to ask your dealer what he knows about the local water quality. You may even want to call the local water department to see what they can tell you. In addition to the advice I am about to present, you also may need to review Chapter 17 on water chemistry for information on how to deal with your tap water.

The one thing that almost all of you will need is a good dechlorinator. Unless you draw your water from your own well, you probably have chlorinated tap water. The simplest dechlorinators are solutions of sodium thiosulfate. You add it to the tank, and it instantly neutralizes the chlorine. These days, most water conditioners include ingredients that do other tasks, too.

Chlorine and Chloramines

Chlorine is added to the water in municipal water supplies to kill microscopic organisms. It does its job well, but if you have ever been swimming in a chlorinated swimming pool, you know that chlorine also is rough on mucous membranes, such as the eyes and nose. It does the same thing to fish, but they have an added disadvantage. Their gills are exposed to the chlorinated water, and chlorine damages gills.

So we need to remove chlorine from the tap water. The easiest way to do so is to purchase and use one of the many commercial tap water conditioners. Your dealer will carry many brands, all inexpensive. To remove chlorine, you dose the product in drops per gallon or teaspoons per 10 gallons, depending on the brand. It's quick and easy.

In a few areas around the country, the local water supplies have high levels of dissolved organic matter. Chlorine can combine with these to form carcinogenic substances (trihalomethanes). To prevent that, some municipal water supplies add both chlorine and ammonia to the water. These two combine into new compounds called chloramines. Chloramines also disinfect water, but don't combine with organic matter.

Your dechlorinating water conditioner will neutralize both chlorine and chloramines. However, when chloramines are neutralized, the ammonia is released! We know how dangerous ammonia is to fish. If you have a well-established tank, it probably will not be a big deal. Your biological filtration will quickly neutralize the ammonia. In a new, uncycled tank, though, the ammonia could be especially deadly.

Ask your dealer if your local tap water contains chloramines. If it does, you may want to consider adding some zeolite ammo-chips to remove the ammonia, or dechlorinating your water with a product that will neutralize the ammonia, too. Of those, Amquel is the only one that I recommend.

> **Something's Fishy**
> Not all products are created equal. Many products that claim to neutralize chloramine really only handle the chlorine part of the compound. They release the ammonia and do nothing to neutralize it.

Liquid Bandage

Many water conditioners include compounds that provide a *liquid bandage* for your fish. Fish that have been in a fight, or have been recently netted, may have had some of their protective slime rubbed off. This slime is the fish's first defense against disease organisms. Some water conditioners will provide a temporary slime on your fish that will protect it until it regenerates its own body slime.

Heavy Metals

Some water conditioners also remove heavy metals such as zinc, lead, and copper from your tap water. Is that feature important? Probably not.

Aquarium Salt

Many dealers and hobbyists add a bit of aquarium salt to their tanks. Salt can help prevent disease, and some fish just plain do better if there is a bit of salt in the water.

Fish School
Aquarium salt is pure, uniodized sodium chloride. Don't confuse it with sea salt, which has many other ingredients.

There are many formulas to decide how much salt to add, but most will use one teaspoon of salt per gallon of aquarium water. That's 10 teaspoons in a 10-gallon tank, and 55 teaspoons in a 55-gallon tank. (You may want to remember that a cup is 48 teaspoons, to save yourself some measuring!)

Livebearers and African cichlids like higher salt levels. You may want to keep them with two teaspoons per gallon. For cichlids, there are special African cichlid salts that are even better, because they have other ingredients that increase the hardness and pH of the water, just like the fish would find in the wild.

For livebearers, using sea salt instead of aquarium salt does the same thing. Be sure to consider the effect of raising hardness and pH on other denizens of your tank, though.

Fish and Tips
Adding one teaspoon of salt per gallon is often recommended. You may want to add more with certain species, mollies for example. There is not a single species of freshwater fish that will be bothered by two teaspoons of salt per gallon.

Is it necessary to add salt to your tank? Probably not. You may want to see how things work without adding the salt. If the tank does just fine, and it very well may, then don't bother adding salt. If you find livebearers getting clamped fins and shimmies, then you probably need to get some salt in there quickly. Some say salt is rough on plants, but I've kept plants in two teaspoons of salt per gallon and not noticed any problems.

Vitamins and Trace Elements

There are products available whose purpose is to add vitamins and trace elements to the water to make your tank healthier. Frankly, I think those products are a waste of money. Dumping that stuff in the water does little, if anything, for your fish, because fish really don't drink much water. What it does is feed the algae in your tank. If you want more algae, then maybe adding vitamins and trace elements is a good idea. If you think your plants aren't getting enough nutrients, then buy proper fertilizers.

The only place where vitamins may have some benefit is if you soak fish food in them before feeding it to the fish. Even then, the vitamins quickly leach out of the food and into the water.

Gas Saturation

When water is under pressure in your tap, it can absorb more gases. Have you ever drawn a glass of water and noticed that it was cloudy for a minute? Jillions of tiny bubbles eventually float to the top and the water clears. When you fill your aquarium the first time, you may find a layer of bubbles coating the glass after a few minutes. These bubbles are the result of gas saturation.

When water is drawn from the tap, pressure is released. Dissolved gases condense out of solution. If you agitate the water really well as it is drawn, the excess gases will condense out of solution quite quickly. That's why the glass of water clears so fast. When filling an aquarium, though, you may not have agitated the water much. If you filled it with a hose and left the end of the hose underwater as it filled, the water wasn't agitated much. So the gases condense out more slowly, and eventually coat the surfaces in the tank.

Here's the problem. If you place fish into water that is still supersaturated with gases, it is very rough on the fish. These gases may be absorbed into the bloodstream and condense out of solution there. Bubbles build up in the bloodstream and may kill the fish! It's the same kind of situation as when deep sea divers surface too fast and get the bends. When they were deep underwater, they were also under high pressure. More gases were absorbed into their blood. If the diver surfaces too fast, the gases condense into bubbles in their bloodstream. It's very painful and can be fatal.

To prevent gas saturation problems, all you have to do is aerate your water. The first time you fill your tank, it's not a big deal, because the filters will aerate the water—driving out excess gases and ensuring that ample supplies of needed ones are present. However, it is always best to play it safe. Agitate your tap water as you draw it. Are you drawing into a bucket? Set the stream so that a real turmoil results. This will drive off excess gases. If you use a hose to fill a tank, put your finger over the end to make the spray jet out hard, and then spray it against your hand, instead of spraying directly into the tank. This will agitate the water quite well.

Something's Fishy
When refilling a tank via a clean-and-fill system, or any other hose, always make sure to keep the water jet above water. You want to agitate the new water as it enters the tank—both to aerate it and to prevent gas saturation problems.

Vanishing Into Thin Air

Evaporation occurs when water molecules escape into the air. It is a continuous process. Molecules are always in motion, bumping into each other. Sometimes they obtain enough energy to bounce free.

A certain amount of evaporation will occur in every aquarium. How fast it happens will depend on several factors, including the humidity of the air in the room, water temperature, whether the tank is covered or open, and how much circulation occurs at the water surface.

Evaporation is only a problem if you let it go too far. Your tank could eventually go dry! Of course, your fish probably would be dead from neglect long before that happened.

Probably the most important thing you need to know about evaporation is that, when it occurs, only the water leaves. The dissolved waste and minerals remain behind. You will remember that a 25 percent partial water change should be made every two weeks. What if your tank evaporates by 25 percent every two weeks? Is it okay just to top it off with new water? No!

It is not okay because the new water adds more minerals without removing any of the old ones or removing any dissolved waste. If you repeatedly top off a tank without removing any water, the waste and minerals will continue to build up. So when you make your regular partial water changes, make them *in addition* to topping off evaporation.

The Least You Need to Know

➤ Regular partial water changes are essential for the health of your fish.

➤ Consider local conditions before deciding how to condition your tap water.

➤ Almost everyone needs a dechlorinator.

➤ One teaspoon of aquarium salt per gallon may keep your fish healthier.

➤ Do regular partial water changes in addition to topping off for evaporation.

Chapter 19

Foods and Feeding

In This Chapter

➤ Find a balanced diet for your fish

➤ Learn how much to offer at mealtimes

➤ Discover delicious dinners and tasty snacks

➤ Vacation foods and electronic fish feeders

You will enjoy watching your fish for many reasons. Ornamental fish are relaxing and beautiful to watch. But I bet you will soon discover that you enjoy your aquarium the very most when you are feeding the fish. That's because it's a time when you can truly interact with the inhabitants of your tank.

Your fish will soon learn that their meals come from *you*, so they will be flocking to the front of the tank whenever you come near. Yes, your fish will learn to recognize you. If several people regularly feed the fish, they may come rushing forward to greet any human that is nearby. However, if you are their only caterer, you may be the only one who gets that excited response when you approach the tank. It'll make you feel loved.

Still, it is not just the attention of the fish you will enjoy at feeding time. You also will get a major kick out of watching the little critters eat. I love watching tetras flash to the surface to grab a flake of food, before shooting back down below as if avoiding some imaginary predator. And it is comical to hear the little tiger barbs, with their poor manners, noisily snapping up food at the surface. They could beat a three-foot carp in a lip-smacking contest. Watching the corydoras cats jamming their faces into the gravel in search of some delectable morsel, or two platies playing tug-of-war with a blackworm, is also quite entertaining.

You can interact with your fish at mealtime.

Fishin' for Nutrition

Nutrition is a cornerstone of successful fishkeeping. You can do everything else right, but if you don't offer the proper types of food and in sufficient quantities, your fish will not survive for long. Most of the species available will take flake foods quite readily, but others may require live foods to survive.

It is your responsibility to find out what diet is required by the species you want to buy, *before* you purchase them. A good dealer will alert you, if you choose a species with specialized dietary requirements, but you can't necessarily count on that happening.

I am not going to bore you with pages and pages about proteins, carbohydrates, and fats. Just like humans, fish need these various nutrients in the proper quantities and proportions to stay healthy. Just as with human foods, most fish food packages will list percentages of crude protein, crude fat, crude fiber, and moisture. Crude protein is not the same as digestible protein, so these figures are really pretty useless, anyway.

Many prepared fish foods on your dealer's shelves will provide a well-balanced diet for most species, all by themselves. However, there is no one food that will be perfect for all fish. Some species prefer more animal matter in their diet. Others prefer more plant-based foods. So if you offer only one food, although all will eat it, the food may be balanced for only a few of the species in your tank.

The Spice of Life

When customers ask me what is the best food for their fish, I always give them the same answer. "Variety." Offering a variety of foods is absolutely the best way to go. It lets individual species pick the foods that best suit them. Besides, it gives everyone a chance to have a more stimulating diet.

My fish at home get a good selection of foods. I tend to keep about a half dozen or so varieties of dried foods around, including flakes, pellets, and freeze-dried foods. Also, there are always at least a couple of varieties of frozen foods in the freezer for them, and I occasionally bring home some live foods, too. Every meal is something different for the fish at my house. Ideally, it will be the same at yours.

The Designated Feeder

I recommend that *only one person* be in charge of feeding the fish. Or perhaps, one person could be responsible for giving them breakfast every day, and someone else could be responsible for giving them their dinner every day. The reason for this is that you are not just feeding the fish—you are feeding the tank. The more food that goes into the tank, the more polluted it will become. If no one has the designated responsibility for feeding the fish, things go wrong. Either the fish don't get fed enough, or perhaps not at all, or everyone who walks by throws in some food and feedings get doubled, tripled, or worse. Besides, if you designate yourself to be the sole person responsible for feeding, guess who the fish will be happiest to see come near their tank?

> **Fish and Tips**
> Ask if your dealer carries feeding rings. These are floating plastic rings, about two inches in diameter. When you sprinkle food inside them, they keep the food from drifting all over the tank and getting lost. You can monitor the quantity of food better, and there is less chance for waste. You can also try making one from a loop of air line tubing.

Don't Stuff Them to the Gills

How often should you feed your fish? Usually twice a day is best. I like to feed my fish when I get up in the morning, and again in the evening when I come home from work. Work out a feeding schedule that fits your own schedule, and don't worry too much if you have to alter it occasionally. The fish won't complain . . . much. If they miss the occasional meal, don't try to make it up at the next feeding. A fish's stomach can only hold so much food at once. Extra food is going to go uneaten and pollute the tank.

Learning how much food to feed is sometimes difficult. People often say to offer just a pinch of food, but how much is a pinch? Your pinch may be quite a bit different from mine. It may consist of just a couple of flakes or a couple of hundred flakes. Let's talk about some guidelines to help you learn how much food to offer.

One old rule of feeding says that a fish's stomach is about the same size as its eye. If you base the amount of food you offer on the size of the fish's eye, you won't overdo it. Most fish will be able to eat more than this, but they don't need to and it can be excessive.

Another rule is to offer two typical one-quarter-inch flakes to each fish at each feeding. Obviously, the rule is based on the fish being the typical size that you would find in a community tank. This rule won't work if you're feeding fish that are a foot long.

Rule 1: A fish's stomach is about the size of its eye.

Rule 2: Two flakes per fish, twice daily, is right for most fish in a community tank.

Fish and Tips
When you buy your first batch of fish, ask your dealer to show you how much to feed. Don't settle for him giving a rule or saying "a pinch." Ask him to spread some food in his hand to show you how much is right.

My favorite rule of feeding is based on a time limit. Offer only what the fish can eat in three minutes. If there is any food *at all* at the end of that time, you have overfed them. Even better, offer what they will eat in 30 seconds to a minute. There are a couple of exceptions that are allowable here. For example, some pelleted foods for bottom dwellers may take more than three minutes to soften up enough to be eaten. That is fine, as long as the pellets are consumed in a reasonable time—say half an hour. Also, this rule applies to packaged foods. If you are feeding live foods, some of them may be able to escape or hide for longer than three minutes. Again, that is okay, if they are eaten within a reasonable time.

Rule 3: There should be no food left after three minutes, or you have overfed.

Using these three rules, or a combination of them, should give you a very good estimate of how much to feed. Until you learn just how much that typically would be, be sure to err on the side of underfeeding. That is, offer a small quantity of food, and if the fish snap it up quickly, offer a little more. You can do that until you get a better idea of how much is safe to offer all at once. It is very important not to overfeed, *especially* in a new tank.

Your dealer probably will carry a veritable smorgasbord for your fish. Dry prepared foods are most popular because they are more convenient, but your fish will do better if you also offer choices from the selection of live and frozen foods that your dealer stocks.

Flaky Choices

Most hobbyists start out with at least one variety of flake food. Flake foods contain an amalgamation of ingredients that were mixed into a porridge, and then cooked and dried into thin sheets. These sheets are broken into bits and packaged. No doubt you are familiar with this type of food. Most people start out with a brand of flake *staple food*. Staple foods provide balanced nutrition for most kinds of fish.

Don't limit your fish to staple food. There are many other flake foods that can help you provide interest and better-balanced nutrition. There are flakes containing a high concentration of *Spirulina* algae to provide extra vegetable content to herbivorous fish, and there are

Fish and Tips
You can kill your fish by overfeeding, but it is not overeating that will kill them. Rather, it is the resulting pollution from uneaten food that causes problems. Remember that you are not just feeding the fish, you are feeding the tank.

Fish and Tips
When feeding flakes, pellets, or other dry foods to your fish, do not sprinkle the food directly from the can into your tank. Instead, sprinkle first into the palm of your hand, and then sprinkle that into the tank. That way, if you accidentally sprinkle too much, you can take corrective action rather than having excess food pollute your tank.

Fish and Tips

An inexpensive way to offer a variety of foods, without buying several types at once, is to purchase one of the multi-packs available. There are cans of flakes that have four compartments and a special dispenser top that you turn to choose the flavor you want to offer at that meal. Recently, some frozen foods have become available in multi-flavor cube-packs, too.

Fish and Tips

Freeze-dried tubifex worms come in cubes. A fun way to offer them is to reach into the tank and press the cube against the glass, squeezing the air bubbles out. The cube will stick to the glass and you will then have a front row seat to watch all the fish nibbling at it. Fish aren't very smart, so the first time you do this, they probably won't all come rushing up to eat. But after that, watch out!

flakes containing brine shrimp or other ingredients to treat the more carnivorous varieties of fish. Also popular are flakes containing natural color-enhancing ingredients. These foods can help bring out the colors in your fish, making them look their best. Growth flakes are available for small fish, and some varieties of food come in a large size flake, for feeding the bigger fish you keep.

Cold Facts About Freeze-Dried Foods

Freeze-dried foods are other commercial dry foods that you will find convenient. Unlike most dry foods, which are a mix of ingredients that include items fish would never eat in the wild, freeze-dried foods actually consist of preserved aquatic animals that fish would find in their natural environment.

Mosquito larvae, daphnia (a tiny crustacean), tubifex worms, various types of shrimp, and bloodworms (sometimes labeled as red mosquito larvae or red grubs) are commonly available. Once these freeze-dried foods soak up some water, they are very much like offering freshly killed foods. However, your fish probably will gobble them down before they get a chance to soak.

The Low-Down on Bottom Feeders

Some foods come in pellet or tablet form. Tablet foods are for bottom dwellers. They sink straight to the bottom, where scavengers can get at them. There are algae tablets for plecostomus and other algae-eating fish, there are staple tablets for all fish, and there is even a brand of tablet made largely from compressed freeze-dried foods.

Pelleted foods may be either sinking or floating varieties. Sometimes, both types are mixed in the same package. Choose according to which fish you want to feed. Floating pellets can help top dwellers get their fair share, while sinking pellets do the same for scavengers. Pellets are also a convenient way to feed large fish.

You will find pelleted foods available for any type of fish that eats dry prepared foods, but there is an especially good selection available for goldfish and koi, and for cichlids.

Fresh From the Freezer

Hopefully, your dealer will stock a large supply of frozen fish foods, too. These days, many dealers have glass-fronted display freezers, similar to those found in grocery stores.

If the store is small, though, it may keep only a tiny selection of foods in the back-room freezer, and require that you request them. Most stores carry frozen brine shrimp, which is the old standby. When I was a kid, it was the only frozen fish food you could find.

These days, there are many other frozen fish foods available, including glassworms (*Chaoborus* larvae), daphnia, tubifex worms, bloodworms, and mosquito larvae—and those are just the freshwater fish foods.

Frozen foods come either in flat-packs or cube-packs. Flat-packs are self-sealing plastic bags with a block of food frozen inside. To feed these foods, you can either break off a chunk and toss it in the tank, or squeeze some out the edge of the plastic wrapper and swirl it in the tank until a sufficient quantity melts free. Of course, if you toss in a chunk, you can still swirl it around to get bits to melt free to keep the more voracious feeders from hogging it.

> **Something's Fishy**
> SNIFF! SNIFF!
> If you feed blood-worms (*Chironomus* insect larvae) to your fish—and I highly recommend that you do—be careful not to touch your face and be sure to wash your hands afterward. Fish love this natural food, but some humans are allergic to bloodworms.

Cube-packs offer even more convenience. They come in clear plastic flip-top trays that resemble miniature ice cube trays. They cost slightly more than flat-packs, but they are much simpler to use. You simply push on the back to pop out the number of cubes you need, much like popping cold medicine out of one of those foil packs, and then toss the cubes into the tank. The fish do the rest.

Now Appearing Live

Frozen foods are the next best thing to live foods, which are the best of all. Live foods not only offer the most natural, freshest ingredients, they also put on a show. If you want to see your fish have a good time, offer live foods. Your fish will go nuts for them.

Unfortunately, you will have a harder time finding live foods. It seems most stores don't carry them. Perhaps they just don't have room for them. After all, it takes vat or refrigerator space to store these foods. Or maybe the store's distributor doesn't stock them, and the store doesn't need the large quantities that would enable them to buy direct. If it is a small store, they may not have enough clientele to justify the overhead to carry live foods. Live foods require maintenance to keep them alive, just like any other animal. Or maybe the store doesn't have the expertise to keep them properly.

Following are some live foods you can find in pet stores. Some are foods that almost all fish will eat. Others will be useful only if you have large carnivorous fish. So take note.

Blackworms

(*Limnodrilus spp.*) These are an excellent food for most small to medium fish. Blackworms are one to two inches long, and as big around as a pencil lead. In the wild, they live in mud with their heads poking out, where they filter out bacteria and debris as food. The ones in the stores are farm raised. Fish absolutely love them and they are especially good for bottom dwellers, such as cory cats and spiny eels. Live blackworms typically sell by the portion, which may contain several hundred worms.

Store live blackworms in the refrigerator, and change their water every day or two. There is a device called a *worm keeper* that consists of a tray with a very fine mesh bottom that nests on top of a larger outer tray. You fill the lower tray with water, and when it is time to change water, lift the top tray. The water will sift out, leaving just the worms, and then you change the water in the bottom tray. Easy. If you buy small portions, you can just store them in the container in which they are sold.

There are several ways to feed live blackworms to your fish. One way is simply to toss some in the tank and watch the fish munch away. Another is to use a worm feeder. The worm feeder is an inverted, perforated plastic cone that floats at the surface. You put the worms inside, and as they poke their heads and tails out of the holes, the fish yank them out and eat them. The advantage of this method is that fewer worms will find their way into the gravel, where they can hide from the fish.

If you want to feed live blackworms to bottom feeders, you could just toss them in the tank, but the other fish may gobble most before they get to the bottom, and some will dig too deeply to get caught. I like to take a one-inch deep plastic condiment cup, put one-half inch of gravel in it, and then sink it in the gravel at the bottom of the tank. Then, when you put worms in the cup, they will dig into the half inch of gravel, where the other fish can't get to them. The bottom feeders, however, will still be able to root them out easily, and the cup keeps the worms from digging too deep for the bottom feeders to reach. It's not unusual to have a spiny eel take up residence in the cup, waiting for the next meal.

Live foods add action, suspense, and drama to your tank.

Tubifex Worms

These are very similar to blackworms, but much less rarely seen. They have a more reddish color, and when disturbed, clump into mats so tight that you will have a bit of trouble tearing them apart.

Rumor has it that tubificid worms, including blackworms and tubifex, can be carriers of fish disease. These worms live in areas where the water has high organic matter, and can be found in the sludge where sewage enters streams. I do not give much credence to these rumors. I have personally offered regular feedings of blackworms, and occasionally tubifex, to my fish with no negative results. In fact, the opposite has happened. Many of my specimens have turned out to be the largest, most colorful that I've seen of the species anywhere. I also know many professional aquarists and fish farmers who use these foods regularly and swear by them.

Brine Shrimp

(*Artemia spp.*) Though these animals are not something your fish are likely to encounter in the wild, your fish will love them. Brine shrimp live in salt marshes, areas where the water is too salty for most fish. In fact, brine shrimp live in areas where the water may dry up, and they have evolved a unique way to survive this. Their dehydrated eggs can last for many years, hatching when the rains return. I have read accounts of thousand-year-old sediments that still held viable eggs. You also can buy brine shrimp eggs to hatch as food for your baby fish. Don't feed the eggs directly, though. The shells are not digestible.

Adult brine shrimp are rust colored and about one-quarter inch long. They are highly nutritious. If you are lucky enough to have a dealer who carries live, adult brine shrimp, they probably came from a brine shrimp farm.

Brine shrimp are sold by the portion, which may include several hundred of them. If you don't crowd them too much, you can keep brine shrimp at room temperature until fed to the fish. You also can refrigerate them. If you refrigerate brine shrimp, they will stop moving, but regain activity when rewarmed.

Glassworms

(*Chaoborus* larvae) These half-inch animals are an interesting food for your fish. They are the totally transparent larvae of a mosquito-like insect, but the adults don't suck blood. They are a seasonal item, sometimes offered for sale in the winter time. In some areas, millions of them can be fished out from beneath the ice covering northern lakes and ponds. They are great for your fish, but they are predatory. So don't mix them with tiny baby fish. Glassworms should be refrigerated until use.

Fish Tales

In Africa, where adult glassworms hatch out into huge swarms of millions of insects, the adults are often caught in quantity and pressed into edible sticky cakes called *kungu*.

Bloodworms

(*Chironomus* larvae) The name of these animals comes from their bright red color and elongated bodies, but they are not worms. They are the larvae of a harmless insect—a midge. Only recently have I seen live bloodworms offered for sale. Previously, frozen and freeze-dried bloodworms were always available, but never live ones. I'm not sure why, as they can be collected year-round.

Something's Fishy
If you use fish as food for other fish, be aware that there is a risk of introducing disease, unless you first quarantine the feeder fish. Additionally, feeder fish are food, and you should treat them as such. That is, only one meal's worth should be introduced to your tank at a time to avoid overcrowding. Keep the rest in a separate holding tank until needed.

Fish and Tips
Even if a fish doesn't eat algae, part of its natural diet is probably fish or other creatures that do. So before offering goldfish or other feeder fish as food to large carnivorous fish, consider serving algae flakes or other assorted foods to the feeder fish. That way, the stomachs of the feeders will be packed with added nutrition from foods that the large carnivores might not normally eat directly.

Ghost Shrimp

A variety of grass shrimp, these shrimp grow to one and a half inches in length. They are completely transparent, except for their internal organs. The heart can be seen beating inside, and you can always tell what the ghost shrimp last ate, because his stomach will be that color. I like to feed assorted colored flakes to the shrimp at the store, and then laugh at all the pink and green and brown spots I later see swimming around. Some people keep them because they are interesting. Others feed them to larger fish.

Guppies

Since the large-tailed fancy version of this fish has been developed, you don't see common guppies sold much as pets anymore. These days, they mostly get sold as small, inexpensive feeder fish. Millions of them are raised and sold as food for other, larger fish.

Rosy Red Minnows

Rosy reds are a bit bigger than guppies and smaller than goldfish. So if you need a mid-sized feeder fish, this is it. They are also popular as pond fish because of their delicate pink color and peaceful nature.

Goldfish

Yep, this is the cheapest version of the fish that commonly sell as pets or are won in carnivals. Believe it or not, probably 99.5 percent of all goldfish raised are sold as feeders. Most dealers will charge about a dollar for a single, hand-picked, pet-quality specimen. When sold as feeder fish, however, they will be much cheaper, usually several for a dollar, but there is no hand picking. First caught is first sold.

Don't expect to pay feeder price and get to choose the fish you want. Also, feeder fish typically sell without a guarantee.

Earthworms

Various sizes and species of earthworms are sold as bait and fish food. They will be relished as a treat by fish large enough to eat them. Earthworms also can be diced into bits for smaller fish.

Crayfish

Many larger fish will readily eat these. Crayfish are interesting in their own right, but are somewhat predatory and best not kept with smaller fish. Also, they like to dig and can disturb decorations. An adult oscar will have no trouble eating them whole, claws and all.

Mealworms

Commonly sold as food for reptiles and amphibians, mealworms are readily eaten by many fish as well. They drown very quickly, so if you are offering them to a fish that requires its food to be live, don't feed too many at once—or they'll mostly drown before they get eaten.

Crickets

Most pet shops and bait shops carry crickets. Assorted sizes are available, and they are relished by most fish that are large enough to eat them.

Cockroaches

Hey, I hope you don't have access to any of these guys, but if you do, feel free to offer some to your fish. (Don't offer ones that were sprayed with insecticide, of course.)

Fry Foods

No, not fried foods—*fry* foods. Fry are baby fish. If you are raising baby fish, you need foods small enough for them to eat. Finely powered foods and frozen baby brine shrimp are popular choices. You also can hatch your own brine shrimp eggs, and feed the live baby shrimp to your fry.

What to Do on Your Summer Vacation

One great thing about fish is that you can leave them unattended and without food for short periods of time. If you are going to be gone for a weekend, don't worry about them. They will be fine.

Something's Fishy
Never feed more than one meal's worth of food at a time. You cannot throw extra food in your tank when you go on vacation. The food that is not immediately eaten will pollute the tank and kill the fish.

Fish and Tips
When using electronic fish feeders, make sure the flakes or pellets are small enough to fit through the dispenser opening, or it will clog. Also, do not pack food too tightly into the storage hopper, or the food can become compacted and will not be released.

If you're going to be gone longer than two or three days, however, you must make arrangements for the care of your fish. If you have someone you trust—someone who knows how much to feed fish and how to watch for problems and take corrective action—you may want to use that person as a fish sitter while you are away. Come to think of it, it wouldn't hurt to have someone look in on the fish, even if you're just gone for the weekend.

Electronic fish feeders are another option. These are devices that clip on the top of the aquarium. You set the timer, and they dispense meals of dry foods to your fish. Some models automatically feed twice a day. Other models are fully programmable. Electronic fish feeders may seem a bit expensive, but remember that you don't only have to use them when you are on vacation. You can use them to feed dry foods to your fish 365 days per year, and supplement with live and frozen foods at will.

For quick trips, consider using one of the "weekend foods" or "vacation foods" that are sold in the stores, *but only as a last resort*. These are plaster blocks that have food particles distributed within. When you toss one in the tank, the plaster slowly dissolves, exposing food for the fish to nibble at. Typically, you use one per 10 gallons.

However, these products are not good choices, for several reasons. First, there are much more chemicals in them than there is food. These chemicals are dissolving into your water, changing the water chemistry, and the rate of dissolution varies greatly, depending on the pH and hardness of the water in your tank. The little bit of food that is available is only going to be available to fish that are willing to feed off the bottom. Finally, there is a real question about how long the food stays fresh, once it hits the tank and gets wet. I often wonder if vacation food isn't rotten after the first day.

The Least You Need to Know

➤ For best results, offer your fish a variety of foods.

➤ Three minutes after feeding, if any food remains in the tank, you have overfed.

➤ Your fish will put on an extra show if you offer live and frozen foods.

➤ Going away for a weekend? Don't worry about the fish. Going on vacation? Consider buying an electronic fish feeder, or hire a fish sitter.

KNOCK!
KNOCK!

DO NOT ENTER
MAINTENANCE

Chapter 20

Get Into a Routine

When it comes to routine maintenance of your aquarium, the two most important things are to feed the fish and do regular partial water changes. Since I have already devoted complete chapters to those two tasks, this chapter will cover the rest of the things you need to do to maintain your aquarium in tip-top condition.

I will try to set priorities for you by dividing chores into daily, weekly, biweekly, monthly, and quarterly duties. Of course, these are just guidelines. Most chores should be done more often if necessary, or less often if not necessary. You should take care of problems as you see them occur. If I tell you to replace your fluorescent bulb once a year and it burns out in six months, I hope you would not wait another six months to replace it! Use your common sense.

Daily Duties

There are some things you need to do for your fish every day. They'll thank you for it.

➤ **Turn on the aquarium light.** If you purchase a timer, this will be taken care of automatically. The timer also will turn off the lights at the time you program.

➤ **Check the environment.** Make sure filters are running, bubblers are bubbling, and heaters are heating. Is the temperature of the tank where it belongs?

Fish and Tips
If you have to spend more than five or 10 minutes per week to maintain your aquarium, you are probably doing something wrong or fiddling with it too much.

➤ **Check the fish.** Take a quick look to see if there are any symptoms of disease. When you first turn on the lights, many fish will still be sleepy. A fish that is lethargic first thing in the morning may not be having any problems. If you see such a fish, give it some time to wake up and then check again.

➤ **Look for dead fish.** When fish die, they usually die at night. The best time to check for dead ones is first thing in the morning. Look carefully. Dead fish don't always float to the top. Sometimes they wedge in plants, behind or practically under rocks, or just drift about on the bottom. The current may even wash a dead body around.

Something's Fishy
Dead fish should be removed immediately so that they don't spread disease or pollute the tank.

Look carefully at the surface of the tank, search the bottom, and then scan mid-water for corpses drifting about or lodged in the plants. You may even want to count to see if anyone is missing. Sometimes the dead body is dried up on your carpet! Fish can jump. I don't want you to get the idea that you should expect to find dead fish often. You shouldn't. In fact, it should be such a rare thing that you will soon quit looking for dead fish altogether. I never look for them in my tank anymore, but hey, you should do as I say, not as I do.

➤ **Feed the fish twice.** If you forget this item, you will spend more time dealing with the previous item. I recommend feeding once in the morning and once in the evening. Don't forget to close the lid afterwards, so the fish don't jump out.

➤ **Check for leaks.** I put this one here for those of you who are paranoid. Leaks are rare. If you ever get one, it will be obvious.

➤ **Run water tests.** I recommend testing the water in your new tank daily for the first couple of weeks. After that, you can move it to the weekly checklist. Once you are satisfied that parameters are remaining stable between water changes, you can move the water tests to the biweekly checklist.

Weekly Work List

There really aren't any required weekly duties. However, there are some things it wouldn't hurt to check—either to play it safe or just to keep the tank in peak condition.

➤ **Check filters.** Most filters will not need to be cleaned weekly, but it depends on the type of filter you have and the bioload in the tank. So it is a good idea to give the filter a quick look each week. If it seems too dirty, or if it is clogged enough to restrict flow, clean it.

➤ **Clean strainers.** Bits of plant leaves and other debris can clog the intake strainers of many filters. Be sure your strainers are clear.

➤ **Replant loosened plants.** Here and there, plants may float loose. Perhaps a fish dug them up, or you knocked them loose while netting a fish or scrubbing algae. Simply replant where you want them to go.

➤ **Run water tests.** After your tank has finished cycling, test the water weekly for a few weeks. Once you are satisfied that parameters are staying stable between water changes, you can move the water tests to the biweekly checklist.

> **Fish and Tips**
> Water changes are extremely important, but time passes quickly and it may be hard to remember when you did the last one. I suggest you set up a system where you plan your water changes on your days off that are closest to the first and the 15th of the month. It's easier to remember.

➤ **Clean the glass.** Take a quick look to see if algae is building up on the inside glass. If so, take a scrubber pad and wipe it away. Also, look at the outside glass to see if there are water spots that need to be wiped away. If so, a paper towel will work. I usually dip one corner in the aquarium to moisten it, and then clean the outside glass. Plain water is all you need, but it is okay to use window cleaning solutions on the *outside* glass. If you do, be very careful not to get any in the tank. Ammonia kills fish!

Biweekly Business

Every other week, you have more chores, which only take a few minutes, so don't worry!

➤ **Run water tests.** Once your tank is established and stable, it should be fine to test the water biweekly. Run the tests right before you make your water change to establish a baseline.

➤ **Use the gravel vacuum to make a 25 percent water change.** Religious partial water changes are the very best thing for your fish. Don't skip them. Using a gravel vacuum to do the chore will remove solid waste from the gravel bed, too. Don't forget to dechlorinate the new water and make sure it is the same temperature as the water already in the tank.

➤ **Clean filters.** A biweekly cleaning schedule works best for most filters. If your filter gets too dirty faster than that, you may be overfeeding or have an overcrowded tank. Or you may have an undersized filter for the application. Some filters will go longer than two weeks before they need cleaning. Canister filters can usually go a month or more.

Monthly Missions

Once a month your system needs a routine checkup. Make sure you look for the following:

➤ **Check airstones.** If you have any air-operated filters or devices, check the airstones at least monthly. Besides the reduction in output, clogged filters wear out the diaphragms in air pumps much quicker. Several things clog airstones. The most likely causes are algae and the build-up of calcium carbonate, but cigarette smoke is another cause. If there are smokers in the house, your air pump is blowing that air through your aquarium 24 hours a day.

➤ **Prune your plants.** If you plant them, they will grow. Some plants grow so fast that you may need to prune them weekly. With most, though, monthly pruning will be plenty. It is entirely your call. You may want to prune regularly to give your tank a tight, manicured look. It's like painting a picture. You prune plants back to fit the space exactly the way you want.

Fish and Tips
Most clogged airstones must be replaced. However, there are glass bead varieties that can be cleaned by soaking them in a bleach solution. Be sure to rinse thoroughly.

➤ **Clean your filter's impeller.** Motorized filters use impellers to drive the water. Slime can build up on the impeller, and hairs or bits of plant leaves can tangle around the axle, reducing efficiency.

Customers often bring in filters that quit working, thinking they had a breakdown. Nine times out of 10, I clean the crud out of the impeller and the filter starts right up. The ironic thing is that the filters usually quit while turned off for cleaning. People clean the media, but don't clean the impeller. So while the filter is off, slime on the moving parts makes them stick together and the filter can't restart. You may even want to clean the impeller every time you clean the filter.

➤ **Clean the glass canopy or full-hood.** As water splashes, the underside of your aquarium's top will get wet. Since your light unit is on top, algae will thrive there. It is a good idea to wipe the underside of the glass with an algae scrubber pad. It may be necessary to use a razor blade to scrape some loose. Keeping the underside of the glass clean will allow more light to pass to let you see your fish and to keep the plants healthy.

Quarterly Chores

Hey, it's only four times a year! When you consider how much pleasure your fish give you in three months, it's a fair exchange.

➤ **Replace light bulbs.** Replace incandescent bulbs when they burn out. They usually have a short life span of around three months. Fluorescent bulbs and metal halide bulbs will last much longer. They may even burn for years, but they will lose much of their intensity within the first six months. Ideally, those bulbs should be re-placed at least yearly, whether they are still burning or not.

➤ **Check the air filter on the air pump.** Many brands of pumps have small felt air filters on the underside. Check to see if the filter is clogging with dust. If so, you may be able to wash and reuse it, but it is probably better to buy a replacement.

➤ **Clean filter tubes.** (This one is optional.) A thin layer of algae growing inside the lift-tubes of your undergravel filter or the intake tube of your power filter can be left there. It is harmless. If the growth is thicker, or if bits of plant stems and leaves have accumulated, you definitely need to clean the tubes to prevent restricted flow. Always check the intake stems of power filters when you clean or change the media. There are brushes that you can buy to clean inside filter tubes.

> **Fish and Tips**
> Fluorescent bulbs should be replaced yearly. The best way is to do it on a rotating basis. For example, if you have four bulbs over your tank, replace one every three months. It is easier on your budget, and it maintains a more stable level of light.

> **Fish and Tips**
> You can use vinegar to help remove mineral deposits from your equipment. The acetic acid in the vinegar will dissolve some of the minerals. Don't get vinegar in your aquarium, though!

➤ **Give a thorough exterior cleaning.** Most people dust off their aquarium when they dust the other furniture in the room, and that is sufficient most times. However, splashing water can cause dirt and dust to stick, and evaporating water may leave mineral deposits. So you may want to give your tank's top a more thorough clean-ing. You can use an old toothbrush to get into nooks and crannies. The toothbrush also works well for scrubbing deposits that have accumulated around the tank frame.

Routine Maintenance Checklist

Daily Duties

- ✔ Turn on the aquarium light.
- ✔ Check the environment.
- ✔ Check the fish.
- ✔ Look for dead fish.
- ✔ Feed the fish twice.
- ✔ Check for leaks.
- ✔ Run water tests daily until the tank cycles.

Weekly Work List

- ✔ Check filters.
- ✔ Clean strainers.
- ✔ Replant loosened plants.
- ✔ Run water tests weekly until the tank is stable.
- ✔ Clean the glass inside and out.

Biweekly Business

- ✔ Run water tests *before* each water change.
- ✔ Make a 25 percent water change with the gravel vacuum.
- ✔ Clean filters.

Monthly Missions

- ✔ Check airstones.
- ✔ Prune your plants.
- ✔ Clean your filter's impeller.
- ✔ Clean the glass canopy or full-hood.
- ✔ Replace the activated carbon in your filter.

Quarterly Chores

- ✔ Replace light bulbs that are due.
- ✔ Check the air filter on the air pump.
- ✔ Clean filter tubes (optional).
- ✔ Give a thorough exterior cleaning.

Filter Maintenance

Your filter cleans the tank. You clean the filter. Filters don't remove waste from the system, they only separate it. It is your job to remove the waste. Usually, you do so by replacing filter media, but sometimes you rinse and reuse the media. Following are some common types of filters and typical methods for cleaning them.

Undergravel Filters

Undergravel filters are the easiest and least expensive to maintain. The gravel functions as the filter media, and you clean it with a gravel vacuum when you make your partial water changes. Since you have to siphon water to make your partial water change anyway, using a gravel vacuum is no extra work at all. There is no filter media to change. However, don't forget to replace your airstones as needed.

Use the gravel vacuum to clean around plants and rocks, removing as much debris from the gravel as possible. If you draw out the allotted amount of water before you clean the whole bottom, don't worry about it. Just take up where you left off at the next water change.

Fish and Tips
Some brands of undergravel filters come with replaceable cartridges of activated carbon that fit on top of the lift-tubes. If your filter has these, it is really better to run without them—they restrict water flow—and use a small outside power filter to provide chemical filtration, instead.

Outside Power Filters

There are many brands of outside power filters. Most use special filter media that won't fit other filters. However, there are two basic categories of outside power filters. One group uses replaceable, slide-in filter cartridges. Others have reusable sponge filter media.

All outside power filters have magnetic impellers. Don't forget to remove the impeller occasionally and take a small filter brush to clean inside the impeller-well. If slime builds up in there, the filter can stop. Be careful not to get sand in the well. You also may need to use a filter brush to clean inside intake tubes and strainers.

Cartridge filter media. There are many brands of these in many sizes. The basic design is a flat polyester filter cartridge, about the size of a slice of bread. Some brands of cartridges have activated carbon inside. Other brands have a coating of activated carbon applied directly onto the polyester fibers. The best of these coated cartridges are refillable, and allow you to add extra activated carbon, or zeolite, or perhaps even water softening resins inside.

Cartridge filters are designed to be easy to clean. You slide out the dirty filter cartridge and pop in a new,

Fish and Tips
Most outside power filters use proprietary filter cartridges. When you go shopping for filter media, be sure you know what brand and model filter you have, or you may buy the wrong media.

clean one. It doesn't get much easier than that. Still, there is a disadvantage to that ease of use. When you throw away your filter media, you also throw away the helpful bacteria that colonized the media. So you temporarily reduce the biological filtration capacity of your tank.

There are a couple of things you can do to help, though. Larger outside power filters may have two cartridges, instead of one. If so, it is better to change them on a rotating basis, instead of replacing both cartridges at once. That way, you retain the helpful bacteria on one cartridge, while the other recolonizes. If you use the refillable cartridges, you may want to replace the outer polyester media one time, and the activated carbon the next.

Fish and Tips
The lid of most outside power filters can be used as a tray to carry the used filter media to the sink or trash without dripping.

Rotating the two types of media retains helpful bacteria. It's a bit of a pain to do, though, and definitely not as easy as tossing out one cartridge and popping in another.

Sponge filter media. One very popular brand uses a separate filter sponge and a bag of activated carbon. When the sponge gets dirty, you rinse it and reuse it . . . forever. Rinse the sponge with water that is close to aquarium temperature, so that you don't kill the helpful bacteria living on the sponge. You want to rinse out the debris, not sterilize the sponge.

The bags of activated carbon should be replaced at least monthly. Activated carbon can only adsorb so much waste and then it is no good. Worse, if you don't change your activated carbon often enough, and your pH drops, substances may be released back into the water.

You can buy pre-sized bags of activated carbon to fit your model of filter, or you can buy net filter bags and bulk activated carbon and bag your own. If you buy bulk carbon, get the good stuff. The price will usually reflect the quality. Good activated carbon will have a dull luster and relatively rough finish. Avoid the cheap, glassy black filter carbons. They are nothing more than crushed coal and are close to worthless. There are some excellent brands of activated carbon that come in pellet form. I highly recommend those.

Fish Tales

Activated carbon works in an unusual way. The manufacturing process forms millions of microscopic capillaries in each grain of activated carbon, greatly increasing the surface area of each particle. The exposed carbon on this surface bonds with organic matter, collecting it. The process is called adsorption.

Canister Filters

There are several brands of these. Follow the manufacturer's instructions for advice on disassembly and for recommendations on getting the best performance. When cleaning filter media, you should also take time to clean the impeller assembly and make sure that intake and output valves are not clogged with plant stems and leaves.

Filter compartments. My favorite canister filters have separate plastic compartments inside. One uses ceramic noodle filter media, another holds activated carbon, and a third holds a filter sponge. At cleaning time, the ceramic noodles and sponge get rinsed and reused forever. The activated carbon should be replaced at each filter change.

Filter sleeves. Some brands have a central core around which you wrap a replaceable filter sleeve. One type of sleeve is soft polyester, another resembles an oil filter for a car. The type that looks like an oil filter will filter finer particles. Both types should be replaced when dirty.

Fish School
Adsorption is the process whereby substances are taken up by binding to the surface of a solid. *Absorption* is the process whereby substances are taken up by soaking into internal recesses, as with a sponge.

Open design. At least one brand of canister filter has a single large compartment for filter media. There are several types that can be used, all having unpronounceable German names. Follow the manufacturer's recommendations for best results.

Fluidized Bed Filters

Since these filters aren't intended to collect dirt, there is little maintenance involved. The most common chore will be to make sure the intake on the powerhead is clean. Bits of plants and other debris can clog it up and reduce flow. Over time, some sand will disappear from the filter and will need to be replaced.

Trickle Filters

Trickle filters are also easy to maintain. There will usually be a pre-filter sponge of some type in the overflow box. Rinse it out as needed. There often is a polyester filter pad at the entry to the sump, which should be cleaned or replaced, too. Of course, if you have bags of activated carbon in the sump, they should be replaced at least monthly.

If your filter uses bio-balls, give them a quick rinse if they start to accumulate crud. This will rarely be necessary, though. If your filter uses the DLS filter media, you probably should unroll the media and rinse it out every month or so.

Other Filters

What about maintenance on other types of filters?

➤ **Box or corner filters.** When the polyester media gets dirty, replace it. Replace the activated carbon at least monthly. If you have a model that uses an airstone, be sure to replace it when the flow slows, or you'll damage your air pump.

➤ **Internal cartridge filters.** Replace the cartridge at least monthly.

➤ **Sponge filters.** Rinse them with water that is close to aquarium temperature. The sponge should last a long, long time. If you see the sponge starting to collapse, or notice reduced output, it is a sign that the sponge needs cleaning. Depending on the bioload in your tank, you may need to do it weekly, biweekly, or monthly.

➤ **Powerheads.** Though not really filters, they power many filters. Keep an eye to be sure that the intake strainers don't become clogged. Sometimes you will need to disassemble the powerhead to remove crud that gets inside.

The Least You Need to Know

➤ Feed the fish twice daily, and check for sick, lethargic, or dead fish.

➤ Change 25 percent of the water every other week.

➤ Replace fluorescent bulbs at least yearly.

➤ Clean filters as needed, but replace the activated carbon monthly.

Chapter 21

Hey, Let's Breed!

In This Chapter

➤ Conditioning brood stock

➤ Livebearers and egglayers

➤ Baby foods for new arrivals

➤ Weird ways that fish breed

Most people keep fish just for the fun of watching them. They are pretty to look at and relaxing to watch. However, if you really want to see interesting behavior, you should try to breed some of your fish. Fish propagate themselves in so many unusual ways that you will surely be amazed.

Most hobbyists breed fish just for the fun of it, and to stock their tanks cheaply. For others, it's a competition. Most aquarium societies have Breeders Award Programs, which give points for species spawned. Points accumulate based on the number of species and the difficulty. Many fish have never bred in captivity. You could be the first!

Still others spawn fish to support their hobby. Angelfish and fancy guppies usually find a ready market at your local pet store. Some dealers give cash, some give credit. Either way, you may never have to buy fish food again.

Livebearers Are Easy

Breeding livebearers is easy. It is so easy that stopping them from breeding is more of a feat. Females are probably already pregnant when you buy them, so you may not even have to buy a male right away.

Fish School
Livebearers are fish that give birth to live young.

The best way to keep livebearers is to keep at least two females for each male. The males want to mate all day long. By keeping extra females, males can divide their attentions—giving the poor females some rest.

Baby livebearers will naturally develop into a ratio of two females for every male. Usually. Mother Nature has a certain amount of control over this, though. For example, did you know that raising platies in crowded conditions will result in the young fish growing to a smaller size, and that most of them will turn out to be male? It is Mother Nature's natural method of population control. Smaller fish are less able to compete with existing full-sized adults for mates, and the low ratio of females will decrease the number of new fry being born. Cool, huh? High levels of dissolved organic matter and pheromones excreted by the fish are what control this process.

Five Easy Pisces

Most hobbyists have their first experience at breeding fish with one of these five popular types of livebearers:

➤ Guppies

➤ Mollies

➤ Platies

➤ Swordtails

➤ Variatus

There are a few other livebearers, such as half-beaks and the four-eyed fish, that are rarely seen.

Almost Permanently Pregnant

Livebearers can be prolific little devils, delivering from six to over a hundred young in a single batch. Plus, they can do this every four to six weeks. The number of fry delivered will range widely. Several factors come into play. The age of the fish is the most important: Young females deliver fewer fry than larger, older females. Conditioning also is a factor: Good water quality and proper nutrition are necessary for a fish to reproduce.

Fish Tales

Female livebearers are able to store sperm. One mating can result in several batches of fry.

Most fry of livebearers are around one quarter inch long when born. This is quite a bit larger than many other baby fish, but still plenty small enough to be eaten by most fish in your tank. Even the parents show little restraint in eating their own fry. It's probably a good thing that baby fish make good snacks for the other fish, because your tank would otherwise soon be overrun with them.

Maternity Ward

If you want some babies to survive, all you have to do is make sure there are hiding places for them. If your tank is well planted, a few fry will survive here and there. It is quite common to have several generations of livebearers living happily in an aquarium.

However, if you want to save the maximum number of babies, plan to set up a separate tank. Livebearers do not exhibit parental care. The only way to guarantee that the fry won't be eaten is to get them away from the adults. Usually, this means isolating the adult female before she gives birth. There are several ways to do this. The best would be to set up a separate maternity ward tank and toss mama in there with lots of plants. After she delivers, you can return her to the main tank.

Fish Tales

Mollies tend to have larger young than the other livebearers, with babies being between a quarter- and a half-inch long. That is still small enough for most fish to eat. Mollies, though, have less of a tendency to eat their own.

Another option is to use a net breeder or breeding trap. The net breeder is a net basket that hangs inside your tank. Place the female inside and, when she delivers, move the babies to a separate aquarium. If you get the style with a coarse mesh, the babies will swim right out. Let the female rest a day or so before returning her to the main tank.

Breeding traps are usually clear plastic boxes with an upper and lower compartment. The pregnant female goes into the top compartment. A V-shaped bottom with a slot at the bottom of the V separates the two compartments. When fry are born, they fall through the slot into the lower compartment, where mama can't get at them to eat them. There are also versions that have a fully slotted bottom.

I'm So Happy, I Could Lay an Egg

Most species of fish don't have live young. Instead, they lay eggs, and they do it in a multitude of interesting ways. I don't have room in this book to get into every detail of breeding fish, but I can run through some common ways that egglayers spawn. Here are the main groups I will discuss, many of which exhibit some parental care for the young:

➤ Egg scatterers

➤ Egg positioners

➤ Bubblenest builders

➤ Mouthbrooders

Some species of egglayers will spawn in a community tank, and if they exhibit parental care, some young may survive. Usually, though, the eggs and fry end up as snacks for the other fish. So to try your hand at breeding most egglayers, you will want to set up a special tank.

Egg Scatterers

Many fish, perhaps most species, simply scatter their eggs and let nature take its course. The males may chase the females through the plants, with adhesive-coated eggs scattering and sticking wherever they touch. Some species lay non-adhesive eggs that fall to the bottom and lodge between bits of gravel and debris for protection.

The serpae tetra is a popular variety that scatters adhesive eggs. It is quite common to see males driving the females into the weeds on sunny mornings, their bodies bumping together as the female sheds eggs and the male sheds sperm. The eggs stick to the plants or any other object they touch. Usually, other fish in the tank are not far behind, picking at the plants to snack on any eggs that catch their eyes. So, while this fish may spawn regularly in your tank, it is very rare to have eggs survive long enough to hatch into fry. Even if they do, the fry are readily eaten, too.

If you want to spawn serpae tetras and raise the young, you need to do so in a separate tank. The best way is to separate the males and females for a couple of weeks, feeding them heavily to condition them, and then toss them together in a five- or 10-gallon aquarium with lots of fine-leafed plants. Remove the adults after spawning occurs. The fry of this species are much smaller than livebearer fry, perhaps only one 16th of an inch long.

Zebra danios are popular fish that are very easy to spawn. Their eggs are non-adhesive and fall to the bottom. The easiest way to spawn zebras is to set up a 10-gallon aquarium and hang a coarse-mesh net breeder inside. Use dechlorinated tap water of the right temperature, and fill the tank to the point where only one inch of the net is under water. Put the breeding stock into the net breeder. The next morning, check the bottom of the tank and it probably will be covered with eggs. Remove the parents.

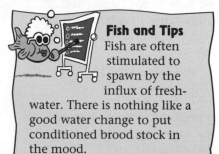

Fish and Tips
Fish are often stimulated to spawn by the influx of fresh-water. There is nothing like a good water change to put conditioned brood stock in the mood.

Instead of using a net breeder, another method is to cover the bottom of your tank with marbles two or three layers deep. The eggs fall through, but the parents don't follow. Remove the breeder fish after the eggs are laid.

Fish Tales

The splashing tetra (*Copella arnoldi*) is quite unusual in its mating behavior. The male and female jump out of the water and cling to the underside of an overhead plant leaf (or the aquarium cover), where they deposit eggs and sperm. Afterwards, the male occasionally splashes the eggs to keep them moist until they hatch a few days later.

Egg Positioners

The fish in this group will prepare a spot to lay their adhesive eggs. They may even exhibit parental care of the eggs and young. The cichlids fall into this category. Typical behavior is to pick a rock, a cave, or sometimes a piece of driftwood or a wide smooth plant leaf, and clean it meticulously. The fish breed in pairs, carefully arranging their eggs in the spot they cleaned. Most egg positioners will guard the eggs. Some guard the fry, too. It's a lot of fun watching the parents protect their brood. My mom still comments on how much she enjoyed watching my convict cichlids herding their fry when I was young.

Fish Tales

Discus fish spawn in typical cichlid fashion. They also care for their young, but they go an extra step. The body slime of the parents is the first food for the fry.

The kribensis is an easy cichlid to spawn. They usually will spawn right in your community tank. The pair will pick a secluded spot near a rock or piece of driftwood. The spot will be carefully cleaned for placement of the eggs. Both male and female will share duties guarding the eggs, and will continue parental care after the fry hatch. I have a pair of kribensis herding a school of babies in my 20-gallon tank at this very moment.

Most fry (which are similar in size to livebearer fry) won't survive in the community tank. They won't find enough food, they will be eaten, and the filters will grab them. Still, a few sometimes survive. It is best to move them to another tank, as they will suffer the brunt of the adults' aggression during the next spawning attempt.

A pair of kribensis guarding their fry in my tank.

Bubblenest Builders

This group of fish includes the betta (Siamese fighting fish) and other gouramies. These fish are easy to breed, but rarely spawn in the community tank. There is too much commotion and too much current in there. You really need to set up a special aquarium if you want to spawn bubblenest builders.

The betta displays typical behavior for fish in this group. The male will pick a secluded spot among the plants in shallow water and build a thick, frothy mound at the surface. The mound is about three inches across and a half-inch high, and is composed of mucous bubbles that he blows. Bits of plant leaves may be mixed in to help anchor the structure. Many hobbyists cut a plastic foam cup in half and float it at the surface to give the male a good spot to build his nest.

Once the male builds his nest, he will try to attract any nearby females with a showy display. He spreads his fins and flares his gills and does a little dance for her. If she is in condition and likes his style, she'll follow him back to the nest.

More unusual behavior is to come. Unlike most egglaying fish, which merely take turns laying or fertilizing eggs, or swim side by side releasing both eggs and sperm simultaneously, the betta is much more romantic. The male and female curve their bodies and embrace each other in a position that most resembles two hands in a handshake. In the midst of this hug a few eggs will be released and fertilized. The male will break away, retrieve the eggs in his mouth before they fall to the bottom, and spit them up into his bubblenest. He'll then return to his lady and give her some more hugs. After each embrace, more eggs are spit into the nest until the process is complete and several hundred eggs may be in the nest.

But this is where the romance ends. Having gotten his one night stand, the male chases the female off. He may even kill her if she doesn't leave. He now takes up position under his nest and keeps it in good repair. If any eggs fall loose, he retrieves them in his mouth and spits them back into the nest.

After a day or so, the eggs hatch, and extremely tiny fry hang in the nest with only their tales protruding. When I say tiny, I mean *tiny*. You must look very closely to see these transparent baby fish. It will be a few more days before they absorb their yolk sacs and become free-swimming. The male will guard the young for a time, but it is usually best to remove him and raise the fry separately to prevent him from eating them.

Mouthbrooders

Some species do more than just guard their eggs and young—they also provide shelter for them. Yes, mouthbrooders really do carry the eggs and babies in their mouths. Most mouthbrooding species are cichlids and spawn in typical cichlid fashion. The difference is that one parent immediately picks up the eggs and carries them in its mouth. While the eggs are incubating, the adult fish will not accept any food.

Fish Tales

Some species of *Synodontis* catfish are known to lay their eggs in the nests of African cichlids. The mouthbrooding cichlids hatch the young catfish in their mouths along with their own young.

Eventually, the eggs hatch and the fry will venture out of the adult's mouth. Often the fry will continue to receive parental care. It is an odd sight to see several dozen scared baby fish go flying back into an adult fish's mouth. It looks as if they are being gobbled up.

Fish Tales

Fry of mouthbrooders tend to be larger than those of other fish. Many African cichlids release fry that are nearly an inch long. The arowana releases fry that are three inches long.

Get Into Condition

If you want to have luck breeding fish, the most important thing is to be sure that you have good breeding stock. Pick fish that show proper shape and good color. Make sure they are in top condition with good weight, especially the females. If they aren't egg-laden, you aren't going to have much luck getting them to breed.

253

Conditioning your fish before breeding attempts is very important. Feed them well and with a variety of foods to get them in condition. In nature, fish breed during the season when insects or similar foods are highly abundant. Aquarium fish breed best when they get good nutrition, and especially if you offer lots of live and frozen foods.

Fish and Tips

Most fish spawn in the morning. So you usually can't expect results from your match-making until the next day.

With many egglaying species, you may want to separate the males and females to condition them. It is a good way to get spawnings of maximum size. Feed the fish well and keep the water quality good, and the fish will quickly come into top condition. Since absence makes the heart grow fonder, when you put the males and females back together, they are likely to be a lot more excited about it. A good water change will arouse them even more. If things don't go the way you plan, separate the sexes and try again.

Shooting Blanks

There are many reasons fish won't breed for you. Here are a few to note:

➤ *Immaturity*. This may be the most common reason. A fish that is too young or too small *can't* spawn.

➤ *Lack of proper conditioning*. Even an adult fish needs to be in shape to produce lots of young.

➤ *Lack of proper conditions*. Are you sure you are providing the right environment for this fish?

➤ *Sterility*. Yep, it happens with fish, too.

➤ *Incompatibility*. Hey, even fish are sometimes so ugly that only their mothers can love them.

➤ *Poor water quality*. It's hard to get interested in sex if you are living in a toilet.

Fish and Tips

Before you attempt to breed fish, be sure they are old enough to do so. Most fish sold in stores are still juveniles. They are too young and too small to breed. Let them grow before attempting to use them as brood stock.

➤ *No privacy*. Some fish need seclusion to spawn.

➤ *Not enough room*. For species that like to go flying through the plants or big open spaces, the only option you may have given them is to bang their heads on the glass headboards of your tank.

➤ *Not enough partners*. Many fish spawn in schools. They won't be turned on if you only have two.

➤ *Lack of the proper trigger*. Many species that have never spawned in captivity fall into this category. Something is lacking to put them in the mood, and no one has been able to figure out what it is.

The trigger may be something quite simple, but difficult or impossible to provide in the aquarium. For example, what if the fish only spawns in water that is 20 feet deep or deeper? What if it is the cycle of the moon that sets them to spawning? Or seasonal changes in length of daylight?

How does the rain factor into the equation? There are species of frogs that only spawn when it is raining. Maybe there are fish like that, too. For that matter, rain has many effects on fish in the wild. A big rain equals a big water change. That's why many fish spawn when you change water. Rain washes nutrients into the water that may be a trigger. Perhaps going from clear to muddy water is the trigger. Or, perhaps the time of year when insects are most abundant as food is the trigger.

Fish Tales

Many species of killifish (*Aphyosemion spp.* and others) live in swampy areas and mud puddles. Since these habitats often dry out, the eggs of the fish can survived dried in the mud until the next rainy season. In fact, the eggs of many species *must* go through a dry resting stage, or they won't hatch.

How about temperature changes? We normally recommend against rapid temperature changes in the aquarium, but rains bring temperature change. It is well documented that rapid temperature changes are a big factor in getting corydoras cats to spawn. Throwing a bucket of cold water on two dogs may break things up, but it gets corydoras cats excited.

The Difference Between Boys and Girls

If you want to breed fish, you must know how to sex them. Following are some guidelines.

Sexing Livebearers

Sexing adult livebearers is very easy. Just look at the anal fin. As it matures, the anal fin of an adult male collapses to form a tube. This tube is called the *gonopodium*. It transfers sperm to the female's vent during mating. Females retain the fan shaped anal fin, and develop larger size and heavier bodies. Juveniles all look alike, with both sexes outwardly resembling females.

Another feature that appears in females is the *gravid spot*. This is a triangular patch just above the fish's vent. It is where the eggs develop within the fish. On some species, the gravid spot turns dark as the babies develop and get nearer to delivery. On some lighter colored species, the spot won't darken but you will be able to see the eyes of the baby fish inside. When the eyes are well developed, the fish is very close to giving birth.

Sexual differences of male and female livebearers.

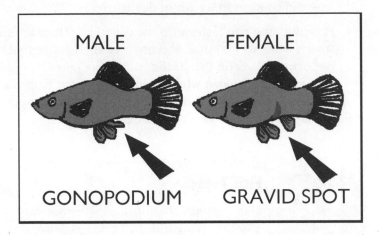

Anyway, looking at the anal fin is the best way to sex a livebearer, because it works for all of them. If a fish has a gonopodium, it is a male. Period. Immature males may outwardly appear female, but a partially formed gonopodium will tip you off that you are merely looking at an immature fish.

To make it even easier, the males of most livebearer species have obvious secondary sexual characteristics. Male guppies have lots of color and fancier fins than females. Male swordtails have the infamous swords, and some species of male mollies have huge sail-like dorsal fins. Male platies and variatus are usually more colorful than their female counterparts.

Sexing Egglayers

This is a much broader group of fishes than the livebearers, so I can't give you a rule that applies to them all. Many egglayers, in fact, are unsexable. They know how to tell each other apart, but we sure don't!

For the species that are sexable, though, males will usually have more color than females. In territorial species, males probably will get larger than females. In non-territorial species, it is usually the other way around, with the females being larger and heavier bodied. (Big girls can carry more eggs.) In some species, the males get longer, more pointed tips on the dorsal and anal fins. Some male plecostomus get big bushy whiskers or brushes on their pectoral fins. Male goldfish get white bumps on their gill plates during breeding season. The list goes on and on.

Fish Tales

If you really want to learn how to sex your egglaying species, you must do further research. I highly recommend the *Baensch Aquarium Atlas*. It comes as a three-volume set, and each volume is around 1,000 pages, so there is lots of information there on all aspects of fishkeeping, but especially about species of fish. Almost every species has a page all to itself.

Sex Changes Without a Scalpel

Here's a weird topic. Did you know that many fish change sex? For example, sometimes female swordtails will develop a gonopodium and a sword on their tail.

Transsexual fish are much more common in saltwater, though. For example, *Anthias* start their lives as fully functional females. A single male will have a whole harem of them. If he should die or disappear, the largest female in the group will change into a fully functional male.

It works the other way with the popular clownfish. They start out as males. When two pair off, the largest turns into a female. If she should die, the male will turn into a female and find himself a new male mate. Welcome to the wild and wacky world of fish!

Bringing Up Baby

Raising baby fish is usually a simple task. There are a few simple needs to meet, and if you meet them, the fry will live and grow.

First off, feed the proper foods. Fry are small. Some are tiny. Livebearers and cichlid fry will take baby brine shrimp, but the fry of most egglayers are too small for that. Heck, some are smaller than the baby brine shrimp!

There are some finely powdered foods available for fry, usually available as egglayer and livebearer formulas. The egglayer formula is the most fine and even the smallest fry can take it. Livebearer formula is slightly coarser, but still so fine that livebearers will quickly outgrow it.

Feed your babies often. If you keep their little stomachs full, fry grow really fast. Feed at least three times a day, but you could feed 10 times, if you want. Of course, feed less per feeding, if you do. The best way is to offer just enough to let them nibble and keep their stomachs full.

Something's Fishy
Avoid the liquid fry foods. They provide more pollution than nutrition.

Change the water often. Change some every day, if you can. Lack of water changes stunts the growth of fry. In a 10-gallon fry tank, I recommend changing at least a gallon per day. Use an air line to siphon debris from the tank bottom in the process.

Keep the fry warm. A temperature around 80°F (27°C) is good. At first, you need to keep the fry a bit crowded, so that they can find food. You would have to dump lots of food into a large tank to allow a few fry to find enough. This would pollute the tank. But as the fry grow, move them to larger tanks and give them plenty of space.

The Least You Need to Know

➤ With livebearers, keep two females for each male.

➤ Unless you set up a separate breeding tank, chances are the adults in your tank will eat all the fry.

➤ Choose good brood stock.

➤ Condition your breeders.

➤ Water changes are aphrodisiacs.

Chapter 22

Plants and the Wet Green Thumb

Picture a bare, undecorated aquarium with an assortment of pretty fish swimming in it. The fish have attractive though somewhat washed out colors, and they swim around lazily. There is not much for them to do. The tank has a dull appearance. There is not much color and there is little action. The water may even be slightly cloudy.

Now, picture the same aquarium lushly decorated with plants. A multitude of greens, browns, and reds grab your eye. Ribbon-shaped leaves flutter in the crystal clear current, and strings of tiny oxygen bubbles waft to the surface as plants photosynthesize in the dappled light. Serpae tetras chase each other through the foliage, rubbing against it to deposit their eggs and displaying their most brilliant ruby breeding colors. A black molly nibbles algae from the edge of a plant leaf. A wood shrimp clings to a stem, reaching into the water flow to grab tasty morsels as they filter by.

There is as much difference between those two tanks as between an old black-and-white photo and a Technicolor movie on the big screen. The difference is plants!

Plants make a tank come alive. They give a natural and more pleasing appearance to your aquarium. They make your fish more comfortable, too—providing places to hide, areas to explore, and sites for breeding. You want your fish to feel like they are at home, not in a bare jail cell.

Gloria the plant lady shows off one of her prize creations.

Be Enlightened About Lighting

Intense, full-spectrum light is absolutely the most important factor in growing thick, lush plants. Without strong light, your plants will either die or grow into emaciated, spindly versions of their former selves.

Plants need light to photosynthesize. Unfortunately, the typical single-strip light and fluorescent full-hood provide enough light to see the fish, but they do not provide enough light for most species of plants to prosper. Without intense light, you will be greatly limited in the number of species of plants that you can keep alive.

Fish and Tips
To retain their color, reddish plants require the highest amount of light, and some also need extra iron fertilization.

When it comes to lighting, you must provide three things for maximum plant growth:

➤ Proper spectral color

➤ Sufficient duration

➤ Effective intensity

While almost any kind of light bulb, in sufficient quantity, will grow plants, some are much better at it than others. Full-spectrum light is the best. Full-spectrum bulbs contain a complete range of colors of the visible spectrum, and a bit of the invisible spectrum, too. Full-spectrum bulbs will give off light that appears white, but may have accents in particular parts of the spectrum. Plants make particular use of red and blue wavelengths, so many full-spectrum bulbs have extra peaks in those colors.

Twelve hours of light per day works quite well. Anywhere from 10 to 14 hours of light per day is acceptable. Twenty-four hours of light will not help your plants, and may be detrimental. Like animals, plants have a daily metabolic rhythm. After a period of time, they quit photosynthesizing and rest, whether the lights are on or not.

It's Light or Death

There is no substitute for providing sufficient light intensity. You cannot take a bulb with poor spectral output and run it longer to get the proper effect. It just won't work. Be bright and buy bright lights!

So, how much light is needed? A good general rule of thumb is to use two to five watts of fluorescent light per gallon. I give a range because some species require more light than others, and because taller tanks will require more light than shallow tanks. The farther light travels, the more spread out and less concentrated it becomes.

You may recall the *inverse square law* from high school physics class. It states that the intensity of light decreases by the square of the distance. Put simply, if light travels twice as far, it will have one fourth the intensity. If it travels three times as far, it will have one ninth the intensity, and so on. So if your one-foot-deep tank needs a certain amount of light to grow plants properly, a tank that is two feet tall will need four times the light, and a tank that is three feet tall will need nine times the light.

Using the two to five watt per gallon rule, you can see that a 10-gallon tank would require 20 to 50 watts of light. Since this size aquarium is relatively shallow—only 12 inches tall—using the low end of that scale should work out just fine. In other words, at least 20 watts of light should be plenty.

Fish and Tips
Fluorescent bulbs lose intensity as they age. While the bulb itself may continue to glow for three years, it will have lost half its intensity within the first six to 12 months. So change your bulbs at least once a year. Changing them on a rotating basis, rather than all at once, is best.

According to the rule, a 55-gallon tank would require 110 to 275 watts of light. Since this tank is almost twice as tall as a 10- gallon, which means it will take almost four times as much light to reach the bottom with the same intensity, you might want to work off the higher end of that formula. In reality, though, you probably will only have room for four 40-watt fluorescent bulbs. In fact, the chart that follows compares the number of bulbs in a typical fluorescent full-hood with the number recommended to keep plants properly. You'll see that the standard equipment often doesn't measure up. Of course, you could go with compact fluorescents or metal halide lighting to achieve the higher wattage ratings.

Typical Lighting vs. What Plants Really Need

Tank Size (Gals.)	L × W × H (inches)	Typical Full-Hood (# bulbs × watts)	Standard Fluorescents (# bulbs × watts)	Compact Fluorescents (# bulbs × watts)	Halide (# bulbs × watts)
			Minimum Lighting for Lush Growth		
Standard Rectangular Tanks					
2.5	12 × 6 × 8	N/A	1 × 8w	1 × 9w	N/A
5.5	16 × 8 × 10	1 × 8w	2 × 8w	2 × 9w	N/A
10	20 × 10 × 12	1 × 14w	2 × 14w	1 × 28w	N/A
15	24 × 12 × 12	1 × 15w	2 × 15w	1 × 28w	N/A
20XH	20 × 10 × 24	1 × 14w	4 × 15w	2 × 28w	1 × 150w
20H	24 × 12 × 16	1 × 15w	2 × 20w	1 × 55w	1 × 150w
20L	30 × 12 × 12	1 × 20w	2 × 20w	1 × 55w	1 × 150w
29	30 × 12 × 18	1 × 20w	3 × 20w	1 × 55w	1 × 150w
30	36 × 13 × 16	1 × 30w	2 × 30w	1 × 55w	1 × 150w
40	48 × 13 × 16	1 × 40w	2 × 40w	3 × 28w	1 × 150w
44	22 × 22 × 24	2 × 15w	6 × 15w	4 × 28w	1 × 150w
45	36 × 12 × 24	1 × 30w	3 × 30w	2 × 55w	1 × 175w
55	48 × 13 × 20	1 × 40w	3 × 40w	2 × 55w	1 × 175w
58	36 × 18 × 21	1 × 30w	3 × 30w	2 × 55w	1 × 175w
75	48 × 18 × 21	1 × 40w	4 × 40w	2 × 96w	1 × 250w
89	36 × 24 × 24	2 × 30w	6 × 30w	2 × 96w	1 × 250w
90	48 × 18 × 24	1 × 40w	4 × 40w	3 × 96w	1 × 250w
100	72 × 18 × 18	2 × 30w	8 × 30w	4 × 96w	2 × 150w
110	60 × 18 × 24	1 × 40w	6 × 40w	6 × 55w	2 × 150w
120	48 × 24 × 24	2 × 40w	6 × 40w	6 × 55w	2 × 150w
125	72 × 18 × 22	2 × 30w	8 × 30w	4 × 96w	2 × 175w
135	72 × 18 × 24	2 × 30w	8 × 30w	4 × 96w	2 × 175w
150	72 × 18 × 28	2 × 30w	10 × 30w	6 × 96w	2 × 250w
180L	96 × 18 × 24	2 × 40w	10 × 40w	6 × 96w	3 × 175w
180W	72 × 24 × 24	2 × 30w	12 × 30w	6 × 96w	2 × 250w
200	84 × 24 × 24	2 × 30w	14 × 30w	6 × 96w	3 × 175w
220	84 × 24 × 25	2 × 30w	14 × 30w	6 × 96w	3 × 175w
265	84 × 24 × 30	2 × 30w	16 × 30w	8 × 96w	3 × 250w
Hexagons*					
10	14 × 12 × 18	1 × 8w	2 × 8w	2 × 9w	N/A
14	14 × 14 × 20	1 × 8w	3 × 8w	3 × 9w	N/A
20	18 × 16 × 20	1 × 14w	3 × 14w	2 × 28w	1 × 150w
27	18 × 18 × 24	1 × 15w	3 × 15w	2 × 28w	1 × 150w

Tank Size (Gals.)	L × W × H (inches)	Minimum Lighting for Lush Growth			
		Typical Full-Hood (# bulbs × watts)	Standard Fluorescents (# bulbs × watts)	Compact Fluorescents (# bulbs × watts)	Halide (# bulbs × watts)
35	23 × 20 × 24	1 × 15w	3 × 15w	2 × 28w	1 × 150w
45	22 × 22 × 24	1 × 15w	4 × 15w	3 × 28w	1 × 150w
60	22 × 22 × 30	1 × 15w	6 × 15w	4 × 28w	1 × 150w
*Flat-Back Hexagons**					
18	24 × 12 × 16	1 × 15w	2 × 20w	1 × 55w	1 × 150w
23	24 × 12 × 20	1 × 15w	2 × 20w	1 × 55w	1 × 150w
26	36 × 12 × 16	1 × 30w	2 × 30w	1 × 55w	1 × 150w
33	36 × 13 × 20	1 × 30w	2 × 30w	1 × 55w	1 × 150w
52	48 × 13 × 20	1 × 40w	3 × 40w	2 × 55w	1 × 175w

* L = diameter measured corner to corner; W = diameter measured pane to pane.

Fertilizers: Step Carefully

Plants need food. They draw nutrients from the water through their leaves. They draw nutrients from the substrate through their roots. If there is sufficient light and nutrients, the plants will grow.

As plants grow, they change the conditions in your tank. Sometimes the change is for the better. For example, plants can use the carbon dioxide fish excrete. They also absorb phosphates and nitrates. So in some ways, they improve the water quality. However, with the presence of luxuriant plant growth, your tank may become depleted of necessary nutrients and trace elements. These nutrients need to be replenished to keep the plants prospering.

There are two basic things you can do to replenish these depleted nutrients. The first is to keep up with your regular partial water changes. Partial water changes remove waste-laden water and replace it with clean water. In the process, some needed trace elements will be replenished. The other thing you can do to replace or supplement these nutrients is to add aquatic plant fertilizers.

Do You Need to Fertilize?

Before I talk about fertilizers, you must first realize that you may not need them at all. It all depends on your local conditions. Your local tap water may be full of nitrates, phosphates, iron, and who knows what. You may find your plants grow like crazy without adding fertilizers, and that regular partial water changes are all you need. Fish excrete waste, which provides nutrients, so the fish bioload in your aquarium also will be a factor.

If you have only a very few plants, it is probably wise not to fertilize the tank. Over-fertilization can poison a tank directly, or it could just turn your aquarium into a big algae farm. Algae are plants, too. So, if the nutrients are there, and you don't have enough of other plants to use them, the algae will happily feast away on what is available.

Fish and Tips
Live plants compete with algae for the same nutrients. In fact, they tend to out-compete the algae. A heavily planted aquarium is much less likely to have algae problems.

Use the condition of your plants to judge the need for fertilizer. If the light is strong but the growth is slow, you may need more fertilizer. If the leaves develop yellow spots or die back, nutrients may be lacking. If you get involved in keeping planted aquariums, I would recommend that you also purchase a book dedicated to aquatic plants and their care.

What's Available?

Let's look at some common types of fertilizer that you will find at the local shop.

➤ *Laterite.* This is an iron-rich clay. It comes in several forms, including crumbled soil, molded sticks, balls, or tablets. Laterite is usually a one-time treatment. The crumbled soil is mixed into the lower layer of gravel when you first set up the tank, to provide iron and nutrients to the plant roots. However, the balls, molded sticks, and tablets may be used any time as a supplement.

➤ *Granulated.* There is at least one brand of fertilizer that looks much like natural aquarium gravel. You mix it in the gravel, and it is a slow release fertilizer for roots.

➤ *Tablets.* Break these into smaller bits and push them into the gravel near the plant roots. Typically, tablets are used when you make your water changes.

➤ *Liquid.* These mixes are especially good for plants that draw nutrients through their leaves. Liquid fertilizers are usually dosed when you make water changes. Most brands are low in phosphates and nitrates to help prevent algae problems. Liquid iron supplements are especially recommended.

➤ *Carbon dioxide.* Adding CO_2 can be beneficial to all plants. If you add carbon dioxide, you may even find yourself having luck with previously difficult species. The most common way of administering CO_2 is to purchase a kit that contains a small, refillable pressurized cylinder and some type of device for delivering the carbon dioxide to the tank. The output may feed into the input of a canister filter, or it may feed into an inverted plastic bell that goes inside the aquarium.

Starting From the Bottom Up

Strong light is the most important factor in growing vibrant plants. So you really need to start at the top if you want to succeed with your planted aquarium. However, I assume that you already have the proper light setup, so I am now going to show you my favorite method for setting up a planted tank. For that, we start at the bottom.

Most books on planted aquaria recommend against the use of undergravel filters. Some will go so far as to say that you cannot properly grow plants in a tank that has undergravel filtration. Baloney! I've done it, as have many others. However, I agree that there are disadvantages to having an undergravel filter in a heavily planted tank.

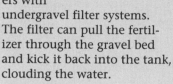

Something's Fishy
Do not use laterite fertilizers with undergravel filter systems. The filter can pull the fertilizer through the gravel bed and kick it back into the tank, clouding the water.

Undergravel filters can draw fertilizer out of the substrate and kick it back into the tank. Undergravel filters are difficult to clean with a gravel vacuum when there is heavy plant growth, because the plants get in the way of the maintenance. Undergravel filters reduce anaerobic activity in the gravel bed, but some anaerobic activity can be beneficial to plants. So when I set up a tank that I expect to be heavily planted, I don't use undergravel filters, though I normally hold them in high regard.

The first thing I do for my planted tank is to purchase the proper amount of laterite for the particular size aquarium. The packages will tell you what size tank they treat. I mix the laterite with clean aquarium gravel to make a one-inch deep layer on the bottom of the tank.

Next, I add more gravel. Elsewhere in the book, I have recommended keeping a 1.5- to 2-inch deep layer of gravel. For planted tanks, though, it is best to put in more. You want lots of room for plant roots to grow. You also want to have enough gravel on top of the layer with the laterite to keep it from getting into the water and turning things muddy. So I recommend adding more gravel until you have at least three inches total depth. For bigger tanks, I go four to five inches. (That works out to 20 to 25 pounds of gravel per square foot of bottom.)

Good Water Current Is a Breeze

Since I don't use an undergravel filter for this setup, you are probably wondering what I've chosen instead. My favorite choice is to use a canister filter. One reason I like them is that most of the components are outside the tank, so they are unobtrusive. Mainly, though, I like canister filters because they are more versatile when it comes to directing the output. Most brands give you the option of having a single large jet of water return to the tank, or of using a perforated spray bar to create several jets.

I prefer to use the spray bar, but instead of mounting it at the back of the tank, like most people do, I mount it at the front. I mount it high enough so that the top frame hides it. If necessary, I purchase additional spray bars and connect them together so that they stretch the entire length of the front of the tank. Then I twist the various sections of spray

Fish and Tips
Water movement is helpful to plants. Some like it more than others, but all benefit from having some water current. Bits of dead leaves are washed away, food particles are kept from settling and rotting among the leaves, and some types of algae growth are inhibited by the flexing of plant leaves in the current.

bar to point them where I need current. Some will spray across the surface for circulation and aeration. Some will point more toward the bottom to keep the debris blowing toward the filter intake.

An added benefit of this method is that, by directing the current from front to back instead of back to front, it helps keep the plants standing up straight. Assuming you planted your large plants in the rear of the tank, when the current is piped from behind, it blows the plants over. The taller ones shade the lower ones, starving them of light. By piping water from the front toward the back, it helps keep the tall plants pushed back a bit, so that the lower plants and the plants in front can get light, too. It also keeps heavy plant growth from completely overgrowing the surface and choking out the influx of fresh oxygen.

The rest of the installation of a heavily planted aquarium is the same as described in Chapter 10 on assembling an aquarium.

Dig Those Crazy Plants

You probably have an idea of what you want your tank to look like. But even if you are wading right in without a preplanned decoration scheme, this part is fun. The placement of the plants will be up to you. You are going to paint your own three-dimensional landscape masterpiece.

Try to make your setup look natural. Group species of plants together, don't make a symmetrical display, don't plant in rows, and (in most cases) put taller plants to the back.

Fish and Tips
New arrivals will look a bit scraggly at first. Once planted, it will usually take a day or so for them to reorient, pointing toward the light with leaves fully spread.

Perhaps you have a plant that would make a good centerpiece, although you don't want to plant it exactly in the center of the tank. Setting it to one side will look more natural. You can leave one large, open space for the fish to swim, or make several smaller connected spaces. Be creative!

It would be easy for me to tell you to just shove the plants down in the gravel and tamp the gravel around them to hold them down, but it isn't always that simple. Plants grow in different ways, and they root in different ways, too. So let me give you a few pointers on planting plants.

Bunch Plants

Bunch plants are usually hardy, fast growing species. Typically, they sell by the clump—a bunch—and you will receive maybe eight stems of plant with a rubber band or lead weight around the bottom to hold them together.

Bunch plants are quite versatile. You can plant each stem singly, or plant the whole bunch as a group, or break the bunch up into two or more smaller groups. Whatever looks good to you is going to be perfect for your tank. Most bunch plants eventually will grow roots, but since what you are buying are clippings off larger plants, the roots will likely not be there yet. To plant, simply push about one inch of the stem into the gravel and tamp gravel around the plant to hold it in place.

Fish and Tips
Always remove the lead weights and rubber bands from the bottom of your bunches of plants before planting. You may even want to take scissors and trim off the bottom inch of plant material that those bindings damaged.

Crown Plants

Crown plants consist of roots and acentral base (crown) from which all leaf stems radiate in a rosette. Swordplants are a good example. With these plants, it is important to plant at the right depth, which is with the crown no more than a quarter inch deep into the gravel. You want all leaf parts to be above the gravel line, and only the roots to be under the gravel.

Crown plants will often come with extensive root systems. You may even need to take some scissors and trim the roots down to an inch or two in length. The easiest way to plant these is to first plant them a little deeper than ideal, then tug gently until the base (crown) of the plant is above the gravel line. Then tamp down the gravel around the plant to firmly hold the roots in place.

Floating Plants

There is not much to figure out here. With floating plants, there is nothing to plant. Just toss them in the tank, and they float around. Your main concern is to be sure the plant is right side up, if it has a top and bottom. Watersprite, for example, has a top and bottom (roots dangle from the bottom), while riccia, wolffia, and hornwort do not produce roots. They tumble with the current.

Something's Fishy
SNIFF! SNIFF!
Don't go over-board on the floating plants. Since they grow right at the surface, they block much of the light that would otherwise shine on the plants down below. If your floating plants get overgrown, don't be afraid to harvest some from the tank so that the other plants can prosper, too.

To Pot or Not

Many crown plants and some bunch plants can be purchased potted. These are usually plants that are grown hydroponically. That is, the plant is grown above water, with the root ball submerged in nutrient-soaked media inside a pot. Inside the pot is rock wool, which holds the nutrient solution, and the plant grows out of that. The pot has perforations so that roots can grow out of the sides and bottom of the pot.

I listed potted plants separately, only because you need to decide if you want to keep the plant in the pot or not. The pot does have advantages in a couple of situations. For example, if you think you will be transplanting the plant often, having it in a pot makes it easier to move the plant around without disturbing the main portion of the roots. Additionally, if you have fish that dig a lot, keeping the plant in the pot may help protect its roots.

Usually, though, it is best to get rid of the pot and the rock wool inside. They restrict the plant's growth. Discard them and plant the specimen directly into the gravel.

Fit and Trimmed

Once your tank becomes established, you will need to do some occasional trimming and replanting. Pruning plants gets rid of dead leaves, reshapes a plant to fit its environment, removes extra growth that is blocking the light, and removes growth that is sparse or spindly.

When bunch plants get too long, you can prune them by pinching off the tops. In fact, you can improve the appearance of many species in this manner, because two stems will grow from the pinch point. So the plant should get bushier with the proper trimming. Plus, you can plant the part that you pinched off and it will form a brand new stem.

Sometimes the stems of bunch plants lose the lower leaves. This may be caused by damage, old age, or lack of light in the lower part of the tank. In any case, you may want to trim these plants by digging them out, pinching off the scraggly bottom portion, and then replanting the leafy top.

With crown plants, the only trimming you want to do is to remove dead leaves. Always pinch them off as close to the bottom as possible. If you see a leaf dying on a crown plant, it is better to remove it immediately rather than waiting for the whole leaf to wilt. As long as the leaf is partially alive, it saps strength from the rest of the plant.

It is not uncommon for some species to shed leaves when transplanted—especially some crown plants, and especially if they grew emersed (above the water). Many of the species of plants that you buy can grow either aquatically or terrestrially. They often develop different types of leaves for each environment, and may shed them when the conditions switch. It is not something to be alarmed about. A healthy plant will grow new leaves faster than it sheds the old ones.

The Least You Need to Know

> ➤ Plants need *intense,* full-spectrum light.
> ➤ Deeper gravel gives more room for roots.
> ➤ Fertilize, but don't overdo it.
> ➤ Be sure there is sufficient current to keep plants free of debris.

Part 5
Problems in Paradise

We all wish life was easy and perfect, but it's not. Sometimes problems arise. Your aquarium, of course, should be almost problem-free. Do it right, and you will have the same fish and plants for years.

Still, problems may occur, so in this part I will talk about some common problems and how to deal with them. You will learn how to prevent excessive algae growth, and what to do if your preventive efforts fail. You will learn about some common fish diseases and how to medicate them. Even better, you will learn how to prevent disease by eliminating stress to your fish. Finally, I will talk about what to do when you find that there is a bully in your tank.

Chapter 23

Aw, Gee! Is That Algae?

In This Chapter

➤ Learn what algae is

➤ Discover what causes it

➤ Find out how to control it

What's fuzzy and slimy and green all over?

1. A moldy, rotten orange

2. The mustache of a guy with a really bad cold

3. A tank with an algae problem

Algae is something every aquarist has to deal with. If nothing else, it will occasionally need to be wiped from the glass to give you the clearest view of your fish. And for some hobbyists, algae will grow in epidemic proportions and be a continuous battle. In this chapter I'll explain what algae is, if it's harmful, how to prevent it from getting out of hand and what to do if it does.

What's It All About, Algae?

Algae are simple plants. Unlike "higher" plants (higher in the evolutionary sense), they have no vascular systems. However, algae come in multitudes of forms and colors. There are single-celled, free-swimming forms that make your water look like pea soup. There are slimy and hairy forms, and there are leafy forms. You can find green, brown, and even red algae. Even the ocean's giant kelp, which grow several hundred feet long, are types of algae. Several hundred feet long? And they say algae isn't a higher plant form!

When aquarists think of algae, they usually think of it as a pest. It can be, but it really isn't. Algae exists in every aquatic system, and even if you start out with a sterile tank, spores in the air will introduce algae to the system. Algae is everywhere, and is a natural, normal part of an ecosystem.

Now, it is true that algae can take over a tank and be a problem. Still, rather than think of algae as a pest, it's better to think of it as a signpost. It can tell you a lot about the condition of your tank. Use algae as an indicator. Algae will not grow out of balance, unless there is something out of balance in the system.

Fish School

Algae (*AL-jee*) is plural for alga (*AL-guh*). Alga may be used to refer to a single algal (*AL-gul*) organism, or to a single species. Algae is plural for both. There is no such word as "algaes."

In fact, that overabundance of algae *may* be doing you a favor. Think about it. If your tank is so loaded with nutrients that you are growing bumper crops of algae, what would that tank be like without the algae? The algae are removing those nutrients and storing them, until you remove the algae. If the algae weren't binding up those nutrients, your fish would be swimming in a soup with a stronger organic content. That is not good.

The Good, the Bad, and the Ugly

There are some good things to be said about algae. It absorbs excess nutrients from the water. It provides a snack for some types of fish. It photosynthesizes carbon dioxide into oxygen, and it keeps a tank from looking unnaturally clean and sterile.

The main reason we don't want algae growth to get out of control is that algae can be ugly. It grows on the glass and obstructs our view of the fish. It can overgrow other plants and choke them out. It can clog filter systems.

Fish and Tips

Algae need light and nutrients to prosper. So if you have algae growing out of control in your aquarium, it's a sign that you have too much light on the tank or too many nutrients in the water—the latter is much more likely. It also may mean you have too few fish that eat algae.

Algae comes in many forms. Sometimes what looks like a little dirt is really algae. On the other hand, many things that we think are algae are not.

The very first "algae" encountered by most aquarists is brown film or brown slime. It first appears as brownish or rust color specks on the glass, rocks, and so forth. As it progresses, it develops into a thin film. The first thing I want to say about brown slime is that it actually isn't algae at all. It is colonies of diatoms (*DIE-uh-toms*), which are microscopic organisms with silica skeletons.

The second thing I want to say about brown slime is don't worry about it. It is completely natural and is temporary. If it obstructs your view, wipe it away. Better yet, toss a pleco or some otocinclus in there, and they probably will clear it away within a day.

The next type of algae that you are likely to see is a thin green film. It may develop on the glass, rocks, or plant leaves. Again, algae-eating fish will normally take care of this algae with no problem.

When this single-celled, free-floating algae gets a foothold in a tank, it can be a major pain. It turns the water green like pea soup, and may even make it difficult to see more than a couple of inches into the tank. Fortunately, the problem isn't too common, but it does tend to crop up in new tanks more than old, established ones. I'll discuss ways to control green water and other algae later in this chapter.

Hair or thread algae are species that grow into green threads that are several inches long. They don't attach, but grow into tangled clusters.

Brush or beard algae may appear dull green or blue-gray, but are actually types of red algae. These algae commonly grow in clumps on the edge of large plant leaves or on driftwood. Brush and beard algae are tough and difficult to control.

Characterized by thick greasy blue-green sheets growing on top the gravel, on plants, and sometimes on the glass, blue-green algae is not algae at all! It is colonies of cyanobacteria. Sometimes it will have mustard brown colors mixed in, as well. This is also a tough one to control, because it is toxic and few creatures will eat it.

Fish and Tips
When brown film is seen in established aquaria, it is generally regarded as a sign that light levels are too low. Perhaps the light bulbs are old and have lost their intensity. Increasing the light will cause the brown film to disappear.

Fish and Tips
The easiest way to distinguish blue-green algae from green slime algae is to flick at it with your fingers. Sheets of blue-green algae will normally peel away quite easily when you direct some current toward them. Green slime algae requires rubbing or scrubbing.

Red slime types of algae are rare in freshwater tanks, as the pH is too low to support them. However, they may turn up in African cichlid or other specialty tanks, where the pH is kept at higher levels.

Green dot algae is not common in new tanks. It develops as pinpoint green dots that grow to pinhead size on glass and hard-leafed plants. Green dot algae is tougher than most algae, so algae-eating fish may have a hard time removing it. You may have to put a bit of muscle behind your algae scrubber pad to get it to come off, too! A razor blade will remove it from the glass quite easily, though.

Black spot algae, though it looks black, is really a type of red algae that grows in tiny spots that develop into larger, mottled colonies.

Light Plus Nutrients Equals Algae

Remembering that algae can be an indicator of an imbalance, it's interesting to note that some people have problems with certain types of algae, while others fight with different species. In fact, you may find that you have a certain type of algae growing out of control in only one of your tanks.

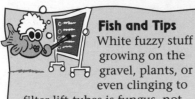

Fish and Tips
White fuzzy stuff growing on the gravel, plants, or even clinging to filter lift-tubes is fungus, not algae. It is almost certainly the result of overfeeding. Uneaten food gets trapped in the gravel. Fungus grows on it and spreads elsewhere. Feed less and increase tank maintenance.

Many factors are involved in this phenomenon. The length of time the tank has been established is one factor. There is a natural succession that takes place in any ecosystem. That is, certain organisms move into a territory first, and once established, help create conditions that make it ideal for other organisms to follow. Succession happens in nature, and in the aquarium, too. Brown slime tends to be found in new tanks, green slime comes next, and brush algae is more likely to be found in older, well-established aquariums.

Excess algae growth can be blamed on two things—too much light (or too much of the wrong wavelength), and too many nutrients. Controlling one or both factors can create conditions unsuitable for algae growth. Of course, it needs to be done in such a way that you don't starve the other plants and animals in your system of light and nutrients, too.

Light

Algae need light to photosynthesize. Without light, they die. Controlling the amount and type of light also may control your algae problem. Review your lighting situation. Based on the chart in Chapter 22, do you have enough light to grow plants well? Can you cut back a bit to inhibit algae? Would running your light for fewer hours per day be beneficial? Are you using the proper full-spectrum bulbs, or did you pick a bulb of the wrong spectrum to save money?

Is your tank near a window? Direct sunlight can contribute to algae growth. Mind you, I only said that because I feel required to—I'm not really happy about it. You see, every fish book ever written offers the possibility that algae is caused by a tank getting too much sunlight. In a few paragraphs, I'll tell you why the "avoid direct sunlight" rule is often a bunch of baloney.

Nutrients

Like all living things, plants need food. They take in nutrients through their roots and through their leaves. If your system has nutrient overload, algae is going to get a foothold. Is the tank overcrowded? Excess fish waste adds nutrients to the tank. Are you over fertilizing or fertilizing when it isn't necessary?

Shortages of nutrients may cause algae, too. You see, if there are nutrients in the water, some plant form will use them. If they are in the proper balance to grow desirable aquatic plants, those plants should prosper and out-compete the algae. However, if the nutrients are insufficient for higher plant forms, or if they are in the wrong proportions, conditions may be created that are more beneficial for the algae, and so the algae may get the upper hand.

Are you keeping up with your scheduled maintenance, particularly your partial water changes? Partial water changes remove dissolved waste and replace depleted trace elements. Even if your aquatic plants are growing well and algae isn't present, those plants are removing nutrients from the water, and therefore, changing the quality of that water. Without regular partial water changes to stabilize things, water quality will deteriorate and may create conditions that are more suitable for algae growth.

Run some water tests. If your tank suddenly has an algae problem, are any of the water quality parameters testing at abnormal levels? Checking pH, general hardness, carbonate hardness, nitrate, and phosphate may give you a clue.

> **Fish and Tips**
> Even if you are doing nothing different, a sudden bloom of algae may be linked to changes in your local tap water. Seasonal variances, including heavy rains, can affect the chemistry of your local water. Using test kits to regularly monitor your water quality can help you troubleshoot your tank.

Plants as Competitors

A few paragraphs back, I suggested that the common advice to avoid direct sunlight for your tank may be a bunch of baloney. In fact, my favorite place to put a tank is smack dab in the middle of a window, so that it *can* get some direct sunlight! Am I loony? Don't answer that! (Don't ask anyone who knows me, either, okay?)

The reason I like to put my tanks near a window is that I like to keep lots of live plants. Sunlight is good for plants. They thrive on it. If you have lots of live plants in your tank, direct sunlight will benefit them. If you don't have lots of live plants, algae will use the light instead. Live plants compete with algae for light and nutrients. Even better, they tend to out-compete the algae. So if you provide proper conditions to grow plants, and have enough of them, algae is rarely going to be a problem for you.

> **Fish and Tips**
> The Siamese flying fox is one of the few species that will eat beard and brush algae. You may want to review Chapter 12 on popular species of fish for more details on these fish.

The real question should not be if the tank gets sunlight. The question should be about whether you plan to keep lots of live plants, if it does.

When, despite your best efforts, algae does crop up, there are plenty of ways to control it.

Herbivores You'll Adore

The easiest way to control algae is to get some live-in janitors. All you have to do is buy a few algae-eating critters. Not only will they help control algae problems, but you'll have fun watching them do it.

Algae-eating fish are the first, best defense. There are several species of fish that eat algae. The ones I most recommend are the various varieties of plecostomus (suckermouth cats) and otocinclus (the pygmy sucker cats).

Even kissing gouramies and mollies like to nibble at algae. They are not as good at clearing it away as the catfish, though. In fact, most fish will eat a bit of it here and there.

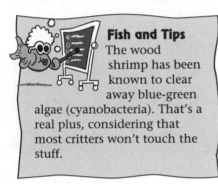

Fish and Tips
The wood shrimp has been known to clear away blue-green algae (cyanobacteria). That's a real plus, considering that most critters won't touch the stuff.

Shrimp are good at reaching places that the algae-eating fish can't reach. There are several species of shrimp that are sold for aquariums. All will nibble at algae to one extent or the other. Ghost shrimp and Malaysian rainbow shrimp are good ones for nibbling at beard and brush algae.

All snails will eat some algae. Some are better than others, though. Avoid apple snails and Colombian ramshorn snails if you have live plants. They want to eat the plants, too. Even the smaller species of ramshorn and pond snails are sometimes to blame for munching softer plants. If you add snails to your tank, do it because you want to watch them. Don't expect them to be all that great at eating algae.

Die, Algae! Die!

Unfortunately, the natural method of algae control doesn't always work, or isn't always enough. You may have lots of live plants to compete with the algae, and a good complement of grazers to nibble at it, but all this still may not be enough. In that case, you are going to have to pitch in and deal with some algae yourself.

You know you have an algae problem when . . .

. . . your plecostomus weighs 50 pounds and is only six months old!

. . . you need a weed whacker to clean the glass.

. . . you wish they hadn't banned Agent Orange.

. . . you have to scrape the *outside* of the tank

. . . every algae-eater you buy chokes to death.

. . . the Jolly Green Giant thinks you're cute.

Even in the best situation, you will occasionally need to wipe algae from your glass. I highly recommend the algae scrubber pads sold in pet stores. Buy the ones without the handles, as they are much easier to use on the hard-to-reach spots. The scrubber pad can be used on the glass, and on some rocks and decorations. For really tough algae on the glass, a razor blade type of scraper works well.

There are several sizes and styles of bottle brushes designed for cleaning algae from filter tubes. There are rigid versions for straight tubes and flexible versions for getting into the bends of siphon and intake tubes. If necessary, you also can remove ornaments from your tank and take them to the sink to scrub with any soap-free household brush.

Bleach can be another option. I hesitate to recommend this, because you can easily kill your fish. However, non-living decorations can be *removed from the tank*, scrubbed and then given a short soak in a solution of bleach—say, one cup of bleach per gallon of water. Afterwards, be sure to rinse the decorations well. Even better, soak them in a bucket with some extra dechlorinator to neutralize any bleach that you missed, before returning the items to the tank. *Never put bleach into your tank* or use it to clean live plants. Use bleach at your own risk!

There are several products on the market that are specifically designed to kill algae in the tank. Used as directed, they are *normally* safe to put in with the fish. However, I recommend using algicides *only as a last resort*, as they may kill your plants. Use algicides at your own risk!

> **Something's Fishy**
> If your snails over-multiply, consider buying a clown loach. This peaceful, attractive fish loves to eat them. *Do not* buy the snail-killing potions! They may kill your plants. Plus, all those dead snails will pollute the tank and kill fish. You also can squash the occasional snail against the aquarium glass, and the fish will all nibble at the meat.

> **Something's Fishy**
> Never use household sponges or scrubbing pads to clean inside your tank. They may contain soap or chemicals. This applies even to brand new ones. For example, put a brand new cellulose sponge in a sink of water and squeeze it a few times. Look at how much suds!

Other chemicals, called flocculents, can be added to the water where they will cause small particulates to clump into larger particles that can be more easily removed by the filter system. They also help with green water problems that are caused by free-floating algae.

If you're in the mood to spend some money, you might consider ultraviolet sterilization. These units use intense UV light to kill the algae that causes green water. As water passes through the unit, the ultraviolet light kills organisms. UV sterilizers only kill the type of algae that causes green water. They won't work on algae in the tank, because exposing fish, plants, and yourself to this light is extremely dangerous. The bulbs can cause permanent blindness and death to you and your pets! UV sterilizers are rarely used for green water control in aquaria, though. Pond applications are more common.

Making It Perfectly Clear

Turbidity (cloudiness) and discolored water are problems sometimes encountered in the aquarium. Since one type of algae is a possible cause, I've decided to talk about cloudy water in this chapter. However, cloudy water can have several causes:

➤ Single-celled, free-floating algae cause green cloudiness.

➤ Bacterial blooms can cause gray cloudiness (milkiness).

➤ Suspended particulates also may cause gray cloudiness.

Something's Fishy
Algicides may kill your plants. Additionally, if the algicide works, a large quantity of dead algae will pollute your tank. So if you do use one of these products, scrape and remove as much algae as possible before the treatment.

Do not confuse cloudy (turbid) water with discolored water. Cloudy water has an opacity. That is, depending upon how turbid it is, you can't easily see through it. If the water is only slightly cloudy, you will be able to see everything in the tank, but there will be a haze. If the water is very cloudy, it may be so opaque that you can only see the fish and decorations that are closest to the glass. The haze obscures the rest.

Discolored water, on the other hand, is perfectly transparent. It just isn't colorless. Tannins released from driftwood, for example, can turn water yellowish or even brown. Medications may turn water green, yellow, or even purple. Making partial water changes and using activated carbon in the filter system can remove these colors from the water.

Green Water

This is the "pea soup" condition caused by unicellular free-floating algae. There are so many of them in suspension that they form a green haze. Green water can be particularly difficult to cure. It may appear suddenly, with no obvious cause, and it may disappear just as quickly.

In evaluating this problem, here are some questions I typically ask:

➤ How much light does the tank receive, and for how long each day? Usually the problem can be traced to too much light. Maybe the person leaves the aquarium light on 24 hours a day. Cutting back on light may be the simple solution.

➤ Are there live plants in the tank? How many? You will recall that plants compete with algae for nutrients. A tank with few or no plants is much more likely to have algae problems. Adding live plants may help.

➤ How many fish are there and what size are they? The more fish, the more waste. The more waste, the more nutrients for algae. The fish load may need to be reduced.

➤ How much food is offered? Coupled with the question above, I can estimate the bioload in the tank. It may help me judge if the nutrient level is too high. Cutting back on feeding may help.

➤ How often are water changes done? I use this question to get an idea of balance in the tank. On one hand, water changes are good. They remove waste and they replace trace elements. Not changing enough water can lead to algae problems. On the other hand, changing water can sometimes make green water problems worse. If the nutrients in the tap water are a factor—say local levels of phosphate and nitrate are high—then changing water may bring more nutrients for the algae.

➤ What type of filtration is on the tank? This question helps me evaluate whether the filtration is adequate, and if the filter is being cleaned often enough. Another reason that I ask this question is that I've noticed a trend: People with green water problems almost always use a particular brand of filter that uses a slide-in filter cartridge. I haven't confirmed this, but it may be the activated carbon used in that brand that contributes to the problem. You see, some activated carbons are washed with phosphoric acid in the manufacturing process. This causes them to release some phosphates when used.

Anyway, to treat green water, try reducing light or reducing nutrients first. Try adding live plants. If those methods don't work, then try one of the flocculating products. If that fails, an algicide may be necessary.

Or, you could just be patient. Eventually, green water will clear on its own. It uses up nutrients and dies back, or microscopic organisms that eat it will eventually clear it away.

Milky Water

Bacterial bloom is one cause of cloudy water. It is more common in new tanks, and many refer to it as "new tank syndrome." An established aquarium has a healthy balance of bacteria and microorganisms. A new tank does not. With the right combination of nutrients in the water, some types of bacteria may supermultiply as they feed on the nutrients. There may be so many bacteria that they will cloud the tank.

This problem will usually fix itself in a couple of days, or it may take a week or so. The bacteria deplete the nutrients and die off. So the best way to deal with bacterial bloom is to wait it out. Of course, be sure that you aren't contributing to it by overfeeding.

Fish and Tips
Using sodium biphosphate to reduce pH may contribute to algae problems. Algae can use phosphates as food.

Fish and Tips
There are some products on the market that are designed to introduce helpful bacteria to a new tank. Frankly, I think they are of little value. However, if you do use them, be aware that they may cause temporary cloudiness. If this happens, discontinue use.

Suspended particulates are another cause of cloudy water. Usually, the particulates will be single-celled algae or the bacteria that have bloomed, as I just described. However, the particulates may be microscopic debris. For example, they could be dust from new aquarium gravel that wasn't properly rinsed before it was introduced into the tank. You may want to try flocculents to combat this problem.

The Least You Need to Know

➤ Algae is natural and is not necessarily a pest.

➤ An overabundance of algae signals that light and nutrients are out of balance.

➤ Live plants compete with algae for nutrients. Heavily planted tanks are less likely to develop algae problems.

➤ Herbivores, particularly algae-eating fish, are the best control for most algae problems.

➤ Keep an algae scrubber pad on hand for touch-ups.

Chapter 24

Stress and Disease

In This Chapter

➤ How stress affects your fish

➤ Danger signals you should watch for

➤ Common diseases of aquarium fish

➤ Typical treatments and preferred medications

➤ Quarantining new arrivals

➤ Euthanising terminal cases

If you play your cards right, this chapter could end up being for informational purposes only. It is entirely possible to set up an aquarium and never have a fish get sick or die of anything but old age. I've done it often and you can, too. If you follow the basic rules laid out in this book, problems will be few and, perhaps, nonexistent.

However, it would be silly to set up an aquarium and not learn how to watch for warning signs or how to deal with problems. Most fish diseases are easy to cure. So let's talk about disease.

First off, what is it that causes diseases and death in your fish? Your first instinct may be to say that germs are the cause. Sometimes that is true, but usually when disease organisms get a foothold in your fish tank it is not so much that they are a cause—more likely, they are an effect. You probably noticed that I titled this chapter "Stress and Disease." Notice that I mentioned stress before I mentioned disease.

Don't Stress Me Out!

Stress is the major cause of disease and death in fish. How do I define stress? Basically, stress is anything that makes your fish unhappy. When your fish are under stress, they will be more susceptible to disease. Pathogens are everywhere. There is no avoiding them. However, happy, healthy fish are normally able to fight them off quite easily. Their immune systems do their jobs well, and the fish stay healthy. Stressed out fish have compromised immune systems.

What are some things that can cause stress in a fish? It shouldn't be surprising that the things that stress your fish are the same things that stress you and me. Overcrowding, hunger, overheating, chills, lack of rest, loud noise, bullies, and living in filth are a few examples. These things can be enough to make a person, or a fish, sick.

Let's look at the common stressors, one by one.

➤ *Hunger.* A fish that is getting insufficient nutrition is a fish with lowered immunity. A starving fish is also more likely to try to take a nip out of someone else. Additionally, a starving fish is more likely to be singled out as a weak fish, and attacked by the others in the aquarium.

➤ *Overcrowding.* Thisstressor will cause territories to overlap more, resulting in more fights. It also will cause the tank to have higher waste levels. I probably don't have to tell you why high waste levels in a tank would be stressful. Can you imagine living in your own toilet, waiting until your owner came around every few weeks and gave it a partial flush? Eeeuuuww! High waste levels can poison a fish directly, create breeding grounds for pathogens, affect appetite, and compromise immunity.

➤ *Rapid temperature changes.* Human beings are more likely to get sick in the spring and fall when the weather is changing. Fish are more likely to get sick when subjected to extremes in temperature, too. A proper aquarium heater helps prevent dramatic temperature changes. When making water changes, you also need to match the temperature of the new water to that of the old water.

➤ *Lack of rest.* Fish don't sleep quite the way we do, but they do go into a resting state. It is important that they get the chance. Be sure to turn out the lights on your tank at night. Can you imagine what it would be like if the lights were on 24 hours a day and you couldn't even close your eyes because you had no eyelids?

➤ *Loud noises.* It is probably not a good idea to put your stereo speakers next to an aquarium. Keep your woofers and tweeters a distance from the tank. Also, don't play that music so loud! Your fish will appreciate it and your so will your neighbors. Setting the aquarium on top of the television is probably a bad idea, as well. Besides the problem of sound from the TV vibrating through the tank, if your tank ever leaks, some serious damage could be done.

➤ *Bullies.* Constant nips not only do physical damage, they keep a fish from getting adequate nutrition and rest. Further, wounds make easy entry points for infections. It is not uncommon for fish to jump out of an aquarium. While there are many reasons for this to happen—and suicide is probably not one of them—being chased by bullies is a primary cause. Mixing compatible species will prevent this problem.

Something's Fishy
Water carries sound better than air, so don't tap on the aquarium glass. It's like screaming in a fish's ear.

What's Wrong With That Fishy in the Window?

In Chapter 11 on picking your first fish, I discussed ways to spot a healthy fish. In this chapter, let's talk about the ways to spot a sick or stressed fish. Fish are fairly good at giving warning signs of impending doom. You just need to know what to watch for. Following are some danger signals.

➤ *Listlessness.* When a fish that is normally active suddenly starts lying around or hiding, it's a sign that something is amiss. Causes of listlessness include deteriorated water quality, parasites, overeating, injury, and incorrect water temperatures. Be aware that some territorial species may be quite active in your tank when first introduced, but once they settle in they will pick a spot and stay there. That is normal. Some, like oscars, go to the other extreme. They may lie on their side as if they are dying when first introduced to a tank. Also, livebearers about to give birth may take to hiding or resting in preparation. Again, that would be normal behavior.

➤ *Loss of appetite.* If your fish stops eating, unless you have just stuffed him with a heavy meal, it's a bad sign. Most fish are hungry practically all of the time. Poor water quality, bullies, disease, and spoiled food are possible causes of loss of appetite.

➤ *Color changes.* Many things can cause a fish to change color. Some of them are good. Some are bad. Fish will change color to blend into the background. That is, take a fish from a light colored tank and throw it into a tank with a darker background and its colors will usually deepen. It's Mother Nature's way of camouflaging the fish from predators. Also, a fish that is about to breed is usually going to take on darker, brighter colors. This is good! The fish is happy.

Watch, though, for color changes that seem abnormal or have no apparent reasonable cause. If a fish's color suddenly fades, it is probably

Fish and Tips
Be aware that many fish will not eat when first introduced to an aquarium. It is not uncommon for some species to skip meals for a day or two. I've seen large piranhas go six weeks before they would take food in a new aquarium—those big sissies!

283

under some type of stress—though, if it fades over time, it may be diet related. If discolored patches develop, the fish may be coming down with a disease.

Some species will change pattern drastically, say from blotched to striped, when excited. Also, most fish will fade at night. Anyway, be sure you are familiar with what is normal for the species you keep.

Fish Tales

The gold tetra (*Hemigrammus rodwayi*) gets its color from a harmless parasite. Brass tetra is another name for this interesting fish.

➤ *Clamped fins.* The fins of most species will be spread and erect when healthy. If these fish suddenly start keeping their fins folded against the body, it is a danger signal. Other fish, like the popular algae-eating plecostomus, will normally keep their fins folded, erecting them only when swimming or when excited.

➤ *Shimmies.* Sometimes clamped fins are accompanied by shimmying. This symptom is best described as the fish swimming in one place, wagging its body from side to side. Mostly, we see this problem with livebearing fish, but gouramies or others may get it, too. Common causes are low temperature or incorrect water chemistry.

➤ *Distended gills.* A fish that is holding its gills open is a fish that is having major troubles. Many things can cause this, including gill parasites, toxins in the water, and gill damage. High ammonia levels or low pH levels are major causes.

➤ *Rapid breathing or gasping at the surface.* Both are signs that a fish is not getting sufficient oxygen. Possible causes are low dissolved oxygen levels in the tank, high waste levels that prevent proper exchange of oxygen, gill damage from parasites, or the presence of toxins in the water.

➤ *Split or frayed fins.* Split fins are usually a result of a fight. In most cases, nothing needs to be done. The fins will heal nicely without help. However, if the edges of the fins become ragged or show signs of decay, it could be a sign of disease or even poor water quality.

➤ *Sores and wounds.* Again, aggression is usually the cause, but advanced infections also can open sores on your fish.

➤ *Cloudy eyes.* There are some diseases that cause this problem, but it is more likely to be due to insufficient water changes resulting in low pH or high ammonia. Occasionally, the problem may be cataracts.

➤ *Swollen stomach.* A swollen stomach may indicate gluttony, a female fish full of roe, internal parasites, or it could mean that your fish has fluid build-up from the disease dropsy.

➤ *Emaciated stomach.* If a fish is losing weight, be sure you are offering the proper diet. Poor water quality can affect appetite, and parasites are a likely cause of skinny fish.

➤ *Bent spine.* A fish with a bent spine was probably born that way, and will likely live a full life. However, a fish that develops a bent spine later in life is probably suffering from a diet deficiency or an injury.

➤ *White slimy patches.* Your fish excretes extra slime as a defense against infection. The problem is a little hard to diagnose without a microscope, because protozoa, bacteria, flukes, and just plain lousy water quality can all cause a fish to slime up.

➤ *Obvious infection.* I'll talk in more detail about this in a moment, but you will need to learn to recognize the common types of disease that may infect your fish.

➤ *Erratic or unusual behavior.* Get to know what is normal for the species you keep, and you will catch problems much earlier. For example, a bottom feeder that suddenly spends all of its time hanging around at the surface is exhibiting unusual behavior.

Fish Tales

The dwarf rasbora (*Rasbora maculatus*) is a pretty red fish with large black dots. It stays under an inch in length, so it isn't safe to mix with many fish.

Make It a Habit to Check the Habitat

If you spot any of the warning signs I just listed, what do you do first? That's right, curse aloud—unless there are kids nearby. Next, visually check the environment. Remember that stress is the most common cause of problems, so here are some questions to ask yourself:

➤ Has an air line become disconnected?

➤ Is a filter clogged?

➤ When was the last water change?

➤ What is the current water temperature?

➤ Is there a bully in the tank?

➤ Is the tank too dirty?

➤ Are there obvious symptoms of infection?

You're not done checking the environment, yet. Even if there are no obvious equipment problems or any signs of disease, you should run your water tests for pH, ammonia, and nitrite. You cannot measure water quality by looking at it with the naked eye. Test the water!

Obviously, if your water tests show that the water quality is out of whack, you will need to take corrective action. See Chapters 16 and 17 on water quality and cycling a new tank for help with that. Sometimes a partial water change is all your fish need to correct a problem.

Also obvious, if there are visible signs of infection you will need to medicate your fish. Let me tell you about some common diseases. Afterward, I'll discuss various treatments.

Dots, Spots, Patches, and Fuzz

Most diseases of aquarium fish will show up as dots, spots, patches, or fuzz somewhere on the outside of the fish. Some diseases are quite easy to identify by sight. Others will require some educated guesswork, unless you have access to a decent microscope.

Most aquarium fish diseases can be classified into the following categories:

➤ Protozoan

➤ Bacterial

➤ Fungal

➤ Parasitic

➤ Viral

Ick! My Fish Has Ich

There are many nasty protozoans that attack fish. Some of them are true parasites, but some are merely opportunistic organisms taking advantage of already sick or dying fish.

Probably the most well known protozoan parasite of fish is ich. Ich is so well known that many new hobbyists seem to want to diagnose every disease as ich. Ich is pronounced *ick* and is short for the name of the offending organism, *Ichthyophthirius multifilius*. Most hobbyists see this parasite at one time or another, so let's talk about how to characterize the symptoms of ich.

Imagine, if you will, that you are holding your fish in one hand and a salt shaker in the other. Now, imagine that you sprinkle some salt on the fish. You have just visualized the exact appearance of a fish infected with ich—except, of course, that you won't be holding a slimy fish in your hand. Ick!

Ich appears as a spattering of tiny white dots the size of salt crystals. It may first present itself as a dot or two on the fins or body, and later spread. If left untreated long enough, the fish will begin to look more slimy than dotted. This is due to massive tissue damage—the fish will then produce extra body slime, seeking some relief. If your fish gets to this state, the odds of saving it will be much lower. Too much damage will have been done.

This marble hatchetfish has an ich infection.

However, you are not going to let your fish get to that state, are you? Ich is quite easy to spot, and if you catch it early and provide proper treatment, you shouldn't lose a single fish to it. Ever! I wish all fish diseases were as easy to treat as ich.

Before I talk about possible treatments, I need to discuss the life cycle of the parasite. When ich first infects your fish, you won't notice it. It is too small. Only after it has had a couple of days to grow will you see the white dots. When attached to the fish in this encysted feeding stage, the parasite is called a theront.

Once full grown, it will drop off the fish, fall to the bottom of the tank, and attach itself to objects there. The ich parasite is now in the tomite stage. This is the reproduction stage, and the organism will divide into up to a thousand baby ich parasites ready to start the next generation of ich in your tank.

After a day or two, depending on the temperature, these swarmers (now known as trophonts) release into the water to seek a new host. Without treatment, the whole cycle starts over. Only this time, there will be many more parasites and your fish will get a much more severe (probably lethal) infection.

The lifecycle of the ich parasite, Ichthyophthirius multifilius. 1) infected fish, 2) theront drops off, 3) tomite attaches, 4) tomite divides, 5) trophonts seek new host.

Treating Ich

As I said before, ich is a very easy disease to treat. There are many effective drugs available, but there is something you need to keep in mind. These drugs don't kill the parasite when it is attached to the fish or when it is in the encysted reproduction stage on the bottom of the tank. The medication only works on the free-swimming stages of the parasite. Therefore, it is important that you don't stop treating the fish when the last dot disappears. Treat for at least one more day to be sure you get all the trophonts.

You will find many brands of ich medication on the market. Some are more effective than others, and some are safer than others. Most will contain various combinations of formalin (dilute formaldehyde), malachite green (a dye), or a solution of copper.

My favorite is a straight malachite green formulation. I've been using it for over 30 years. It works. It's relatively safe, and it's usually the cheapest choice. It will turn your water slightly blue at first, but the color will fade away within a few hours. Note, though, that some tetras and scaleless bottom fish can be sensitive to this medication, and it should only be used at half dosage with those fish. Follow the manufacturer's instructions for dosage of the brand you choose.

Formalin-malachite green formulations are also quite popular. I sometimes use this combination to treat other, more difficult protozoal infestations. In combination, formalin and malachite green have a synergistic effect, meaning the two ingredients are safer and stronger together than when used alone.

If this is so, why don't I use this combination for ich, too? It's because I find that ich is plenty easy to treat, and that using malachite green alone requires no extra water changes during treatment. Formalin, on the other hand, does more harm to the biological filtration in the tank, may cloud the water, and stinks. Formalin and malachite green are both known carcinogens, but I don't worry about stuff like that in the dosages I'm exposed to. Anyway, after treating with a product that contains formalin, you will need to change some water to get your water quality back in order.

There are some copper formulations available for treating ich, but I don't much like them. Their efficacy depends on such factors as whether they are chelated (pronounced *KEY-lay-ted*) and the hardness of your water. Copper medications are dangerous if you have soft water. Copper is hard on plants, too. In other words, they may work, but they also may be dangerous or useless.

> **Something's Fishy**
> Always remove activated carbon from your filters during treatment with medications. Activated carbon adsorbs medications, leaving them unavailable to cure the fish. Do not turn off the filters, though! Just remove the carbon and leave them running without it. After the treatment, replacing the activated carbon will help remove leftover medication from the tank.

Other Nasty Protozoans

Anyway, ich is like the Mother of All Parasitic Protozoans. It is comparatively large and easy to spot. There are many other protozoal infections of fish, though, and most of them are so small that you would need a microscope to diagnose them. Unfortunately, instead of obvious dots, they may produce slimy patches that look more like bacterial infections. Without a microscope, it is easy to misdiagnose a disease.

Other protozoans you may want to read about are *Oodinium* (velvet disease), *Hexamita*, *Tetrahymena*, *Ichthyobodo* (costia), *Chilodinella*, and my favorite, *Trichodina*. Trichodina is my favorite because the parasites look like little flying saucers under the microscope, and I'm a big sci-fi fan. Formalin, malachite green, copper, and metronidazole are common treatments for controlling the above protozoans—most of which are fairly easy to kill. Tetrahymena, though, is one tough little parasite. If your fish catches that one, good luck.

Bacterial Infections

Bacteria are much smaller than protozoa, but they tend to grow in colonies, so resulting infections may be more easily visible to your eye than protozoal infections. Typically, bacterial infections will show as slimy patches developing on the skin of the fish. Sometimes they will be bloody. Fin rot (as opposed to split or damaged fins) and mouth rot (often erroneously called mouth fungus) will probably be due to bacterial infections.

Antibiotics will be necessary to treat bacterial infections. It is important that you treat quickly, too, as these infections can spread very quickly. Some will kill your fish within hours of the symptoms first appearing!

Your pet store probably will carry a variety of antibiotics. Some are effective. Some are not. In a moment, I will steer you toward the better ones, but you must remember that

Fish School
In the fish hobby, the term "antibiotics" commonly refers to both true antibiotics and antibacterials. Technically, antibiotics are substances derived from living organisms. For example, penicillin comes from a mold. Antibacterials are compounds created in the laboratory. Both will destroy microorganisms.

the best you can do is take an educated *guess* about which is the right choice. Why? Because no antibiotic treats every bacterial infection. They all will be effective against some bacteria, but not against others.

In fact, many antibiotics don't kill bacteria in the first place! Instead, they mess up the reproductive ability of the bacteria, so that the bacteria stop multiplying. This lets the immune system of the host catch up and do the job of eliminating the infection.

Positive and Negative

As you read the packaging of the various antibiotics on your dealer's shelves, you will notice that the terms "gram-positive" and "gram-negative" come up occasionally. What does this mean? Well, you need a microscope to see bacteria, and even then, they are colorless and hard to observe. So a long time ago, a man invented a procedure for staining bacteria so that you could see them under the microscope. Just as all medications don't kill all species of bacteria, stains don't affect all bacteria equally either. This man, whose last name was Gram, came up with a procedure that stains most bacteria. Consequently, the stains became known as Gram's stain. The bacteria most affected by the stain turn purple and are called gram-positive. The others, being relatively unaffected, turn pink and are considered gram-negative.

Why is this important? It's not likely that you are going to be staining and fixing samples to view under the microscope. The reason it is important is that most bacterial fish diseases just happen to be gram-negative. So antibiotics that are gram-positive will probably not be good choices to treat your fish. You will want to steer toward gram-negative antibiotics.

Fish and Tips
Some antibiotics come as tablets, some as gel-caps. The tablets can usually be dropped directly into the aquarium without crushing. The gel-caps should be opened, and the powder inside should be poured into the aquarium. Dispose of the empty capsules.

This is not to say that gram-positive antibiotics will necessarily be useless. In fact, some antibiotics will have some effect on both gram-negative and gram-positive bacteria. This brings us to another reason you may want to avoid gram-positive antibiotics. It just so happens that the helpful nitrifying bacteria in your filter bed are gram-positive. So the wrong medication may not only do little to cure your fish, it may have a destructive effect on your biological filtration.

A Cure for What Ails

Now I'm going to point you toward some effective antibiotics to try if the need arises. Since there are many brands out there and I have no way of knowing which ones your local shops carry, I'll give you the names of the active ingredients. I recommend you avoid choosing medications that don't list the active ingredients. For one thing, you won't know what you are getting. For another, if that medication doesn't work, how do you know that the next thing you try isn't the same medicine under a different brand name?

Here are some of my favorite antibiotics:

➤ *Kanamycin sulphate.* Many antibiotics don't absorb well and treat only the outside of the fish. Gram-negative kanamycin absorbs well and doesn't discolor the water. It's even stronger (synergistic) when combined with oxolinic acid.

➤ *Furan drugs.* This is a whole group of drugs, including furazolidone, nitrofurantoin, nifurpurinol, and nitrofurazone. These drugs are effective. They will discolor the water a bit, turning it various shades of green or brown. Furan drugs can be carcinogenic, so handle them carefully. Furans treat both gram-negative and gram-positive bacteria.

➤ *Sulfa drugs.* Again, this is a whole group of drugs, including sulfamethazine, sulfamerazine, sulfathiozole, and sulfaisoxazole. The most common way to find these is in combinations sold as "tri-sulfa" or "triple sulfa." Sulfas treat both gram-negative and gram-positive bacteria.

➤ *Chloramphenicol.* This is a good one, but you probably won't run across it. Due to some side effects it can have on humans, it is much more highly regulated. Chloramphenicol is gram-negative.

➤ *Minocyline.* This is a well-absorbed, gram-negative drug.

➤ *Neomycin sulphate.* This treats both gram-negative and gram-positive bacteria.

Here are some other, less favorable medications you may find. These may be more effective if used in combination with another gram-negative antibiotic, as listed above.

Fish and Tips
If you buy the powdered or gel-cap form of tri-sulfa, as opposed to tablets, it is very helpful to mix the powder in a jar of water before adding it to the tank, because the powder tends to float and may not dissolve properly.

Fish and Tips
If you choose tetracycline as a treatment, you may want to use the oral form. You can purchase "medicated flake" fish food that contains this drug. The advantage of oral medication is that it puts the drug inside the fish, where it will do the most good. Of course, your fish must be eating for it to work.

Something's Fishy
Do not use antibiotics as a preventive. This can result in the development of resistant strains of bacteria. If resistant bacteria should infect your fish, you will have a much harder time curing them.

➤ *Oxytetracycline hydrochloride.* Also known as tetracycline and Terramycin, this drug has been overused as a preventive in the Far East, so there are many resistant strains of bacteria, which reduces its effectiveness. It treats gram-negative and gram-positive bacteria.

➤ *Penicillin.* This drug is gram-positive.

➤ *Ampicillin.* This drug is also gram-positive.

➤ *Erythromycin.* A gram-positive drug, this one has been shown to have some temporary negative effect on biological filtration.

A Fungus Among Us

Before I discuss fungus infections, I want to be sure that we have our terminology straight. When I say fungus, I mean *true* fungus. Unfortunately, the term "fungus" is commonly misapplied in the aquarium trade to diseases that are actually bacterial infections, such as "mouth fungus."

True fungus, caused by the organism *Saprolegnia*, is quite distinctive from the various bacterial infections that often get mislabeled as fungus. True fungus is fuzzy. In advanced stages, it is even hairy looking. It looks a bit like a dandelion head that has gone to seed. Assuming your eyesight is decent, you will be able to see actual filaments. True fungus is the fuzzy stuff that you see growing on dead, rotting fish, or perhaps on uneaten fish food that is lying about the tank.

Fish Tales

If your fish seems to have hair growing on it, it is:

a. Just reaching puberty.

b. Evolving into a mammal.

c. Infected with true fungus.

True fungus is a secondary infection. The spores that produce it are everywhere, but a healthy, undamaged fish will never catch it. True fungus infects dead tissue. So if you have a fish that has dead tissue from an injury, it may contract fungus. If your fish has an advanced protozoal or bacterial infection that has caused tissue to die, fungus may set in as well.

This disease is difficult to treat, probably because you can't cure dead tissue. It sets roots deep into the flesh of the fish, which may make the situation worse by killing more tissue. There are some medications that may help. They can retard the growth of the fungus. These include sodium chlorite solutions, methylene blue, and potassium perman-ganate. Formalin and malachite green combinations may have some effect, as well.

One treatment involves netting the fish and dabbing some mercurochrome or Betadine directly onto the infected area. In severe cases, I find it helps to take some tweezers and try to pull off as much of the fungus as possible before applying the treatment.

False Fungus

You may also run across a protozoan masquerading as a fungus. It's the *Epistylis,* a proto-zoan shaped like the stem and flower of a tulip. It usually grows in colonies. Sometimes, it can be found infecting fish—particularly growing as a tuft on the edge, or at the base of the fins. Unfortunately, a colony of epistylis can become large enough that it looks fuzzy like a colony of fungus. In fact, fungus may be growing right along with the protozoan. Anyway, formalin-malachite green will clear up epistylis in a few days. So if your fungus medication doesn't seem to be working, you may want to treat with formalin-malachite green or another antiprotozoal remedy.

The Worms Go In, the Worms Go Out

Worms are not just good food for fish. Sometimes, fish are good food for worms! Of course, we're not talking about the same type of worms that you would feed your fish. There are many worm species that are internal or external parasites of fish.

It should come as no surprise that fish, like many other animals, can get tapeworms and other intestinal worms. Unfortunately, it is difficult to diagnose these problems without sacrificing a fish and examining the contents of its guts under the microscope. If your fish has internal worms, the odds are that they are present in low numbers. Generally, no action is needed. A healthy fish can live just fine with an occasional parasite. In severe infections, you can try to medicate.

You probably will have a hard time finding worm medication for your fish. There just aren't many commercial preparations available for fish, without going through a veteri-narian. Treating internal worms isn't easy. Picking the right medication and delivering it where it can work is difficult. Butyl tin oxide, praziquantel, piperazine, levamisole, mebendezole, flubendazole, and mebendazole are common ingredients.

Just a Fluke

The flukes are an interesting group of worms. Many have an encysted larval form that is just plain untreatable. If the numbers present are low, it's no big deal. If the fish is heavily infested, its chances are not so good.

Another interesting thing about some flukes is that they are digenetic or trigenetic. That means their lifecycle includes two or three different host animals. For example, a shore bird gets infected when it eats an infected fish. The bird passes fluke eggs in its droppings that hatch in the water and infect snails. The snails, in turn, are eaten by fish, starting the cycle anew. This is a complicated and amazing process, but the good news is that your fish is not likely to get eaten by a bird. So if it can survive in harmony with the few flukes it has on board, those flukes will never be able to breed. The infection stops right there.

Most of the types of worm that infect fish, infest them from the inside. However, some types live on the skin and gills. Skin and gill flukes are sort of like microscopic leeches. They have grasping hooks at one end and a mouth at the other. They move about your fish in inchworm fashion.

Something's Fishy
Always be careful when handling medications and chemicals. Be careful not to inhale dust from them, and always wash your hands afterwards to play it safe. You never know what might be toxic or what may cause an allergic reaction.

It will take a microscope to make a definite diagnosis, but if your fish scratches on rocks, or if the gills have become distended, it may be infested with flukes. Also, bloody patches may result from a heavy infestation. Fortunately, skin and gill flukes are easy to treat. There are several medications on the market. Praziquantel, various organo-phosphates, fenbendazol, flubendazole, mebendazole, potassium permanganate, or copper can be used. Check with your dealer.

Professionals often use Dylox, an herbicide, for treating external flukes. If you find a medication that lists trichlorofon or dimethyl trichloro hydroxethyl phosphonate (with some numbers mixed in the formula), it is probably a good bet. But be careful! This stuff is carcinogenic.

Other Assorted Maladies

Fish can also get sick in other ways. I'll look at some of the most common problems and how to treat them.

Swimbladder Problems

This manifests itself as a buoyancy problem, with the fish swimming loop-de-loops, or floating upside down, or having trouble rising from the bottom of the tank.

The swimbladder is a gas-filled balloon inside most species of fish. It lets the fish maintain the proper buoyancy in the water, and it helps keep the fish in an upright position. However, the swimbladder sometimes fails. There are many possible causes for this, including infection, injury, genetic defects, rapid temperature changes, and so forth. The condition is normally not contagious, but is rarely treatable.

Fancy goldfish are probably the most commonly afflicted. By breeding that fat egg-shaped body into them, their swimbladders have become genetically distorted. So it doesn't take much to throw them out of whack. Some aquarists have suggested that too much dry food is the cause of swimbladder problems with this fish, and that adding more of the aquatic plant anacharis to the diet helps. Also, feeding crushed peas or cooked spinach is sometimes suggested. Further, feeding smaller meals may help, because an overly full stomach will press on the swimbladder, affecting its function. Finally, feeding foods that sink may help prevent the fish from swallowing excess air.

A swimbladder problem is not to be confused with a fish that is somersaulting in its death throes. A fish with swimbladder problems may die soon, too, or it may last a good long time with the condition. You just never know.

Fish and Tips

Tiger barbs often have buoyancy problems after a meal. They are voracious feeders and may swallow lots of air with their meal. Normally, they will stop their unnatural bobbing after the meal digests.

Popeye

Sometimes things go wrong, and it's enough to make your fish's eyes bug out! Popeye is a condition where gas or fluid builds up behind the eye, popping it from its socket. Sometimes an antibiotic will help this condition. Sometimes it goes away on its own.

Fish Tales

The four-eyed fish (*Anableps anableps*) gets its name from its special eyes and their figure-eight shaped pupils. This surface dweller swims with the top half of its eyes protruding from the water. It can watch for insect prey above and below the waterline simultaneously.

Dropsy

This condition is not so much a disease as it is a symptom. The fish swells with fluids, and if you look at it from above, you will see the scales standing out on edge giving a pine cone appearance. The tank water may be too hard or the fish may have an infection. Raising the salt level to two or three teaspoons per gallon may help, along with the addition of a good antibiotic.

Hole in the Head

The common name for this disease, more correctly called head and lateral line erosion (or HLLE), describes a typical symptom. Fish have sensory pores on their faces and running down their sides is a row of tiny pores that form the lateral line. Sometimes, these pores become irritated and develop into pale open pits. There may be a bit of exudate (that's stuff oozing out—aren't you sorry you asked?).

Over the years, many things have been blamed for causing HLLE. Some early hobbyists saw strands of exudate coming from the sores, leading them to blame the problem on worms. Others claimed that the protozoan *Hexamita* was the cause. Still others have blamed diet, induced voltage from aquarium pumps, viruses, and so on. The truth is that no one really knows. Except the worm theory, there is probably some truth to all of the other possibilities.

However, I will tell you this. In over 30 years, I have never seen a freshwater fish develop HLLE when kept in stores with central filter systems. In fact, I've seen many fish cured of the problem, with no additional treatment, when put into these systems. Also, the only freshwater fish that seem to get HLLE are large fish in crowded conditions.

I firmly believe that water quality is the biggest single cause of HLLE. Central systems in stores usually have excellent water quality because the water changes take place continuously. Also, customers whose fish develop HLLE almost always have low pH, high ammonia levels, or both. Living in waste is bad, and big fish put out lots of waste!

So if you have a fish that develops this problem, change more water, more often. If you aren't varying the diet, do so. Better nutrition is always good. You may want to treat with metronidazole, in case there is a secondary Hexamita infection.

Viral Infection

Fish also get viruses, but we know little about them and there are no treatments available anyway. So, this will be a short topic! The only viral infection that you may be able to identify is *lymphocystis*. This disease is not very common, but it does show up on certain species with some regularity. The virus causes cartilaginous tissue to rapidly multiply, forming little nodules. Usually, the nodules form on the rays of the fins, but sometimes on the body, too. They start out looking like ich. That is, you will see isolated single dots first. As the disease progresses, the dots develop into cauliflower-like growths.

The bad news is that there is no treatment for lymphocystis. However, extra water changes may help. The problem is more common on salt-loving species, so be sure you have met their needs in that regard. Sometimes, you can take a razor blade, scrape off the nodules (*very carefully!*), dab the wound with mercurochrome, and the problem may not return.

The good news is that lymphocystis will usually spontaneously remit in a few weeks. So your fish should eventually cure itself. Technically, the disease is considered contagious. In my experience, though, that is rarely the case.

Anyway, there are many other diseases that your fish can get. If you'd like to learn more, I recommend you check your pet shop for *The Manual of Fish Health* by Dr. Chris Andrews, published by Tetra Press. The book has great photos of sick fish, making it easier for you to identify diseases.

This Is Your Fish on Drugs

You probably will find that your aquarium store has a large selection of fish medications. It will be quite confusing to choose, because every brand and medication is going to make great claims about itself. There are even some brands that make absolutely false claims about what they can do. The fish medication industry isn't as highly regulated as the human medication industry. On one hand, this is bad, because there is less rigorous testing, less quality control, and more exaggerated claims. On the other hand, many of these medications are the same ones given to humans, but are sold at a fraction of the cost that your pharmacist would charge.

I have talked about symptoms, diseases, and possible medications to use. Now, I want to give you some guidelines for using those medications.

➤ Before medicating, check the environment. Be sure the filters are working properly, the temperature is correct, and run some water tests for pH, ammonia, and nitrite.

➤ If it has been more than a week since your last partial water change, change some now. Water changes are very important. Medications degrade water quality. I recommend that you change some water every day during any drug treatment, but minimally I recommend a partial water change before, halfway through, and after treatment is complete.

➤ Remove activated carbon from the filters. Activated carbon removes many medications from the water!

➤ Follow the manufacturer's directions to achieve a therapeutic dose of the medication. Too little of a drug will render it ineffective. Too much and it can be toxic to your fish.

➤ Evaluate the treatment. Watch your fish for changes. I recommend that you treat three days before you evaluate. Then, do the following:

> ➤ If the fish is cured, treatment can be discontinued, although it is better to continue for a full five to seven days, to play it safe.

> ➤ If the fish has improved but is not cured, continue the treatment a bit longer.

> ➤ If the fish is the same or worse, the treatment is not working. Change some water and try a different drug.

Quarantine and Hospitalization

I am about to give you a good piece of advice—advice that you probably will ignore. If you do, don't say I never told you so. Before introducing new fish to your tank (except the very first batch, of course) I recommend that you quarantine them for two weeks in a separate tank. This greatly lessens the chance that you'll introduce a disease to your aquarium.

Fish and Tips
Consider steriliz-ing your nets after each use and between aquariums. Nets can transfer disease. There are commercial preparations you can buy to make a sterilizing net soak, or merely mix some bleach and water in a bucket and let the net soak a bit. Rise *thoroughly* to remove all the bleach.

Something's Fishy
Dispose of dead fish by putting them in a plastic bag and into the trash. Do not flush dead or dying fish down the toilet, as they may carry exotic diseases that could be transferred to native fish via the water supply.

A quarantine tank can be quite simple. It can be a five- or 10-gallon bare aquarium with an el-cheapo filter in it (I prefer sponge filters for this application) and a rock or plant to provide cover for the fish. When you're not using the tank for quarantine, it can be used as a hospital tank to treat a sick fish or let an injured one recover. It also makes a good tank for raising baby fish, when not otherwise in use. You probably can put together a quarantine tank for under $20.

Putting a Fish Out of Its Misery

Sometimes it is necessary to euthanize a fish. If a fish is too badly injured or too ill to save, this is a better choice than letting it die a lingering death. Also, if you have a single sick fish and didn't follow my advice about getting a separate hospital tank, you may want to destroy that fish rather than risk letting it infect the others.

Killing fish is not particularly fun. Here are some common ways to euthanize a fish. Choose the one you find the least distasteful or cruel.

➤ *Freezing.* Put the fish in a plastic bag with some water and freeze it. As it gets colder, its movement will slow until it freezes to death. They say this is the most painless method, but nobody really knows for sure, do they?

➤ *Decapitation.* Lay the fish on a paper towel and crush or whack off its head. Sometimes both are necessary.

➤ *Suffocation.* Put the fish in a glass of Alka-Seltzer. The carbon dioxide will suffocate it.

➤ *Bull's-eye method.* Take a stick of chalk outside and draw a bull's-eye on the sidewalk or a brick wall. Throw the fish hard at the target. If you do it right, it will only take one throw. It is never fun to euthanize fish, but this is my preferred method. Done properly, I feel that it brings the most instantaneous death of any of the methods.

The Least You Need to Know

➤ Overcrowding and other stresses are the primary causes of disease.

➤ Be familiar with warning signs of illness.

➤ When problems appear, check the environment first.

➤ A quarantine tank can prevent the introduction of disease to your community tank.

Chapter 25

Dealing With Aggression

In This Chapter

➤ Things that tick a fish off

➤ Signs of aggression

➤ How to break up fights

➤ Fish first aid

The world is not a peaceful place. The natural order of things is such that the strong dominate the weak, the jerks torment the gentle, and many animals look upon each other as food. The same applies to your aquarium. No matter how carefully you plan the mix of your community, there is always going to be occasional friction. Sometimes it will break out into full-blown fights, resulting in serious injury or death.

In this chapter you will learn why fish behave the way they do. You will learn about the things that tick a fish off, and what you can do when the bullies in your tank start taking everyone else's lunch money.

My Fish Are Mean!

Do you remember the little horror story that I told in Chapter 11 on picking your first fish? Recall that there were fish fighting and killing each other. When fish fight, people tend to get anthropomorphic and say that the fish are mean. I don't really think so. Meanness implies malice for the fun of it. When fish fight, they have important reasons for doing so.

You know your fish is mean when . . .

. . . it is the only fish in the tank that still has both of its eyes.

. . . it has its own Harley parked out front.

. . . it has an impressive human finger collection in the rear corner of its tank.

. . . Charles Manson is its pen pal.

. . . it once shot a man for snoring.

. . . you wake up in the hospital, and opening the lid of the tank is the last thing you can remember.

. . . your friends ask what it eats, and you reply, "Anything it wants!"

. . . Mike Tyson won't come within 50 feet of it, and Robin Givens won't come within a mile.

. . . its tank has wire mesh in the glass.

. . . the dog won't come in the house.

. . . it has its own collection of 2LiveCrew albums, and a boom box in the tank.

This Is My Yard and You Can't Play in It

One reason fish fight is for territory. Many species of fish like to pick a spot and call it home. How big that spot is depends on the species of fish and the size of the fish. As a fish grows, the territory it claims probably will expand, too. When other fish come into its territory, it will drive them out. Usually, this involves a very short, threatening chase—that is the fish equivalent of shouting, "Hey! Get lost! This is *my* yard!"

If the encroacher doesn't move fast enough, or stays around to challenge, then things get nastier. Scales are going to fly and fins are going to get nipped. Think about it. If your neighbors started wandering into your house uninvited, you probably would gently chase them out a time or two. After that, just like the fish, you'd get nastier. Quite a bit nastier. You would start kicking some serious butt!

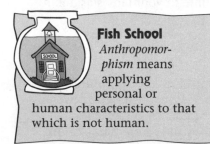

Fish School
Anthropomorphism means applying personal or human characteristics to that which is not human.

That would not make you a mean person. You would merely be protecting your home turf, and that's justifiable behavior—that is, unless the weaponry escalates!

Often, customers will ask me, "What's your most aggressive fish?" I cringe at answering that question—for several reasons. First, I don't really know the answer. It's a judgment call, at best. Second, I think it is better to enjoy fish for their beauty than their viciousness. But mainly, I hate answering that question because I know that, no matter what species I say is the most aggressive one in the store, the very next thing that person is going to ask me is going to start with, "Now, does that get along with…?"

Fish School
An aggressive fish likes to kick butt. A gregarious fish like to snuggle (sort of).

Okay, Some of You Can Play in My Yard

Territoriality is an even more interesting phenomenon than simply staking out a spot and laying claim to it against all others. A fish may guard its home against some species, but not others. What determines this? Generally, a fish is going to be concerned with species that may want to claim the same territory, or with fish that are possible rivals. All others may be left alone entirely.

For example, if a school of tiger barbs comes swimming buy, the Jack Dempsey may ignore them entirely. They don't stake territories, so they are not a threat. Also, they don't look anything like a Jack Dempsey, so they are not rivals for prospective mates. They swim by with impunity. Of course, Mr. Dempsey may be inwardly smirking, thinking about what delicious snacks they will make when he puts on another six months' worth of growth! Jack Dempseys grow much faster and get much larger than tiger barbs.

Some of You Can Play in My Yard Sometimes

However, if another Jack Dempsey comes along, things will be different. Several things may happen:

➤ The newcomer may be seen as a threat and be chased off.

➤ A serious fight may ensue.

➤ If the interloper is of the opposite sex, mating displays may result.

➤ Nothing may happen. Hey, after all, sometimes the neighbors are welcome to come over for a visit!

However, the last option is unlikely unless both fish are juveniles, or grew up together, or have already beaten on each other until they decided to call it a draw.

A fish doesn't have to be of the same species to be considered a threat to another fish's territory. If the fish is of a similar looking or related species, it will have a higher chance of being considered a rival. Earlier in this book, I told a horror story in which a green terror and a Jack Dempsey lived on opposite sides of the tank. They are closely related territorial species that tend to see each other as a threat. Staying away from each other is a good strategy for them. However, their paths will cross sometimes, and as they get accustomed to each other, they are less likely to have spats. They will become habituated.

Another switch that may activate the aggression machine in a fish is sex. Within the species, two fish of the same sex may fight brutally, while the approach of a fish of the opposite sex triggers a courtship display. Actually, it's sometimes hard to tell the difference between aggression and courtship, because courtship in some species involves mock battles. Both participants may get a bit scuffed up before they decide that they are worthy to mate with each other.

Sometimes two species of fish will have completely different shapes, and one may not even be a territorial species, but it could still be seen as a threat. Why? Pattern. For example, the sight of vertical or horizontal bars may be all it takes to elicit a response from another fish. Many species display different color patterns depending on whether they have dominant or submissive status, too.

Who Are You Calling a Chicken?

This brings us to pecking order. Fish have them, too. A pecking order can be interspecies or intraspecies. Once everyone settles into your aquarium, they will all know their place. Some fish will be submissive. Some will be dominant. Some will be ignored entirely. It all depends on a complex interaction of species, size, territoriality, and sex.

Sometimes, pecking at another fish is mere opportunism. Your fish is hungry, it sees a nice fresh filet swimming by, so it takes a nibble. Injured fish are particularly popular targets, though I doubt anyone really knows why. Some say it's because the other fish sense weakness and exploit it. Perhaps it is simply easier to take a bite out of the soft flesh around a wound, or maybe the scent of blood is a draw, or maybe it is just the healthy fish's way of telling the damaged fish to get its sickly butt away from here, and to take its disease with it.

Fish School

In the barnyard, chickens will peck at other chickens that they consider to have lesser status. Likewise, they themselves will be pecked by the more dominant chickens. A hierarchy results, with the most dominant chickens at the top of the *pecking order* and the most submissive at the bottom. Some fish do the same.

Officer, I Didn't See a Thing

It is usually quite easy to spot signs of aggression, but not always. My customers commonly describe symptoms of abused fish, but swear they never see any fights. Just because there are no witnesses doesn't mean it didn't happen. For starters, remember that you won't be watching your aquarium 24 hours a day. So there will be lots of time for the catfish to play while you are away.

Also, when you are in the room, where do you think the fish have their attention? That's right—on you! You are the great Lord and Master of the Fish Food Can, the One Who Sprinkles Manna Down From Heaven. So, when you are around, and particularly when you are close enough to the tank to see what's going on, the fish aren't going to have their minds on misbehaving. They are going to be thinking about pigging out!

Signs of Abuse

It is possible that you will witness fights and be able to identify the guilty parties. Fish that fan their fins and gills while wagging their bodies at each other may be fighting. (Courtship behavior is similar.) But you don't have to witness a fight in progress to tell when a fish has been abused. The fish has plenty of ways of telling you after the fact.

Look for split and ragged fins. When fish bite at each other, torn fins are a common result. If the fins have grayish decaying edges, it could be fin rot, though.

Look for scratches and scrapes. The sharp edges of fins can cause these, or there may even be teeth marks. Sometimes, scratches result from a fish running into objects as it tries to escape or hide.

Torn lips are a sign of aggression. Many fish lock jaws during their tussles. Locking jaws is also a common courtship behavior of cichlids.

Something's Fishy
Got a mean fish that you no longer want? Maybe a friend has a tank for it, or consider trading or donating it to a pet store. *Never* release aquarium fish into the wild! They may decimate local species.

SNIFF! SNIFF!

Obvious wounds also may result. Sometimes an opponent manages to take a pretty good bite! Please note that some infections progress to a point where there are open sores. So be sure that you haven't been overlooking a disease problem.

Watch for missing scales. As fighting fish thrash and bite at each other, scales get jarred loose. I've seen fights that made it look like silver rain was falling in the tank.

Color changes may indicate aggression. Many species display submissive color patterns when bullied.

Finally, a fish that hides may be under attack. Hiding is normal behavior for many species, especially nocturnal ones, but when you find an outgoing fish suddenly se-questering itself, it is a sign that something is stressing it.

Break It Up!

If you do witness a fight, you may want to take action. It will depend upon how much damage occurs. Occasional spats aren't reason for alarm, especially if they inflict little or no damage. Sometimes fish just need to vent their frustrations a little. Sometimes they just need to reinforce their territorial boundaries. Besides, life will be easier for you if the fish can work things out between themselves. Give them a chance to do so, whenever possible.

Fish and Tips
When one fish beats up another, it may be better to move the bully instead of the victim. Often, the bully will merely focus on a new victim. In a way, when you remove its victim, you are rewarding the bully by getting rid of the rival.

However, if things are getting too vicious and if major injuries are starting to appear, you will need to wade in and break things up. Sometimes a couple of taps on the glass will distract the fish. Sometimes the mere sight of you, oh Lord and Master of the Fish Food Can, will distract the fish. Other times, you may need to poke a net handle into the tank to scare the combatants away from each other. Of course, that is no guarantee they won't take up later where they left off.

Even when a fight is serious—when one fish is showing damage—things may still work out. Sometimes a fish just needs to be shown its place in the pecking order. Once it figures that out, peace returns. Be sure to check on the fish, though. Injured fish are targets for more attack by other fish.

In This Corner...

If you decided a fish has had enough, you will need to separate it. Perhaps you can move it to a different tank where the tank mates are more peaceful. You may even want to move the fish to a quarantine tank, where you can preventively medicate the wounds so that infection doesn't set in. (Chapter 24 tells you all about quarantine tanks.)

Usually, though, wounds will readily heal without medication. Fish are hardy characters. Still, it is a good idea to separate the fish so that it can recuperate without further stress and injury. The easiest way to do this is to hang a net breeder in the corner of the tank. Toss the injured fish in the basket, and it will be protected from rivals until it heals.

Fish and Tips
If fighting causes you to separate a fish that you intend to return to the same tank, using a net breeder to isolate the fish has an added advantage. Since the fish remains a part of the community, it won't look or smell unfamiliar when reintroduced. So there will be less chance of new fights.

Joe Aquarist, Fish Paramedic

Here are some things you may want to do for a fish that is badly beaten:

➤ Put it in a quarantine tank with an antibiotic to help prevent bacterial infections.

➤ Use one of the "liquid bandage" water conditioners to help replace its slime coat.

➤ Dab some iodine or mercurochrome on the wounds.

➤ Dim the lights to help the fish relax.

➤ After the victim has rested up and becomes active again, offer some of its favorite live and frozen foods to give it nutrition to heal fastest.

➤ Make sure you have kept up with your water changes. Clean, healthy water is probably the best cure.

When New Neighbors Drop In

The fish most likely to get into a fight is the new fish added to an existing population. The current residents have their territories claimed and their pecking order established. They all know their place in the current fishy society.

The new fish is at a disadvantage, though. It doesn't have a territory of its own. It doesn't have any friends. It gets dumped in with all these strangers and it has to steal some of their living space to survive. The current residents probably won't be too happy about that. They don't want to give up their territories or their places in the social hierarchy. Sometimes, when you add a new fish to the tank, you can almost hear all the others shouting, "Let's get ready to rumble!"

The new fish doesn't look or smell familiar. In fact, it smells like a tasty fish dinner! Even worse for the new fish, it is the great Lord and Master of the Fish Food Can who is dumping the fish into the tank like manna from heaven. So, when the new arrival hits the water, every other fish may think it is feeding time and take a sample nip.

Here are some things you can do to make the transition easier for the new fish:

➤ Feed the existing fish before adding the new one. If their stomachs are full, they will feel less like nipping or fighting.

➤ Consider rearranging decorations in the tank before the addition, especially if you keep territorial species. Since the new fish may have to fight its way into a territory, you can help it out by making it so that *everybody* has to find themselves a new territory. It puts them all on a more even footing.

➤ Introduce a fish late in the day when everyone is settling down and the lights are going out.

➤ Hang around a bit, just to keep an eye on things. Stay until you're satisfied that no one is going to kill the new fish.

> **Fish and Tips**
> A well decorated aquarium helps control aggression by providing lots of hiding places and visual barriers. When it comes to prey and predator, out of sight is out of mind.

Petproofing Your Tank

Sometimes aggression comes from outside. Make sure your tank is on a sturdy stand that can't be knocked over by large dogs. Be sure to have a close-fitting cover on your tank to keep kids and pets out. Cats like to walk across the top and paw at the fish. Make sure they can't catch them.

Not only can pets be a danger to aquariums, but aquariums can be a danger to pets. I once had a parakeet drown while trying to bathe in the outflow of a filter box. The current washed it into the tank where there was no escape! I was heartbroken.

The end.

The Least You Need to Know

➤ Fish fight for good reasons.

➤ Do your best to pick compatible species.

➤ Know the signs of abuse.

➤ Separate bullies from the general population.

➤ Petproof your tank.

Sample Shopping Lists

My friend Elaine once told me that she wished there had been an aquarium book with some sample shopping lists when she started her first tank. It would have been easier if she could have walked into a store with a list of exactly what she needed.

Now there is such a book! Following are some sample shopping lists for a few popular sizes of aquariums. I made it even easier by including some brand names, where appropriate. I chose quality brands that have wide distribution, so you shouldn't have trouble finding any of the items. Still, these are just guidelines—don't be afraid to let your dealer substitute equivalents.

Each shopping list includes:

➤ A list of equipment

➤ A list of hardy live plants that can survive with only a standard full-hood; add more light if you want to keep more diverse plant species

➤ A first batch of hardy fish to cycle the tank

➤ A second batch to fill out the tank, after it has cycled

2.5-Gallon Mini-Tank Shopping List

Equipment	❏ Perfecto 2.5-gallon hexagon aquarium kit (includes undergravel filter and light)
	❏ Whisper 100 air pump
	❏ six-foot air line
	❏ five pounds of aquarium gravel
	❏ 15-watt incandescent aquarium bulb (clear)
	❏ thermometer
	❏ 25-watt heater
	❏ TetraMin fish food
	❏ three-inch aquarium net
	❏ Stress Coat water conditioner
	❏ beginner's book (this one!)
	❏ rocks, driftwood, decorations of your choice
Fish (Batch 1)	❏ one corydoras catfish
Fish (Batch 2)	❏ one male betta *or*
	❏ one pair fancy guppies *or*
	❏ one dwarf gourami (That's right! Two fish in a tank this size is pushing it; consider buying a bigger tank.)
Plants	❏ three vallisneria and one bunch anacharis

10-Gallon Small-Tank Shopping List

Equipment	❏ 10-gallon Perfecto or All-Glass aquarium
	❏ 20-inch full-hood with fluorescent light
	❏ Aqua-Clear Mini power filter
	❏ 50-watt heater
	❏ thermometer
	❏ 15 pounds of aquarium gravel
	❏ TetraMin fish food
	❏ four-inch fish net
	❏ Stress Coat water conditioner
	❏ beginner's book
	❏ rocks, driftwood, decorations of your choice
Fish (Batch 1)	❏ three zebra or pearl danios
	❏ three platies
Fish (Batch 2)	❏ four neon tetras
	❏ two corydoras catfish
	❏ one otocinclus
Plants	❏ six vallisneria
	❏ two bunches anacharis
	❏ two bunches rotala indica
	❏ one amazon swordplant

29-Gallon Medium Tank Shopping List

Equipment	❏ 29-gallon Perfecto or All-Glass aquarium
	❏ 30-inch full-hood with fluorescent light
	❏ Aqua-Clear 200 power filter
	❏ 150-watt heater
	❏ thermometer
	❏ 30 pounds of aquarium gravel
	❏ TetraMin fish food
	❏ five-inch fish net
	❏ Stress Coat water conditioner
	❏ beginner's book
	❏ rocks, driftwood, decorations of your choice
Fish (Batch 1)	❏ three silver or marble hatchets
	❏ three platies
	❏ six black tetras
	❏ three corydoras catfish
Fish (Batch 2)	❏ six neon tetras
	❏ six harlequin rasbora
	❏ three otocinclus *or*
	❏ one small plecostomus
Plants	❏ six vallisneria
	❏ two bunches anacharis
	❏ two bunches rotala indica
	❏ three bunches hygrophila polysperma
	❏ one Amazon swordplant

continued

55-Gallon Large Tank Shopping List

Equipment	❑ 55-gallon Perfecto or All-Glass aquarium
	❑ 48-inch full-hood with 48-inch fluorescent light
	❑ Aqua-Clear 300 power filter
	❑ 60 pounds of aquarium gravel
	❑ 200-watt heater
	❑ thermometer
	❑ TetraMin fish food
	❑ six-inch fish net
	❑ Stress Coat water conditioner
	❑ beginner's book
	❑ rocks, driftwood, decorations of your choice
Fish (Batch 1)	❑ six zebra or pearl danios
	❑ six platies
	❑ six tiger barbs
	❑ 12 serpae tetras
Fish (Batch 2)	❑ 12 large neon tetras
	❑ two kissing gouramies
	❑ one pair kribensis
	❑ three clown loaches
	❑ six corydoras cats
	❑ six otocinclus *or*
	❑ three otocinclus and one small plecostomus
Plants	❑ 12 vallisneria
	❑ two bunches anacharis
	❑ four bunches rotala indica
	❑ four bunches hygrophila polysperma
	❑ one bunch hornwort
	❑ three Amazon swordplants
	❑ six aponogeton instant bulbs

Myths, Mysteries, and Misinformation

Water changes are unnecessary.

This is, perhaps, the most common piece of misinformation out there, although it is contrary to the statements made in every aquarium book ever written. Water changes are essential for your fish to remain in optimum health and to achieve a maximum life span.

Undergravel filter systems don't work.

With undergravel filters, the gravel is the filter media. Like any filter media, if it gets clogged it won't function properly. Use a gravel vacuum when you make partial water changes, and your undergravel filter will do a great job.

Fish don't live long.

One of the Emperor of Japan's koi lived for 226 years. Is that long enough for you? Most small fish live at least three years, and larger ones live around 10 years. A goldfish should live 25 years!

I added dechlorinator, so my water is perfect.

Dechlorinators remove chlorine. That is all that they do. When I ask new hobbyists if they checked their tank's ammonia level, I often get the reply, "I added some of those chlorine drops," as if removing chlorine solves all problems. This brings us to our next bit of popular misinformation.

I don't need test kits.

There is no way you can judge the quality of your tank's water by looking at it. At the very least, you need test kits for ammonia, nitrite, and pH.

I bought these plants in a fish store, so they must be aquatic.

Unfortunately, too many plants sold in some aquarium stores are not aquatic plants at all. Some of them are merely terrestrial plants that take varying amounts of time to drown. Others are bog plants that may survive underwater for a while.

Aquarium full-hoods provide enough light for plants.

The hoods normally supplied with aquariums do not accommodate more than one fluorescent tube, which will not provide sufficient light for most species of aquarium plants. Upgrade the lighting system to really do plants right.

Salt kills corydoras cats.

Baloney! I have kept practically every commercially available species of corydoras at levels of two teaspoons of salt per gallon, with no ill effects. Unfortunately, this myth is printed as fact in many books.

Iodized salt kills fish.

This is another myth printed in many books. The levels of iodine in table salt are harmless to fish, and may even be helpful. In the marine aquarium hobby, reef tank aquarists add iodine supplements for improved growth of their corals.

My dealer wouldn't sell a harmful product.

Fish bowls and tiny novelty tanks may be the best examples of poor products that you will find for sale. Colored light bulbs are another. Studies have shown that they shorten the lives of fish.

Mini-tanks are good starter aquariums.

Sorry, but they are not. Many people believe that it is best to start out small. Then, if successful, they plan to move up to a larger tank. Unfortunately, mini-tanks are more difficult to maintain because they provide less stable environments. Besides, they don't hold enough fish to keep anyone's interest for long.

One inch of fish per gallon is the correct stocking level.

It really depends on the size of the fish. This rule applies only to small, community fish. All you have to do is line up 10 one-inch neon tetras next to one 10-inch oscar to see that there is no way the two are equivalent.

My fish got stuck in a plant and died.

Nope, it didn't happen that way. The fish was already dead or very close to it when it washed into the plant.

My fish got stuck in the filter and died.

Same as above. Your filter can't catch a healthy fish, but it will catch dead and weak, dying ones.

That fish is a killer! I saw it eating another one.

If you saw it attacking and eating a live, healthy fish, then you can call it a killer. If you saw it feeding off a dead or nearly dead fish, it was probably just scavenging. Live fish eat dead fish.

Where to Learn More

Freshwater Aquarium Books

I have shelves and shelves of fish books at home, but here are some of my favorites. Titles followed by an asterisk are readily available through pet stores (possibly by special order). It may take a little hunting to locate the others. Listed retail prices are in U.S. dollars, are approximate, and will vary from dealer to dealer.

Aquarium Atlas, Volumes 1–3* by Dr. Rudiger Riehl, Hans A. Baensch, Tetra Press, 1996, $40 per volume.

> **Subject:** Aquarium keeping, tropical fish, plants
>
> **Rating:** Beginner and up
>
> **Comments:** For detailed information on individual species, these books cannot be beat. Each volume has from 1,000 to 1,200 pages, and most of these are dedicated to describing individual species of fish and plants (one per page). Each book also contains excellent information about general aquarium keeping and fish care. Beginners will love these books, but there is plenty of information for advanced hobbyists, too. I can't think of a better gift than the three-volume set.

Aquarium Plants by Dr. Karel Rataj, Thomas J. Horeman, T.F.H. Publications, 1990, price varies.

> **Subject:** Aquatic and bog plants
>
> **Rating:** Intermediate
>
> **Comments:** This is the aquatic horticulturist's bible. It is the best book for identifying species. It is out of print now, but used copies are not too hard to find.

*The Cichlid Aquarium** by Dr. Paul V. Loiselle, Tetra Press, 1985, $22.

> **Subject:** Cichlids
>
> **Rating:** Advanced
>
> **Comments:** If you are interested in the specialty of cichlid keeping, this book is fantastic. Topics include behavior, habitat, breeding, and much more. I rated it

Advanced because of the liberal use of scientific names and technical jargon, but most beginners will be able to follow it without a problem. There is a wealth of information here, and many color photos make this book useful for species identification.

The Complete Book of Aquarium Plants by Robert Allgayer, Jacques Teton, Ward Lock, Ltd., 1987, $14.95.

Subject: Aquarium plants

Rating: Intermediate

Comments: An excellent resource on the care and identification of aquatic plants.

*Dr. Axelrod's Atlas of Freshwater Aquarium Fishes** (Sixth Edition) by Dr. Herbert Axelrod, Dr. Warren E. Burgess, Neal Pronek, Jerry Walls, T.F.H. Publications, 1989, $70.

Subject: A photographic survey of freshwater aquarium fish

Rating: Beginner

Comments: This is a huge book, containing over 6,000 color photos, most with symbols underneath indicating what the fish eats, how big it gets, and so forth—but that is not the book's strong point. For photo identification of freshwater fish, this book is unbeatable.

*Dr. Axelrod's Mini-Atlas of Freshwater Aquarium Fishes** by Dr. Herbert R. Axelrod, Dr. Warren E. Burgess, Dr. Cliff W. Emmens, Neal Pronek, Jerry G. Walls, Ray Hunziker, T.F.H. Publications, 1987, $28

Subject: A photographic survey of freshwater tropical fish, including care of the freshwater aquarium

Rating: Beginner

Comments: This is a condensed version of *Dr. Axelrod's Atlas of Freshwater Aquarium Fishes*, with an added section on plants, equipment, disease, and other topics. More than 1,800 photos. Although this book is smaller than the regular *Atlas*, the fish that have been omitted are mostly not kept in aquariums, anyway.

Fish Tales

Want to join the club? Contact these two organizations to see if there is an aquarium society in your area: Federation of American Aquarium Societies, 4816 e. 64th St. Indianapolis, IN 46220-4728, (317) 255-2523. Canadian Association of Aquarium Clubs, 298 Creighton Court Waterloo, Ontario, Canada N2K 1W6.

Exotic Aquarium Fishes (19th Edition) by Dr. William T. Innes, Aquariums Incorporated, price negotiable.

> **Subject:** Aquarium keeping, fish identification
>
> **Rating:** Beginner
>
> **Comments:** "The Innes Book" was my favorite book when I was a kid, and remains one of my very favorites. Dr. Innes is considered by many (myself included) to be the father of the aquarium hobby in the U.S. Originally published in 1938, this book underwent many revisions. The book is long out of print, but you may find used copies at garage sales or used book stores. If you find one that is 19th Edition or older, snap it up. There was also a 19th Edition published by Metaframe. T.F.H. Publications eventually bought the rights to this book, and still has an edition in print, but it is nothing like the original. It's smaller and prettier, but is missing a lot. While other fish books have long become outdated, this one still holds up.

Fish and Their Behavior* by Gunther K.H. Zupanc, Tetra Press, 1985, $14.

> **Subject:** Fish behavior
>
> **Rating:** Advanced
>
> **Comments:** This book helps you get inside your fishes' heads, and helps you understand how they think, and why they act the way they do. Both marine and freshwater fish are covered. Interesting reading.

A Fishkeeper's Guide to Aquarium Plants* by Barry James, Tetra Press, 1986, $10.

> **Subject:** Popular plants, plant-keeping
>
> **Rating:** Beginner
>
> **Comments:** The first half of this book covers aquatic plant care. The second half contains photos and facts on individual species. This book is a British import, so there are some references to nonstandard equipment.

A Fishkeeper's Guide to Community Fishes* by Dick Mills, Tetra Press, 1984, $10.

> **Subject:** Compatible aquarium fish
>
> **Rating:** Beginner
>
> **Comments:** Approximately one-third of this book is devoted to installing and maintaining an aquarium. The balance contains photos and descriptions of popular, mostly compatible, aquarium fish. This book is a British import. Although technically accurate, it includes some references to equipment not normally available in North America.

A Fishkeeper's Guide to the Tropical Aquarium* by Dick Mills, Tetra Press, 1984, $10.
> **Subject:** General aquarium-keeping
> **Rating:** Beginner
> **Comments:** The largest part of this book is devoted to equipment set-up, fish care, and breeding. There is a small section with information on individual popular fish species. A British import, it includes some references to equipment that is not normally available in the U.S. or Canada.

Hobbyist Guide to the Natural Aquarium* by Dr. Chris Andrews, Tetra Press, 1991, $10.
> **Subject:** The planted aquarium
> **Rating:** Beginner
> **Comments:** This is an inexpensive starter book for setting up the planted aquarium.

The Manual of Fish Health* by Chris Andrews, Adrian Exell, Dr. Neville Carrington, Tetra Press, 1988, $24.
> **Subject:** Fish disease and treatment
> **Rating:** Beginner
> **Comments:** This book starts off on the right foot by telling you all the things you need to know to keep your fish from getting sick in the first place. It has an excellent section on water quality, a chapter on recognizing warning signs and disease symptoms, and a treatment guide. Plus, it has the best photos I've seen of actual diseased fish, making it invaluable as a diagnosis tool.

Nature Aquarium World* by Takashi Amano, T.F.H. Publications, 1994, $25.
> **Subject:** Landscaped aquariums
> **Rating:** Beginner
> **Comments:** There is nothing else like this book—except for volumes two and three of the same book, which were recently released. Originally published in Japan, this is a picture book of beautifully landscaped aquariums. Mr. Amano has taken the art of aquatic landscaping to a pinnacle. This is not a how-to book, though many photos contain vital statistics about water parameters and so forth. It is more like an art book, with photos having titles like "Scent of Green Wind."

The Optimum Aquarium by Kaspar Horst, Horst E. Kipper, AquaDocumenta (U.S. distributor is Lewis Books), 1986, $24.
> **Subject:** The heavily planted freshwater aquarium
> **Rating:** Advanced
> **Comments:** This book is translated from German, and is partially an advertisement for Dupla products. Dupla is known for its technically advanced products, sold at premium prices. However, that aside, the information is state-of-the-art for the heavily planted aquarium. This is the book for you, if you want to set up a planted tank and you want to do it right.

Tropical Aquarium Fish—Comprehensive Edition* by Dr. Chris Andrews, Dr. Ulrich Baensch, Tetra Press, 1991, $20.

>**Subject:** Popular aquarium fish
>
>**Rating:** Beginner
>
>**Comments:** This is a very good book about identification and care of common freshwater aquarium fish.

Aquarium Magazines

Only a few hobby magazines are available. You may find them in aquarium stores or even at the newsstand, but you'll save money if you subscribe.

Aquarium Fish Magazine
Fancy Publications
P.O. Box 53351
Boulder, CO 80322-3351

Published: Monthly

Price: $24.97 a year

Comments: This magazine is probably the best choice for the beginning freshwater hobbyist, though it has some saltwater content, too. It is full color throughout, beautifully laid out, and filled with articles you can trust. It does lean more to the beginner's end of the hobby, but it has some technical stuff mixed in, and is always written in a way that anyone can follow. Though it is the newest magazine, *Aquarium Fish* has already achieved the widest circulation. The publisher also puts out an annual under the title *Aquarium USA*. I have to admit that I have a soft spot for both the magazine and the annual, and I occasionally write for them.

Tropical Fish Hobbyist
T.F.H. Publications, Inc.
One TFH Plaza
Neptune City, NJ 07753

Published: Monthly

Price: $40 a year

Comments: T.F.H. has been around for 45 years—longer than any of the other fish publishers. It has a real mix of topics. You will find everything from beginner's articles to technical ichthyological stuff written by one of my customers (yes, I'm bragging), Dr. Stanley H. Weitzman at the Smithsonian Institution. This magazine runs more articles on breeding fish and fish collecting expeditions than any of the others. The founder, Dr. Herbert R. Axelrod, is probably the hobby's most well-known celebrity.

Fish Tales

Find it online! Your computer can access many electronic resources that are aquarium related. For example, CompuServe's Fishnet Forum (GO FISHNET) is by far the most complete and my favorite. You can download files, read and post messages, and even chat live with other fish geeks. They even have a fish paramedic service! You can also find information on America Online (GO PET CARE), on the World Wide Web, or on the Usenet.

Freshwater and Marine Aquarium
R/C Modeler Corp.
P.O. Box 487
Sierra Madre, CA 91025

Published: Monthly

Price: $23 a year

Comments: This magazine has a big emphasis on marine aquariums, so it wouldn't be my first choice for new freshwater hobbyists. On the upside, new ideas seem to hit this periodical first. On the downside, the articles are often full of wild conjecture and out-right baloney. Technical editing could be better. They also commit the mortal sin of running April Fools' articles in the April issue, without identifying them as such. If you want mail-order ads, though, this magazine is full of them.

Practical Fishkeeping
Motorsport
550 Honey Locust Rd.
Jonesburg, MO 63351

Published: Bimonthly

Price: $30 a year

Comments: *Practical Fishkeeping* is a British import, and I can't help but notice that the layout sometimes resembles a tabloid newspaper. Still, it is full of excellent information, and almost every issue comes with a free gift.

Glossary

Absorption   The process whereby substances soak into the empty spaces in another substance and are trapped.

Activated carbon   A special, highly porous carbon product used as a chemical filter medium.

Adsorption   The process whereby substances are trapped by chemically bonding with the surface molecules of another substance.

Aggressive   Likes to pick fights.

Algae   Simple-celled microorganisms that photosynthesize. Some scientists classify them as plants, some as single-celled animals (protists).

Alkalinity   Synonym for carbonate hardness (not the same as alkaline pH).

Ammonia   A poisonous waste product excreted by fish and other organisms.

Anthropomorphism   Applying human characteristics to that which is not human.

Antibiotic   A natural substance, produced by an organism, that kills microorganisms (mold, which produces penicillin, is an example). The term is often applied to antibacterials, as well, which are artificial agents.

Aquarium salt   Uniodized salt; pure sodium chloride.

Biological filtration   The use of helpful bacteria to break down waste.

Biotope   A sample of a particular type of environment.

Brackish   Somewhat salty. Brackish water is found where rivers meet the sea.

Break-in period   The time during which a tank is cycling.

Bubblenest   A floating mound of mucous-coated bubbles used by some fish to hide their eggs.

Buffer   A substance that helps resist changes in pH.

Bunch plants   Plants sold by the clump—about eight stems secured with a rubber band or lead weight around the bottom to hold them together. Typically, these are hardy, fast growing species.

Canopy   A glass top for an aquarium. Lights go above. A decorative wooden or acrylic canopy covers the lighting system to hide it from view.

Carcinogen   An agent known to have the ability to cause cancer.

Chemical filtration   The use of chemical compounds to adsorb waste.

Chloramine   A harmful additive found in some municipal water supplies.

Chlorine   A harmful additive found in most municipal water supplies.

Community tank   An aquarium with a mix of compatible, peaceful species. The species are usually small, but large fish can be kept in community tanks, too.

Crown plants   Plants that consist of roots and a central base (crown) from which all leaf stems radiate in a rosette.

Cycling   Breaking in a new aquarium by starting with fewer fish until enough helpful bacteria develop to handle the ammonia and nitrite loads.

Diatoms   Microscopic organisms with silica skeletons. They appear as brown slime and are often mistaken for algae.

Dimorphism   Having two forms; particularly sexual dimorphism, where males and females are visibly distinguishable.

Dither fish   Active schooling fish used to bring shy fish out of hiding. Their presence is a signal that all is clear.

Emersed   Above the water.

Floating plants   Plants that normally float on the surface of the water.

Fry   Singular or plural for baby fish.

Gonopodium   A tube found on the adult male fish that is used to transfer sperm to the female's vent during mating.

Gravid spot   A triangular patch just above the female's vent where the eggs develop within the fish.

Gregarious   Prefers to be part of a group.

Hardness   General water hardness is a measurement of minerals, particularly magnesium and calcium. Carbonate hardness measures buffering capacity.

Horticulture   Growing plants.

Ich   The most well-known fish disease.

Ichthyology   The study of fish.

Livebearers   Fish that give birth to live young.

Marine   Synonym for salt water or seawater.

Mechanical filtration   Separating solid particles, particularly waste, from a solution.

Mouthbrooders   Species that carry their eggs in their mouth to protect them, and also guard the fry in this manner.

New-tank syndrome   The buildup of ammonia and nitrite during the cycling of a new tank. Also used to refer to some cloudy water problems in new tanks.

Nitrate   A non-toxic (in normal levels) product formed by the oxidation of nitrite.

Nitrite   A toxic by-product produced by the conversion of ammonia.

Nitrogen cycle   The process whereby helpful bacteria break down ammonia into nitrite, nitrate, and eventually, nitrogen gas.

Paludarium   The word means "swamp tank." It's a tank that is part land and part water, with plants growing up out of the water—a combination aquarium and terrarium.

Pecking order   A hierarchy where the most dominant one is at the top of the pecking order and the most submissive is at the bottom.

pH   A measurement of the acidity or alkalinity of the water.

Salt creep   The crust that builds up when salt water evaporates, leaving minerals behind. Also, an affectionate term for a saltwater hobbyist.

Synergistic   When two or more ingredients combine to become more effective than either would be if used alone.

Submersed   Below water.

Target fish   A fish introduced to misdirect aggression; particularly used to keep parents guarding fry from beating each other up.

Taxonomy   The scientific classification of organisms. (Kingdom, phylum, class, order, family, genus, and species.) In this book I am most concerned with genus and species, which compose the scientific name.

Terrarium   An enclosure with a land mass in which live plants and animals are kept.

Thermostat   A device that controls temperature (as opposed to a thermometer, which is an instrument that measures temperature).

Vivarium   An enclosure for live plants and animals that is divided into two sections—one for water and one for a land mass.

Index

raising fry, 257-258
rams, 139
ramshorn snail, 161
raphael cat, 137
rapid breathing, danger signals, 284
rasboras
    brilliant rasbora, 148
    harlequin rasbora, 148
    scissortail rasbora, 149
recharging granular activated carbon (GAC), 49
rectangle aquariums, 41
red devil, 163
red empress (African cichlids), 169
red irian rainbowfish, 148
red slime algae, 273
red terror, stripes, 163
red-eye tetras, 152
redtail catfish, 165
red-tail sharks, 149
reducing
    ammonia levels in tank
    Amquel, 200-201
    zeolite, 200
    high nitrite levels, 201-202
relocating aquariums, 189-190
removing mineral deposits, 241
replaceable filter media filters, 94
reproduction. See also breeding
    livebearers
    defined, 321
    sexing, 255-256
    mouthbrooders, 321
    transsexual functions, 257
returning merchandise, 32
rival species, aggression, 301
rock pile aquariums, 18
rocks
    arrangements, 82
    artificial, 85-86
    colors, 82

pH/hardness, 82
potentially harmful effects, 82
quartz, 82
shapes, 82
shifting, 106
texture, 82
types, 82
washing prior, 82
rosy barb, 136
rosy red minnows as food source, 234
rotala indica (plants)
    color, 174
    leaf shape, 174
ruby swordplant (plants)
    color, 176
    leaf shape, 176
rusty (African cichlids), 169

S

salespersons
    advice, 24-25
    level of expertise, 24-25
salt
    aquarium salt, 319
    effects on water pH, 205
    salt creep, 321
salt creep, 14
saltwater aquariums
    American households, 14
    cost of fish, 13-14
    versus freshwater aquariums, 13
    water chemistry, 13-14
scales
    color changes, danger signals, 283
    missing, signs of fighting, 303
scat varieties, 166
scavengers, role in health of tank, 138

schooling behaviors
    minimum number of fish, 124
    predators, 123-124
scientific names versus common names, 131-132
scissortail rasbora, 149
seashells, use warnings, 85
seawater, specific gravity, 19-20
self-sticking backgrounds, 81
separating aggressive fish, 304
serpae tetras, 151
severum varieties, 163
sex of fish, opposite sex aggression, 302
sexing
    egglayers, 256-257
    livebearers, 255-256
sexual dimorphism, 167
shark cat, 166
sharks
    carp family, 149
    iridescent sharks, 150
    prominent dorsals, 149
    rainbow sharks, 149
    red-tail sharks, 149
    tricolor sharks, 150
shimmies, danger signals, 284
shipping fish from dealer to home, 183-184
shopping lists
    2.5-gallon mini-tanks
        equipment, 308-310
        fish, 308
        plants, 308-310
    10-gallon small tanks
        fish, 308
        plants, 308-310
    29-gallon medium tanks
        equipment, 309-310
        fish, 309
        plants, 309-310
    55-gallon large tanks
        equipment, 310